# Welcome to the *EVERYTHING*

These handy, accessible books give you all you need to tackle a difficult project, gain a new hobby, comprehend a fascinating topic, prepare for an exam, or even brush up on something you learned back in school but have since forgotten.

You can read an *EVERYTHING*® book from cover-to-cover or just pick out the information you want from our four useful boxes: e-facts, e-ssentials, e-alerts, and e-questions. We literally give you everything you need to know on the subject, but throw in a lot of fun stuff along the way, too.

We now have well over 100 *EVERYTHING*® books in print, spanning such wide-ranging topics as weddings, pregnancy, wine, learning guitar, one-pot cooking, managing people, and so much more. When you're done reading them all, you can finally say you know *EVERYTHING*®!

**FACTS**

Important sound bytes of information

**SSENTIALS**

Quick handy tips

**ALERT**

Urgent warnings

**QUESTIONS?**

Solutions to common problems

# THE EVERYTHING® Series

Dear Reader,

Welcome to the world of William Shakespeare.

What's that, you say? Shakespeare? Give me a break! What can a 400-year-old, dead white male *possibly* have to say that's relevant to my life? Why do people always try to force *Shakespeare* down my throat like it's good for me?

Of course, if someone made you eat ice cream by forcing you, you'd hate that too. But if only you can find out about ice cream on your own, there are some wonderful tastes and experiences waiting to be discovered.

These days, Shakespeare is a something of an industry. There's too much reverence paid to the Bard—and not enough appreciation. In a very minor way, I want to try to correct that. Good performances of Shakespeare's plays are fantastic, satisfying, roller-coaster dramatic experiences.

My hope is that this book will act as a doorway into a world of paradox and wonder, magic and gore, beautiful poetry, memorable characters, and startling insights into the what makes us tick—be it Hamlet pondering the morality of bloody revenge and suicide, or King Lear's arrogance plunging him into insanity and causing the death of his beloved youngest child.

Shakespeare is not just quoted too often, it's hard not to quote him. He helped to invent the language we now call "English" and we use words and phrases he wrote every day. He is woven into the fabric of our daily lives in ways that are remarkable, and each generation rediscovers him and finds that he has something to say to them.

"All the world's a stage," he said. Without further ado, I bid you welcome to our little theatre. Take a seat, get comfortable, and enjoy the show.

[The curtain rises on a bare stage. A man enters . . .]

# THE
# EVERYTHING®
# SHAKESPEARE
# BOOK

A comprehensive guide to
understanding the comedies,
tragedies, and sonnets of the Bard

Peter Rubie

Adams Media Corporation
Avon, Massachusetts

EDITORIAL
Publishing Director: Gary M. Krebs
Managing Editor: Kate McBride
Copy Chief: Laura MacLaughlin
Acquisitions Editor: Bethany Brown
Development Editor: Lesley Bolton

PRODUCTION
Production Director: Susan Beale
Production Manager: Michelle Roy Kelly
Series Designer: Daria Perreault
Layout and Graphics: Brooke Camfield,
Colleen Cunningham, Rachel Eiben,
Daria Perreault

An Everything® Series Book.
Everything® is a registered trademark of Adams Media Corporation.

Published by Adams Media Corporation
57 Littlefield Street, Avon, MA 02322 U.S.A.
*www.adamsmedia.com*

ISBN: 1-58062-591-6
Printed in the United States of America.

J  I  H  G  F  E  D  C  B  A

**Library of Congress Cataloging-in-Publication Data**
Rubie, Peter.
The everything Shakespeare book / by Peter Rubie.
   p.   cm.   —(Everything series)
Includes index.
ISBN 1-58062-591-6
1. Shakespeare, William, 1564–1616—Handbooks, manuals, etc.
I. Title. II. Series.
PR2894 .R83        2002
822.3'3—dc21        2002006661

Cover Illustrations by Barry Littmann.

*This book is available at quantity discounts for bulk purchases.*
*For information, call 1-800-872-5627.*

**Visit the entire Everything® series at everything.com**

# Contents

# Introduction

In a scene of the special millennium episode of the British comedy show *Blackadder,* the hero, played by Rowan Atkinson, travels back in time to the days of Queen Elizabeth I and meets William Shakespeare walking the corridors of the royal palace. Before Shakespeare realizes what is happening, Blackadder punches him. As the Bard lies on the floor totally mystified, Blackadder says, "This is for every schoolboy and schoolgirl for the next 400 years!" and marches off.

The point being, many a potential fan has been turned off forever by being forced to read Shakespeare at school, or dragged to see a badly staged and acted version of one of his plays. Nearly all of us as schoolchildren were forced to suffer through turgid study sessions of Shakespeare plays because it was "good for us."

There is a light at the end of the tunnel, however. Some producers have staged fantastic versions of Shakespeare's plays with great actors who take what seems to be incomprehensible language and make it sing. Also available are some great radio productions that are sold as audiotapes. If you look carefully you can find not only extracts but also full audio versions of the plays on the Internet for free. If you're going to study a Shakespeare play, you may want get one of these audiotapes and follow along. It's a terrific experience.

There is no question, studying Shakespeare requires some effort. He takes us into a different world, introduces us to some very different people, and makes us listen to them talk in a way that at first seems almost incomprehensible. But the key word here is *almost.* The truth is, his characters are, in fact, very recognizable. You can pick up the newspaper or turn on the TV and see variations on the people he populated his plays with.

Shakespeare's genius was to capture, perhaps for the first time in the English language, the deep and troubling complexities and passions that we are all slave to. It took another 300 years for Sigmund Freud and the advent of psychology to fully appreciate how perceptive were Shakespeare's observations of the human condition. Are the passions of Othello, driven to murder his wife by a blinding jealousy brought on by his consuming love for her, really so different from the guy in New Jersey who arrived at his ex-lover's house on her wedding day and shot her? Most of us can identify with the frustrated passions of a tormented Hamlet. We learn to feel great compassion for a mighty man fallen as King Lear falls further and further into madness, grief, and homelessness. The ambitious and brutal Gordon Gekko, who declares, "Greed is good" in the 1988 Oliver Stone movie *Wall Street* can't hold a candle to the naked, murderous ambitions of Macbeth and his wife.

But more than this—as if this weren't enough—Shakespeare also helped to invent the language we now know as English. He wrote at a time when English was evolving from a form called Middle English, which was part Germanic and part French, into the language we recognize today. He invented words and played with the language. Don't think for a minute that audiences in his day understood everything he wrote any better than we do. He was a challenge then and now. He was a poet with a poet's sensibilities, and his use of language and his inventiveness reflects that.

But he was also an actor and knew well how to entertain the "groundlings" or common folk who flocked to his plays. The scripts are filled with double entendres (dirty jokes), blood, and gore—the end of *Hamlet* is bloodier than even *The Godfather*, and *Titus Andronicus* is a bloodbath with bodies and dismemberments all over the place. He also includes bawdy sex, drunkenness, humorous idiots, and evil characters, who all but twirl their moustaches as they rejoice in revealing their plans of wickedness.

So, let's investigate the world of the man who once wrote "All the world's a stage, and all the men and women merely players" *(As You Like It)*, and see if he can't teach us a thing or two about ourselves and our neighbors while having a good time.

PART 1

# The Life and Times of William Shakespeare

## CHAPTER 1
# *Shakespeare's World*

Shakespeare is an enigma. Back in Elizabethan times not too many people could write, so records are sketchy. However, a bit of detective work in church records, court case records, and a few personal reminiscences gives us the bones of a skeletal life story to which we can conjecture some "meat."

## The Early Years

It is commonly agreed that England's greatest poet and playwright was born and died on the same day of the month, St. George's Day—born on April 23, 1564, and died on April 23, 1616. (It was a notion of the time that great men were born and died on the same date.) His birth date is calculated from an entry in the parish register for a William Shakespeare baptized on April 26; baptisms usually took place about three days after a child's birth because infants often died in those first two days.

 **ESSENTIALS**

Spelling was hit or miss in those days before English was standardized, so Shakespeare's name can also be found spelled as Shackerpere, Shaxpeare, and many other variations. This discrepancy has to be factored into the hunt for the real William Shakespeare.

He was born at Stratford-upon-Avon in the county of Warwickshire about 100 miles north of London. In the mid-sixteenth century, Stratford was a market town of some 1,500 people. In the agrarian society of the time, villages were limited in size by the productivity of the surrounding countryside. They were dependent on rivers and streams to transport local produce such as wool, cheese, and grain. The population of London at the time of Shakespeare's birth was about 100,000 people. In comparison with London, Stratford can be considered the equivalent of a large town.

## Shakespeare's Family

Shakespeare was the eldest son of a glove maker and leather worker, John Shakespeare, and the third child of eight. John was of yeoman stock, which meant his family was reasonably well-off for middle class people, but he still rented his farms and worked them himself. Shakespeare's mother's maiden name was Mary Arden, and her family was from the gentry—that is, they were landlords rather than tenants and lived off the income of their real estate. In fact, John's landlord was

Mary's father. Along with the properties that Mary brought to the marriage and the leather and tanning business, which was a very respectable trade in those days, John also bought and sold grain.

John was active in local government and was appointed to jobs of increasing responsibility culminating in his election as bailiff, or mayor, of Stratford. However, as Shakespeare's fortunes rose, John's began to decline. In 1586 he was replaced as an alderman, and by 1592, he was being rebuked in writing for not attending church and was in fear of being jailed for debt.

Historians speculate that John may have held onto old Roman Catholic beliefs and suffered for it. England had become Protestant under Henry VIII, and after he died, his daughter Queen Mary had tried to reintroduce Catholicism in a rather bloody way. But then Elizabeth I became queen and established the Church of England as a Protestant church once and for all, though she also strove for religious tolerance.

## Shakespeare's Education

As the son of a local official, Shakespeare would have been entitled to free schooling (mandatory schooling was not yet the law), and it is likely he was educated at Stratford Grammar School, which had a reputation as an excellent school. His lessons would have included Latin grammar. After a few years of training in basic literacy, boys of well-off families spent the rest of their education learning to read, recite, and speak Latin and possibly some Greek. The influence of Latin authors such as Pliny, Ovid, and Seneca, as well as Greek authors such as Homer and Plutarch, are clear in Shakespeare's works.

John's debts grew, and the family properties were mortgaged; Shakespeare did not go on to a university, but the grammar school curriculum must have given him a formidable linguistic and literary education. As was common at the time, he attended classes from dawn to dusk six days a week and was probably whipped if he was inattentive or lazy in his studies. Some researchers think that the character of Sir Hugh Evans, in *The Merry Wives of Windsor,* is a caricature of Shakespeare's old headmaster, Thomas Jenkins.

## Marriage and Children

According to the parish records, "William Shagspere" married Anne Hathaway in 1582 when he was eighteen years old. Anne was eight years his senior and from the nearby village of Shottery. Her father Richard was a pretty well-to-do farmer. The couple was forced to ask for a waiver of the banns from the Bishop of Worcester so that the wedding could take place quickly before the holiday season, when marriages weren't performed. Their daughter Susanna was born six months later.

Their marriage does not seem to have been particularly happy, and it may have been what we would now call a "shotgun" wedding, urged on by Shakespeare's father because of the financial improvements to the family that would result from the union. It's also worth remembering that in those days marriage was considered as much a business proposition as a union of two people who had fallen in love. Moreover, historians estimate that one in three Elizabethan brides was pregnant on her wedding day, so this situation was not out of the ordinary by any means.

Anne gave birth to a daughter, Susanna, in 1583. Three years later, in January 1585, Anne gave birth to twins. They were named in honor of two family friends, the baker Hamnet Sadler and his wife Judith. Hamnet Shakespeare died in 1596, at only eleven years old. Some historians think that the lines spoken by Constance in *King John*, which he wrote the following year, refer to Shakespeare's heartsickness at losing his only son:

> Grief fills the room up of my absent child,
> Lies in his bed, walks up and down with me,
> Puts on his pretty looks, repeats his words,
> Remembers me of all his gracious parts,
> Stuffs out his vacant garments with his form;
> Then have I reason to be fond of grief.
> Fare you well. Had you such a loss as I,
> I could give better comfort than you do.

QUESTIONS?

**Is there any connection between Hamnet and Hamlet?**
Some critics have suggested that in *Hamlet*, when Hamlet talks to his father's ghost at the beginning of the play, it is a psychological inversion of Shakespeare talking to his son's ghost. Hamlet's father is also named Hamlet.

## The Effects of War

Not a lot is known of Shakespeare between the ages of eighteen and twenty-five. Some stories say he had to flee Stratford after being caught poaching deer on a nobleman's estate, while others, less fanciful, have him working as a schoolmaster, either in a small town or for the family of a local nobleman. Be that as it may, he arrived in London in 1587 as a member of a troupe of actors called Lord Leicester's Men.

Newly Anglican (i.e., Protestant) London was the capital of a nation at war, engaged in a drawn-out fight with the Catholic Spanish Empire that controlled a great deal of Europe, either directly or by alliance. The Lowlands of the Netherlands (Holland and Flanders) were the battlefields of constant engagements between the armies of Spain and small companies of men from Holland, France, and England.

At sea, meanwhile, Sir Francis Drake and Sir Walter Raleigh among others were harrying Spanish ships bringing back gold and exotic trade goods from the New World. Although really pirates or privateers they received a royal blessing from Elizabeth who turned a blind eye as long as money filled the royal coffers. It all came to a head in 1588, when the English smashed a vastly superior Spanish Armada. The war dragged on, though, and the English lost Calais to the Spanish in 1596. For days, it was said, you could hear the sounds of the cannons as far as London.

Shakespeare wrote a lot about a nation at war or existing in an uneasy peace, while religious strife and bigotry could result in a treason trial and your head stuck on a pike on Traitor's Gate in London. As the medieval guilds (like unions, in some ways) began to founder, unemployment grew, and beggars and homeless people filled the streets and prisons of towns and cities. A kind of "baby boom" also took place as the country recovered from the ravages of the Black Death over the previous 100 years.

**FACTS**

There is information about Shakespeare's activities from 1582 when he married until 1592 when he pops up in London. This time is often called the Lost Years.

But the riches of the Renaissance began to pour forth, and the notion of being an Englishman was steadily taking hold. This growing pride in nationhood and military might, particularly after the defeat of the Armada, is a key to understanding a lot of Shakespeare's work.

## Life in Theater

It is unlikely, but commonly held, that Shakespeare's first job in the theater was holding horses at the stage door. He was probably some sort of stage manager. As he began journeyman play editing and copying, and collaborating with other playwrights and actor managers, he learned his craft.

By 1592 he was well established as an actor/playwright in London. Shakespeare worked at the Globe Theatre and appeared in many small parts. However, a bitter rival, Robert Greene, accused Shakespeare of stealing techniques from other playwrights to further his own career, and added, " . . . there is an upstart crow, beautified with our feathers [that is, he stole our stuff], that with his Tygers hart wrapt in a Players hyde [a possible reference to a line from *King Henry VI, Part III*, an early play, but also referring to Shakespeare as an untalented person pretending to be a playwright and actor], supposes he is as well able to bombast out blanke verse as the best of you [that is, he thinks he's pretty hot stuff as a writer]; and being an absolute Johannes fac totum [that is, Jack-of-all-trades (and the rest of the insult implies a master of none)], is in his own conceit the only Shake-scene in a country [in other words, he *really* thinks he's hot stuff]."

Greene was a university-trained writer who resented the "uneducated" lowlifes like Shakespeare becoming more successful than he. It's easy to think of Shakespeare now as eclipsing his contemporaries, but he wrote alongside other famous names—Marlowe, Kyd, and Jonson, then the younger generation of Webster, Beaumont, and Fletcher.

We don't know exactly what roles Shakespeare played, but authorities on Shakespeare think he probably played "cameo" roles, such as the Ghost in *Hamlet*, and Chorus in *King Henry V*. He seemed to play older men. He is in the cast list of a Jonson play, *Sejanus*.

The troupe did well, no doubt partly as a result of their in-house writer, and performed for Queen Elizabeth I several times a year. They also put on productions in the courtyards of inns for law school professors and students (whose courtyards are known to this day as Inns of Court) and at theaters such as the Swan.

**SSENTIALS**

The sonnets, though some of his most moving and personal pieces, were never written for publication, nor have scholars determined when and to whom they were written.

In 1592 the plague broke out again, and the authorities in London closed all the theaters because of the risk of spreading infection in the audiences. In an attempt to bridge the gap in his sudden loss of income, and probably to get himself a noble patron as well as establish himself as a legitimate poet (poetry was considered a higher calling than playwriting), Shakespeare published two major lyric works, *Venus and Adonis* in 1593 and *The Rape of Lucrece* in 1594.

When the theaters reopened in 1594, the thirty-year-old actor/play-wright joined an acting company led by Richard Burbage, which called itself the Lord Chamberlain's Men.

## The Master of Revels

Anyone involved in the production of plays in Elizabethan England, from the playwright to the theater owners, knew that the Master of Revels was the man to impress and fear, for he auditioned acting troupes, selected the plays they would perform, and controlled the scenery and costumes to be used in each production. During the reign of James I, the Master of Revels reached the apex of his power and had complete authority over both the production and the publication of plays.

The Master of Revels, deputy to the Lord Chamberlain, headed the Revels Office, the department of the royal household responsible for the coordination of theatrical entertainment at court. To perform at court was the goal of every Elizabethan theater company. When the Master of Revels organized an upcoming season of performances he would summon the acting troupes so that they could audition before him and his three subordinate officers. The Master would then choose which companies would perform and which plays they were allowed to produce. If the Master saw fit, he would delete lines or passages and even request that entire scenes be inserted into the original material.

**FACTS**

The Master of Revels's power included issuing licenses to provincial acting troupes, which led to a gradual corruption of the office; it was common for the Master of Revels to earn ten times his yearly salary through bribes. However, following the English Civil War in 1642, the Puritan government closed all the theaters and the Office of the Revels became fruitless; it was formally eliminated by 1737.

Once the Master selected the plays to be produced before the royal court, he arranged for all the required costumes and scenery to be created by his own seamstresses and workmen. Much time and money was spent on the elaborate wardrobes, and only the finest fabrics were used.

## Profile of the Bard

By some accounts Shakespeare was a good-looking, witty young man, probably not unlike Joseph Fiennes's portrayal of him in the 1998 movie *Shakespeare in Love*. He could probably be pretty intense, had a real eye for the dramatic in a situation, was extremely knowledgeable about stagecraft, and likely paid great attention to the world and the people around him, initially listening more than talking.

He probably wasn't above taking someone's idea if he liked it and rewriting it for himself and his company. Shakespeare's version, of course, would have been uniquely his. For example, the *King Lear* story did not have an unhappy ending until Shakespeare rewrote it. In those days, plagiarism wasn't a crime. A lot of his work, for example the stories of Macbeth, King Lear, and Hamlet, can be traced back to stories by Chaucer, Plutarch, Holinshed, and also to folktales.

Shakespeare would likely have been the quiet one in a crowd at first, the one who sat in the corner entertaining himself and perhaps a friend or two by watching everyone coming and going in a room and making pithy, witty comments probably in a low voice. But once the party got going, he was likely just as crazy and passionate as others. Pity the poor guy who had to get into an argument with Shakespeare. A nimble mind, a way with words, and a sharp tongue no doubt helped him win a lot more arguments than perhaps he should have won.

## Shakespeare the Businessman

Most of the records that mention Shakespeare deal with lawsuits. He was a big businessman and the theater was the television of its time. As a result, Shakespeare received proceeds as a percentage owner of the company, as an actor, and as a writer. He was careful with his money (perhaps as a result of lessons learned from his father's misfortunes). He earned fees from his plays, acting in his and other's works, and as the owner or part owner of several theaters and the acting company. He did not own his plays—those were owned by companies such as the King's Men—but he invested his money wisely in real estate in both London and back home in Stratford, and ended up a wealthy man. As he grew older, he still liked to hang out with his theater pals, drinking and swapping stories of days gone by, keeping his hand in, so to speak, while being fairly removed from the hurly-burly of everyday theater life.

**SSENTIALS**   A great deal is still missing from Shakespeare's biography. We have no evidence, for example, that he traveled around the country or abroad, although it's certainly possible given his knowledge of other countries and the things he wrote about in his plays.

## Performing for Royalty

Shakespeare's time spent writing and performing entertainment for Queen Elizabeth and later King James I no doubt helped him write convincingly about royalty, and it is not a stretch of the imagination to think that as the leading playwright and poet of his time, he was often in the company of his "betters," that is, noble men and women and leading political and social figures of the time.

In 1599 the Lord Chamberlain's Men built the Globe Theatre on the south bank of the River Thames near the Swan. It held about 3,000 people—a huge place for its day and none too shabby nowadays—charging a penny for the standing room only groundlings, on up for those with the cash to buy a cushioned seat. Most of the great tragedies, such as *Hamlet* and *King Lear*, were probably performed there for the first time.

In 1603, Queen Elizabeth I died, and she was succeeded by James VI of Scotland, known as James I of England. He took Burbage and company under his wing and the Lord Chamberlain's Men changed its name to the King's Men and soon became established as the premier troupe of the day, performing often at court for King James.

## The Works

Shakespeare wrote for nearly twenty years, and at the height of his powers probably wrote as many as two or even three plays a year. He began writing plays in 1595 and of the thirty-eight plays that comprise the Shakespeare canon, thirty-six were published in the First Folio of 1623. Eighteen plays had been published in his lifetime in the Quarto publications. Scholars have identified evidence of his work in other plays as well.

King Henry VI, King Richard III, Titus Andronicus, and Love's Labour's Lost appear to be among the earliest, followed by The Comedy of Errors, King Richard II, The Two Gentlemen of Verona, and Romeo and Juliet. Then followed The Taming of the Shrew, King John, The Merchant of Venice, A Midsummer Night's Dream, All's Well That Ends Well, King Henry IV, The Merry Wives of Windsor, King Henry V, Much Ado About Nothing, As You Like It, Twelfth Night, Julius Caesar, Hamlet, Troilus and Cressida, Othello, Measure for Measure, Macbeth, King Lear, Timon of Athens, Pericles, Antony and Cleopatra, Coriolanus, Cymbeline, The Winter's Tale, The Tempest, King Henry VIII, Cardenio, and The Two Noble Kinsmen.

**E**SSENTIALS  King Henry VIII may have been a collaboration with John Fletcher, an up-and-coming playwright who was working as a dramatist with the King's Men and who probably also collaborated on Cardenio and The Two Noble Kinsmen.

## The Final Years

Shakespeare retired from writing in 1611, although King Henry VIII was performed at the Globe in London in 1613. During the performance a sound effect cannon was fired in a shed on the roof and the thatching caught fire. Someone tried to douse it with a flagon of ale, which fueled the flames, and the Globe burned to the ground. No one was hurt except a guy whose pants caught fire. The Globe was recently rebuilt, and reopened in 1997.

Shakespeare returned to Stratford to live in a house he had built for his family on his substantial real estate holdings in the area. His daughter Susanna married a Stratford doctor, John Hall, in 1607 and their home, called Hall's Croft, is today preserved as one of the Shakespeare Properties and administered by the Shakespeare Birthplace Trust.

In 1616, a few months after his daughter Judith (Hamnet's twin) was married, Shakespeare died at the age of fifty-three and was buried in the Church of the Holy Trinity, the same church in which he was baptized.

Tradition has it that he died of a fever after an evening's drinking with Ben Jonson and some of his other theater friends. His gravestone bears the words that are thought to be the last words he ever wrote:

Good frend for Jesus sake forebeare,
to digg the dust encloased heare,
Bleste be ye man yt spares thes stones,
And curst be he yt moves my bones.

FACTS

Judith married Thomas Quiney and had three children, all of whom died young without leaving heirs. John and Susanna, who received the bulk of Shakespeare's estate when he died, had a daughter Elizabeth who died in 1670, leaving no heirs.

## CHAPTER 2
# *The Elizabethan Stage*

In order to appreciate both what Shakespeare wrote and why it's as brilliant as it is often said to be, it's useful to know something about the Elizabethan stage and how it developed. It is also important to note that Shakespeare and his companions invented what we now consider the modern theater. Today's Broadway shows are the direct descendents of the early plays presented in Elizabethan theaters.

# The Evolution of Elizabethan Theater

When Shakespeare reached London around 1587, the Elizabethan theater was slowly taking shape. It was evolving from the religious pageants and morality plays of the Middle Ages that had been the norm until then. London at that time was an exciting place for a young dramatist. John Burbage opened the first public theater—the theatre—in Shoreditch (now East London) in 1577. The old religious drama was dying out, but two new plays, written shortly before Shakespeare's birth, *Ralph Roister Doister* (the first regular comedy in English) and *Gorboduc* (the first regular tragedy in English), were helping to shape a new Elizabethan drama.

The precursor of the theater was a type of religious pageant performed on the front steps of cathedrals with repetitions and chants as seen in the *Quem Queritis Trope*. Later, amateur actors took on roles and the stories were broadened for entertainment's sake. One such play depicted the character of Noah's wife as a shrew, though she is not portrayed as such in the Bible. This kind of expansion into entertainment made the church nervous of drama, and it began to keep it at arm's length. Eventually, most of the morality plays were performed only for the nobility because of their abstract concepts.

The Elizabethan theater competed for its audience with public executions where victims were literally hung, and sometimes "drawn and quartered," or butchered. Traitors were beheaded and their heads left to rot on pikes at the city limits. Another form of entertainment for the public was baiting. Dogs were pitted against other dogs or bulls and bears to fight to the death.

# Morality Plays

Roaming groups of acrobats, mimes, and musicians of varying talent performed in the first theater. Their plays, known as mysteries, were heavily influenced by religious morality and took place in inn courtyards, town squares, village halls, and fairgrounds, or anywhere a bunch of boards could be rested on barrels or trestles to create a stage. (That's where the expression "treading the boards" comes from.)

Private performances for noble folk were held in great dining halls lit by tall candles. A curtain ran behind the boards, forming an area hidden from public view where the actors could change costumes and make ready their entrances and exits. They used few props and little scenery, and because the casts were small, actors often played two or more roles during a production.

These morality plays about vice and virtue used archetypes to get their points across. Characters were the vices and virtues—Death, Kindness, Virtue, while the human protagonists were called Everyman. In contrast, as the theater developed throughout the reign of Queen Elizabeth I and went from a traveling fairground act to something housed in a permanent structure, distinctive stories about recognizable characters with sometimes ambiguous purposes and personalities developed.

## The Players

Actors, or as they were called, players, were all men. Women were forbidden to step on the stage, so boys played women's roles, as they still do in Kabuki and Noh theater. (In 1642 the Puritans shut down the theaters for twenty years; when they reopened during the restoration of the monarchy under King Charles II, women were finally allowed to act.)

It is interesting to note that of all the people in Shakespeare's companies, only one, Will Kemp, actually had a performing background. All of the others were from merchant families as was Shakespeare. The itinerant troubadours generally went about their business on the roads. Players needed a license to act, and the "carny" types couldn't do that. Actors were generally considered to be among the lowest of the low in society, akin to cutpurses (thieves), vagabonds, and beggars.

But it's also true that as the theater developed, Elizabethan actors became well skilled in singing, dancing, swordsmanship, throwing knives and axes, juggling, and performing sleight-of-hand tricks. There was no faking it. If a playwright needed a song, a player would sing it: if he needed a thrilling sword fight, there was no fumbling, clumsy jabbing, and poking at arm's length; the players should give the playwright and the audience the real thing without anyone getting hurt. However, the only skill you really needed in order to become an actor was the ability to memorize lines.

**FACTS**

Journeyman actors would be paid five shillings a week, (twenty shillings equals a pound), and more experienced actors would be paid ten shillings a week or fifteen shillings on the road.

The players in *Hamlet,* for example, pretty accurately recreate what acting troupes were like during Shakespeare's time:

HAMLET: Speak the speech, I pray you, as I pronounced it to you, trippingly on the tongue. But if you mouth it, as many of your players do, I had as lief the town-crier spoke my lines. Nor do not saw the air too much with your hand, thus; but use all gently: for in the very torrent, tempest, and, as I may say, whirlwind of your passion, you must acquire and beget a temperance that may give it smoothness. O, it offends me to the soul to hear a robustious periwig-pated fellow tear a passion to tatters, to very rags, to split the ears of the groundlings, who, for the most part, are capable of nothing but inexplicable dumb shows and noise. . . Pray you, avoid it. . . Be not too tame neither, but let your own discretion be your tutor. Suit the action to the word, the word to the action, with this special observance, that you o'erstep not the modesty of nature. For anything so overdone is from the purpose of playing, whose end, both at the first and now, was and is, to hold, as 'twere, the mirror up to nature, to show virtue her own feature, scorn her own image, and the very age and body of the time his form and pressure. Now this overdone or come tardy off, though it make the unskilful laugh, cannot but make the judicious grieve, the censure of the which one must in your allowance o'erweigh a whole theatre of others . . . And let those that play your clowns speak no more than is set down for them; for there be of them that will themselves laugh, to set on some quantity of barren spectators to laugh too, though in the mean time some necessary question of the play be then to be considered. That's villainous, and shows a most pitiful ambition in the fool that uses it.

## The Playwrights

The playwrights were often anonymous hacks, laboring in obscurity either in collaboration with others or in ill-paid anonymity. But even if they had "little Latin and less Greek"—as Ben Jonson, the university-educated playwright said of his contemporary and sometime friend William Shakespeare, the writer who had *not* gone to university—they could still get a copy of Holinshed's history book, *The Chronicles of English History*, North's translation of the Greek writer-philosopher Plutarch's *Lives of Noble Greeks and Romans*, Florio's translation of the Frenchman Montaigne, and many French and Italian romances that were making their way into English.

**SSENTIALS** Shakespeare's knowledge of people combined with his poetic skill made him the greatest of playwrights. In building his plays he seldom wrote a speech that did not forward the action, develop a character, or help the imagination of the spectator.

Shakespeare was also particularly influenced by Golding's translation of the *Metamorphoses*, not to mention the new translations of the Bible. It's from *Metamorphoses* that Shakespeare found the seeds of *Romeo and Juliet*, *Othello*, *Measure for Measure*, *As You Like It*, and *The Winter's Tale*. He transformed old folktales similar to those about King Arthur into dark tales of tragedy: *King Lear* and *Macbeth*.

## Reaching Modern Audiences

Copyright laws did not exist in Shakespeare's time, and playwrights were free to borrow plots and dialogue from other sources. Some experts, for example, think parts of *King Henry VI* were borrowed, while some of his Roman plays such as *Julius Caesar* and *Antony and Cleopatra* have been linked to North's translation of Plutarch's *Lives of Noble Greeks and Romans.* Playwrights thought nothing of wholesale adapting or filching of events, characterization, and even lines from previous works.

As a result, there was no real incentive for acting companies to publish the plays they commissioned until they had stopped acting the play. The versions sold to printers were called quartos and about half of Shakespeare's plays were first published this way, sometimes in pirated editions like the Bad Quarto of *Hamlet.* Not until his companion Ben Jonson oversaw the publishing of his own folio of dramas was publishing plays treated with some care and respect.

A number of Shakespeare's contemporaries still loom large and occasionally their plays are still performed. Chief among them were Ben Jonson and Christopher Marlowe who in their day were in some ways more famous than Shakespeare. Now considered to be Shakespeare's greatest literary rival, Marlowe died in a pub brawl at the age of twenty-nine, leaving behind several famous plays: *Doctor Faustus* (the text of which is very corrupted and has to be reassembled by whoever produces it), *Edward II, The Jew of Malta,* and *Tamburlaine I* and *II.* Shakespeare's work has passed the test of time. It is an important part of most classical educations and it continues to challenge modern day actors and directors who continue to find relevance and meaning in the plays for contemporary audiences.

**SSENTIALS**  Many of Shakespeare's plots seem farfetched. The Elizabethans were romantics who loved poetry. People did not go to the theater to see real life. They wanted to be carried away to other times and places or to a land of fancy. The imaginative reader today loves him for the same reason.

## Little Fame, Little Glory

Just as it is today, the actors, not the authors, were the stars that drew the audiences. Usually, playwrights would propose their ideas to a theater company. If the manager liked the idea the writer would be commissioned to write the play. Sometimes the company manager would come up with the idea and approach a well-known dramatist to put the idea into play form. It was not uncommon for a company to commission several writers to write about the same idea; then the manager would cut and paste the versions into one play, or another writer would be hired to revise the work.

The going rate was about £4 a play (in today's money that would be many times as much, and translated into dollars would be perhaps $700–$1,000). Once sold, a play became the property of the company. Authors of successful plays—ones that ran more than the average ten performances—might get bonuses.

## To Play or Not to Play

As the theater developed, the need for sponsorship from the great lords diminished, except for the license to operate, and actors began to be able to support themselves through their craft. A large part of this independence was due to the growth of theaters in London, a thriving city nestling against the banks of the River Thames since the days of the Romans. As the century drew to a close, ships sailed up the Thames from foreign ports and departed on the turn of the tide as London sent its sons and daughters as far afield as newly colonized Virginia in the New World, while welcoming travelers from all over the known world.

## The Queen's Protection

Presiding over the growth of art and drama and maritime adventure was the aging queen. Elizabeth was childless and unmarried; her advancing age and the likelihood that the throne would soon stand empty threatened the peace and security of the nation with potential civil wars or the imposition of foreign potentates. All of these fears and wonders, in his own way, Shakespeare wrote about.

Most plays were staged during the daytime, and the local authorities often cast an unwelcoming eye on players and their audiences. The city alderman and constables feared that the theaters would become meeting places for mobs and disaffected groups, as well as dangerous centers of infection in times of plague. The Earl of Essex's attempted coup against Queen Elizabeth I was to have begun with a performance of *King Richard II*. Luckily Shakespeare and company suffered no aftereffects except stiff questioning from the authorities.

Meanwhile, disease was constantly forcing the theaters to close and the acting troupes to take to the road. The actors were allowed to follow their vocation under sufferance, however, because the rich, particularly the queen, demanded their entertainment.

## Attacking Moral Purity

The Protestant clergy considered the theater an attack on the moral purity of the populace, particularly the young. In 1583 in his *The Anatomie of Abuses*, religious leader Philip Stubbes declared that far from teaching men and women how to be better people, plays offered instruction in how to lie, cheat, steal, and deceive: "If you will learn to jest, laugh and leer, to grin, to nod, and mow [fornicate]; if you will learn to play the vice, to swear, tear, and blaspheme both Heaven and Earth; if you will learn to become a bawd, unclean, and to deviriginate maids, to deflower honesty wives; if you will learn to murder, flay, kill, pick, steal, rob, and row . . ." Well, you get the idea. The Puritans, to give them their due, also didn't approve of the animal baiting, which took place at the theaters.

Because of the official hostility to plays and players, most companies consisted of about a dozen or so regular players and looked for protection through patronage. Shakespeare began his career with Lord Leicester's Men, then joined a troupe called the Lord Chamberlain's Men with acting stars such as Richard Burbage and Will Kemp, a famous comedic actor. The troupe was renamed the King's Men when James I came to the throne. Rival companies had names such as the Lord Admiral's Men, which starred Edward Alleyn.

# Choice Theaters

In 1576 James Burbage, a former carpenter and then the actor/manager of Lord Leicester's Men, leased a piece of land in Shoreditch, just north of the London city limits, and built the first permanent theater called, appropriately enough, the Theatre. (Burbage's son, Richard, later headed a company of actors with Shakespeare.) A second theater was built nearby the next year. Building permanent theaters within the London city limits was prohibited.

Other theaters on the north bank of the Thames soon followed, including the Curtain and the Fortune. Builders of permanent theaters sought to avoid the interference of the local authorities, so they also built on the south bank of the Thames River in what could be thought of as a sort of "downtown" or entertainment area in Shoreditch, where you could also find brothels, gambling dens, and bull- and bear-baiting arenas. Here you could find the Rose, the Swan, and eventually the Globe flourishing.

**FACTS**

As people entered the Globe theatre, they would drop their admission fee into a box. The practice continues today in the name of the box office at the front of the theater.

In 1598, Richard Burbage lost the lease to his father's theater, which fell into disrepair. In the dead of night, he and his players had to sneak the building timbers off the property before the landowner confiscated them. They dismantled the building, transported it piece by piece across the frozen River Thames, and reassembled it on the south bank of the river and called it the Globe.

The theater provided a good annual profit of several hundred pounds—a comfortable amount for Elizabethan times—for a consortium of people that included Burbage and Shakespeare. In 1613, during a performance of *King Henry VIII* some wadding from one of the stage cannons caught the thatched roof alight, and the theater burned to the ground.

Different companies adopted particular theaters as their "homes" even if they toured the countryside and gave performances in the houses of noble patrons. The Blackfriars, for instance, was a small indoor theater that housed a troupe of boy actors, offering highbrow theater for nobles (as did other boy companies) until it was taken over by Shakespeare's King's Men after the Globe burned down. Scholars speculate that some of Shakespeare's later plays, particularly the more contemplative works such as *The Tempest* and *The Winter's Tale*, may have been composed for the more intimate setting of the Blackfriars, and its richer, more sophisticated audiences.

## Stage Construction

The stage still had little scenery, no front curtain to hide the bare stage, and little or no stage machinery for special effects. A chorus, or dialogue, established the scene. Entrances and exits were through two doorways to the "tiring house" (a corruption of "attiring house") backstage.

### The Stage

However, the theater was by no means a drab affair. A lack of scenery was compensated for by magnificent costumes. Even if the play was supposed to take place in ancient Egypt (*Antony and Cleopatra*) or some mythical far-off Island Kingdom, the audiences knew that the plays were really about themselves, and so there was little attempt to make the costumes fit the time or style of the setting.

**FACTS**

The battle scenes were accompanied by loud bangs and smoke, with braying trumpets sounding the start and announcing the arrival of important characters. Music played a large part in Elizabethan theater, and often incidental music that included jigs and reels and clowning was used, even when the main event was a tragic play such as *King Lear*.

The "dead" were carried off in dramatic flourishes because there was no other way to get the bodies off the stage. Some stages had a curtained alcove, set off to one side, for small, more intimate, or intense scenes, such as the murder of Desdemona in *Othello*. There might also be an open gallery or balcony high up on the back wall of the stage where Romeo could climb up to pursue his love Juliet.

The groundlings were left open to the elements, but the stage was covered by a roof; the exposed underside would sometimes be painted with a moon and stars. A trapdoor in the stage would allow a "ghost" such as in *Macbeth* to arise, or for the gravedigger scene in *Hamlet*.

## The Audience

Unlike the modern theater, where the expensive seats put you almost on the stage, and certainly near the front of the theater, the "cheap seats" weren't seats at all, but a courtyard open to the sky in front of the stage where the groundlings, or common folk, stood. They were usually an opinionated, often drunken, unruly mob of laborers, less-skilled artisans, and prostitutes who lived near the theater and no doubt saw an opportunity to make some money when a play was being performed.

The groundlings stood in a rough circle some sixty feet or more in length in front of a stage that stood some five feet off the ground, was about forty feet in width, and had a jetty-like piece that jutted into the audience as much as twenty feet or more. The vertical walls of the theater in front of the stage had a number of "boxes" or galleries that were reached by steep staircases. On a good day, a packed house could have upwards of 3,000 people in the audience.

Given the nature of the audience, we can presume that feedback was instantaneous, with shouts of encouragement and applause for what worked, and boos and rotten fruit and vegetables thrown onstage for what didn't work. The groundlings would have paid a penny, which was close to a day's wages, to see the play, and they wanted value for their money. The price was at least double for the boxed seats. It's been estimated that a penny would approximate the cost of a movie in a big city today.

## CHAPTER 3
# *Did Shakespeare Write Shakespeare?*

O f all the great writers in the Western literary canon, Shakespeare is unique in the enigma he presents. Despite several hundred years of scholarship, doubts still remain that the Stratford man wrote what we consider to be "The Collected Works of William Shakespeare."

# The Oxfordians and the Stratfordians

Was there really a William Shakespeare of Stratford? Or was Shakespeare someone else, for example, Edward de Vere, the seventeenth Earl of Oxford? Two main schools have arisen: the Oxfordians, who promote the idea of de Vere as the author of the plays and poems (all told, some sixty candidates vie for the honor of writing Shakespeare's works) and the Stratfordians, who contend that Shakespeare wrote Shakespeare.

## The Oxfordian Stance

Sincere and intelligent people have believed that strong evidence exists to prove that Shakespeare did not write Shakespeare. Among them are Walt Whitman, Mark Twain, Sigmund Freud, Helen Keller, Orson Welles, Muriel Spark, Malcolm X, and Supreme Court Justice Harry Blackmun. As Ralph Waldo Emerson put it, "I cannot marry the life to the work."

The Oxfordians claim that those who support the Stratford man are blinded to the evidence by a vested self-interest. More extreme Oxfordians claim that Stratfordians are engaged in an active conspiracy to suppress pro-Oxford evidence. The truth, however, is far more mundane. Oxfordians are not taken seriously by the Shakespeare establishment because most of them do not follow basic standards of scholarship, and the "evidence" they present is either distorted, taken out of context, or flat-out false.

**FACTS**

Thomas Looney's *Shakespeare Identified in Edward de Vere, 17th Earl of Oxford* is the first work to claim de Vere was the Bard. On the flip side of the argument, Dave Kathman's articles, which can be found on the Internet, put forward strong reasons why Shakespeare was really Shakespeare.

## The Stratfordian Argument

The Stratfordians maintain that one of the greatest difficulties with the Earl of Oxford's writing Shakespeare's plays is the fact that de Vere died in 1604, yet still managed to produce some of his greatest plays post-mortem, as it were. These plays include *King Lear* (c. 1605–6), *Macbeth* (c. 1606–7), *Antony and Cleopatra* (c. 1606–7), *Coriolanus* (c. 1608), *Cymbeline* (c. 1608–10), *The Winter's Tale* (c. 1609–11), and *The Tempest* (c. 1611). Most Oxfordians concede that these plays postdate de Vere's death but argue that de Vere wrote the plays before he died, and that they were brought out as needed for performance, sometimes with added contemporary references to events after 1604 in order to make them look timely.

**FACTS**

In 1769, the actor/manager David Garrick staged a Shakespeare Jubilee at Stratford, and from that time on Stratford became the mecca for those pilgrims who worship the Bard.

The problem with this argument is that when you examine the body of Shakespeare's plays as a whole, it's possible to trace a definable stylistic development. As David Bevington, professor of English Language and Literature at the University of Chicago said in a 1989 PBS *Frontline* documentary about this issue:

> The argument [that de Vere wrote Shakespeare] has to posit a conspiracy of staggering proportions. Shakespeare, according to this scenario, agreed to serve as a front man for Oxford because the writing of plays was below the dignity of a great man. Shakespeare's friends in the company agreed to serve up his plays in the years after Oxford's death, publicizing the plays as by Shakespeare. Persons who knew Shakespeare well, like Ben Jonson, went along with the fiction, writing economiastac verses for Shakespeare after his death in 1613. The acting company, especially Shakespeare's colleagues John Heminges and Henry Condell, supervised the publication of all of the plays (except *Pericles*, *Cardenio*, and *The Two Noble Kinsmen*, which are regarded as collaborations) in a handsome Folio volume in 1616, essentially the first of its kind to recognize a dramatist. Many writers poured out their praise for

England's great national poet and playwright, and some of them knew Shakespeare. All of these people had to be either deceived by the presumed coverup or, in many cases, accessories to a hoax.

## Lack of Formal Education

That Shakespeare wasn't Shakespeare didn't occur to anyone before the nineteenth century. Before then, everyone celebrated Shakespeare as the great English writer of genius. The debate can be couched in terms of "class warfare," which is difficult for Americans to grasp.

As a newly emerging Victorian middle class arose and a liberal university education became the distinguishing mark of a gentleman, it became important for people to reinforce the superiority of their own lifestyle by thinking that Shakespeare's plays and poems could have been the work only of a university-educated gentleman rather than the genius of a somewhat self-taught middle-class glover's son. What's more, to add fuel to controversy, writers such as Christopher Marlowe and Ben Jonson *did* attend university, although others, like John Webster and Thomas Dekker, apparently did not.

The point that many scholars miss is that writing is about observing and reflecting the human condition. It is also about reading, and a great deal was being printed for the first time in English around Shakespeare's time, as we've seen. What's more, if you examine the careers of great writers throughout history, their formal academic education was the least relevant aspect of their success as a writer.

**E**SSENTIALS Playwrights did not have to be courtiers themselves to accurately portray court life, just as journalists today can recreate and interpret what happens in the White House or Congress without being administration or elected officials.

In fact, many writers have come primarily from social classes below those of the ruling class. For example, James Joyce, D. H. Lawrence, Harold Pinter, Sam Shepard, John Arden, and Arnold Wesker all came from the working classes or middle classes. In prenineteenth century times, John Webster was the son of a merchant tailor; Edmund Spenser's father was a cloth maker; Christopher Marlowe's father was a shoemaker in Canterbury; Ben Jonson's stepfather was a bricklayer. While these promising young men were well educated at schools such as the Merchant Taylor's School in London and the Westminster School, not all went on to university.

However, these men had enough education to challenge the concept of "knowing their place" and move to thinking "outside the box," as it were, and beyond society's expectations of them, and they became writers in London. There, the theater among other opportunities provided them both employment and intellectual stimulation, and drew them into a world of urbane events. They either observed or became peripheral participants in the goings-on of kings and nobles, and were able to write compelling pictures of courtly life in their plays.

## Is Hard Evidence Needed?

The lack of manuscripts or handwriting samples (we may indeed have some of Shakespeare's handwriting in some additions made to several pages of a play he was either editing or collaborating on called *Sir Thomas More,* which was never produced) and the uncertainties about certain periods of Shakespeare's life are all in keeping with a playwright of the period.

Play scripts, like many movie scripts today, existed so that an acting company could stage a play. The wonder is that so many of Shakespeare's plays were published at all. We have no manuscripts of plays by Marlowe or Jonson or Webster, even though some of their plays rival Shakespeare's in their literary and dramatic qualities and their authorship is not generally questioned.

No one suggests that Marlowe wasn't written by Marlowe or Jonson by Jonson. So why is Shakespeare singled out? The answer lies mainly in his greatness. True geniuses are few and far between, and there are those such as Einstein and Shakespeare who defied their backgrounds as their genius flowered. Shakespeare is among the greatest of our thinkers and creators, and so he is the subject of intense speculation.

## Influence of Society

Some people believe that the question of authorship is inspired by today's society. Today, we live in an era where democracy and being yourself, particularly in the arts, has sometimes come to mean mediocrity and license, with little real artistic merit needed beyond an ability to command attention at the moment.

**SSENTIALS**    Some men known personally to Shakespeare—for example, Francis Meres and Ben Jonson—did recognize his worth. And to argue that an obscure Stratford boy could not have become the Shakespeare of literature is to ignore the mystery of genius.

"Great art" is often defined by how much money something earns, and everyone, as the artist Andy Warhol said, "will get their fifteen minutes of fame." Shakespeare has become an icon of Western literature that must be toppled in order that the rest of us can feel that what we do has some worth.

## Too Many Questions, Not Enough Answers

What could be more exciting than solving a mystery? What happened to the crew of the *Marie Celeste?* Is there a Bermuda triangle? What really happened in the Kennedy assassination? or Who wrote Shakespeare's plays? Such detective work appeals to lawyers and businesspeople who like to pursue Shakespeare as a hobby.

Imagine if you can, that an enthusiastic amateur could show the professional scholars that all of Western culture has been bamboozled over the centuries by a hoax, and that Shakespeare is really the Earl of Oxford.

As David Bevington writes, "If Oxford was so eager that someone should 'Report me and my cause aright/To the unsatisfied,' why did he leave such enigmatic clues? Was the stigma of being a playwright so huge that he could tell no one, not even write it down for his friends? Ultimately the case collapses on lack of motive as well as lack of evidence, for it presupposes a social history of how playwrights got to be playwrights that is simply not in keeping with historical reality."

## Candidates for Shakespeare

Why are there so many candidates, and why should we choose de Vere over such illustrious figures as Francis Bacon or Christopher Marlowe? Actually, of all Elizabethans put forward since the middle of the eighteenth century as the "true Shakespeare," only four have merited serious consideration: Sir Francis Bacon (Lord Verulam), Christopher Marlowe, William Stanley (Sixth Earl of Derby), and Edward de Vere (Seventeenth Earl of Oxford).

Irvin Leigh Matus's *Shakespeare, In Fact* (Continuum, 1994) is a good examination of the authorship question. Charlton Ogburn's *The Mysterious William Shakespeare* is generally considered the most thorough exposition of the Oxfordian case. In 1997, Joseph Sobran's *Alias Shakespeare* introduced many newcomers to the Shakespeare authorship question.

FACTS

Since the 1800s, different scholars have attempted to prove that Shakespeare did not write the plays or that others did. For a long time the leading candidate was Sir Francis Bacon. In fact, nearly every famous Elizabethan has been named. Some people even claim that "Shakespeare" is an assumed name for a whole group of poets and playwrights.

The contest, summed up by *Frontline* correspondent Al Austin, "comes down to this: Those who believe de Vere was Shakespeare must accept an improbable hoax as part of it, a conspiracy of silence involving among others, Queen Elizabeth herself. Those who side with the Stratford man must believe in miracles." Or, it might be added, accept the nature of genius for what it is—a rarity of generational proportions.

## CHAPTER 4
# Shakespeare's Rivals

Shakespeare was not the only playwright of his time, and was not even the most famous for most of his writing career. After the success of the Theatre and the Globe, quite a few theaters sprang up and playwriting became a way to fame and fortune. Would-be playwrights flocked to London, much in the same way that aspiring screenwriters today head to Hollywood.

# Christopher Marlowe

It's generally acknowledged that the greatest of Shakespeare's rivals was Christopher Marlowe (1564–1593). Marlowe was the second child and eldest son of John Marlowe, a Canterbury shoemaker. Nothing is known of his first schooling, but on January 14, 1579, he entered the King's School, Canterbury, as a scholar. A year later he went to Corpus Christi College in Cambridge and received his Bachelor of Arts degree in 1584.

**FACTS**

A group of playwrights who became known as the University Wits sprang up in the closing years of the sixteenth century, all of whom in some way or another helped pave the way for Shakespeare's success. One of the pioneers was John Lyly. Others included Thomas Lodge, George Peele, Christopher Marlowe, Robert Greene, and Thomas Nashe. Another of the Wits, though not university-trained, was Thomas Kyd.

He continued in residence at Cambridge, which may suggest that he was intending to take Anglican orders. However, according to university records, Marlowe disappeared frequently during his last years at college, putting his degree in jeopardy. The university's doubts were apparently set at rest after the Privy Council sent a letter declaring that Marlowe had been employed "on matters touching the benefit of his country"— apparently in Elizabeth I's secret service.

It's likely that a lot of this time was spent in Rheims, France, among the Catholics who were plotting against Queen Elizabeth's Protestant regime. It's also possible that Marlowe fought in the wars in the Low Country after graduation.

## Marlowe's Playwriting Career

What is certain is that by 1587 Marlowe was living in London and had begun his career as a playwright—although he may still have been working for William Cecil in the newly created secret service. Marlowe also earned a dangerous reputation for atheism. In Robert Greene's deathbed tract, *Greenes groats-worth of witte*, he calls Marlowe a "famous gracer of Tragedians" and reproved him for having said, as did Greene himself, "There is no god."

The young poet was quickly in the heady company of poets and adventuring soldiers such as Sir Phillip Sidney and Sir Walter Raleigh. He roomed with fellow playwright Thomas Kyd, and often frequented the taverns of London with the likes of Robert Greene and Thomas Nashe. His magnificent appearance, impulsiveness, and bejeweled costumes soon became the talk of the town.

In a playwriting career that lasted not much more than six years, Marlowe's achievements were remarkable. Before leaving Cambridge he had already written *Tamburlaine the Great* (a two-part play performed by the end of 1587 and published in 1590). He also translated Ovid's *Amores (The Loves)* and the first book of Lucan's *Pharsalia* from Latin. He also cowrote the play *Dido, Queen of Carthage* (published in 1594 with Thomas Nashe). It was *Tamburlaine the Great*, the first notable English play in blank verse, that won him recognition and acclaim. None of his other plays, poems, or translations were published during his life, but his unfinished *Hero and Leander* is considered by many to be one of the finest examples of nondramatic Elizabethan poetry composed before Edmund Spenser's *Faerie Queene*.

**ESSENTIALS**

Scholars argue about the order of plays after *Tamburlaine* was written. Many think *Dr. Faustus* was next, followed by *Edward II* and *The Massacre at Paris*. Marlowe's last play may have been *The Jew of Malta*.

It wasn't until Marlowe and Shakespeare began their careers in the 1580s that dramatic poetry began to flourish. England took pride in its poets, and a new breed of actor appeared that was able and willing to give dramatic life to the new style of play that was developing. The Lord Admiral's company, one of the premier acting companies in London, presented Marlowe's plays. While his contemporaries were watching their work performed by church boys, Marlowe saw his dramas staged by full-chested men such as the seven-foot-tall, outstanding actor Edward Alleyn who played Tamburlaine, Faustus, and Barabbas the Jew.

*Dr. Faustus* is Marlowe's most famous play, but it has survived only in a corrupt form. It was first published in 1604; another version appeared in 1616. Nevertheless, no playwright had previously invoked the world, the flesh, and the devil so magnificently and with such powerful and lyrical language. However, while the acclaim piled up, the money didn't, and Marlowe became more and more restless and irritable until even his friends began to lose patience with him.

## Heresy and Death

In 1593, after pointing out what he considered to be inconsistencies in the Bible, Marlowe fell under suspicion of heresy. His roommate, Thomas Kyd, was tortured into giving evidence against him. On May 18, 1593, the Privy Council issued an order for Marlowe's arrest; two days later the poet was ordered to give daily attendance on their lordships "until he shall be licensed to the contrary."

On May 30, 1593, the twenty-nine-year-old poet went to Dame Eleanore Bull's tavern in Deptford to have dinner with some friends: Ingram Frizer, Nicholas Skeres, and Robert Poley. According to witnesses, there was a quarrel over the bill and Marlowe drew his dagger on Frizer, who defended himself by driving the dagger back into the young poet's eye, mortally wounding him.

## John Lyly

John Lyly (c. 1554–1606) is considered the first English prose stylist to leave a lasting impression upon the language. He was educated at Magdalen College, Oxford, and went to London in 1576. He gained recognition with the publication of two prose romances, *Euphues: The Anatomy of Wit* (1578) and *Euphues and His England* (1580). These poems made him the major writer of the 1580s. *Euphues* is a story told in letters interspersed with general discussions on religion and love. Lyly's style became known as euphuism.

In 1583 he gained control of the first Blackfriars Theatre, in which his comedies were produced. The players in his comedies were the Children of Paul's, a children's company that periodically played for Queen Elizabeth. The finest of his plays is considered to be *Endimion* (1588), which some critics hold as a masterpiece.

**FACTS**

**Lyly's popularity waned with the rise of Thomas Kyd, Christopher Marlowe, and William Shakespeare, and his appeals to Queen Elizabeth for financial relief went unheeded. He had hoped to succeed Edmund Tilney in the court post of Master of the Revels, but Tilney outlived him, and Lyly died a poor and bitter man.**

Lyly's comedies marked an enormous advance in English drama. Their plots are drawn from classical mythology and legend. While his characters are often engaged in euphuistic speeches filled with flowery Renaissance pedantry, the charm and wit of the dialogues and the skillful construction of the plots set standards that younger and more gifted dramatists could not ignore.

## Thomas Kyd

The details of Thomas Kyd's (1558–1594) life are obscure, though it's known that he shared a room with Christopher Marlowe for a while. He is best known for *The Spanish Tragedie* (1589) (sometimes called Hieronimo, or Jeronimo, after its protagonist), which initiated the Elizabethan revenge tragedy genre. The son of a professional copyist or scrivener, Kyd was educated at the Merchant Taylors School in London. There is no evidence that he attended a university before turning to literature. He seems to have been in service for some years with Ferdinando, Lord Strange, the patron of Lord Strange's Men.

It is not known which company first played *The Spanish Tragedie* nor when, but Strange's company played it sixteen times in 1592, and the Admiral's Men revived it in 1597, as did the Chamberlain's Men. The play became the most popular and influential tragedy of its day and was even more popular than Shakespeare's plays. It continued to be performed throughout the Elizabethan period.

Many critics believe that Hieronimo in *The Spanish Tragedie* prepared the way for Shakespeare's psychological study of Hamlet. Kyd did not share Marlowe's towering poetic ability, but his brilliance came from an instinctive grasp of the tragic form and what worked best on the stage. By 1589 he had written a lost *Hamlet*—sometimes referred to as the *Ur-Hamlet*—which may have been the model for Shakespeare's tragedy.

The only other play that can be attributed to Kyd with certainty is *Cornelia* (1594), which was adapted from a French play by Robert Garnier. *Soliman and Perseda* is usually attributed to him as well on the basis of style and the fact that it has the same plot as *The Spanish Tragedie.*

**ESSENTIALS**

Another play sometimes attributed to Kyd is *Arden of Feversham*, a dramatization of a crime that had been reported in Holinshed's *Chronicles*. Kyd's authorship of this play has come into doubt, but if he is indeed the author, then Kyd is the founder of middle-class tragedy as well as the revenge play.

In 1593, after falling under suspicion of heresy, his rooms were searched and certain "atheistical" disputations denying the deity of Jesus Christ were found. He was arrested for atheism and tortured into giving evidence against his roommate, Marlowe. Kyd denied the charge of atheism, claiming the offending evidence belonged to his roommate. The situation is rich with irony. The innovator of the revenge genre may well have been set up by Marlowe. Kyd may have returned the favor, and Marlowe's subsequent death could have been a covertly arranged murder.

Kyd was eventually released from prison, but had been broken by his imprisonment, torture, and disgrace. He died in poverty in December 1594, not yet thirty-six years old, his debt-ridden estate repudiated by his mother.

# Ben Jonson

A close friend of Shakespeare, Ben Jonson (1572–1637) is generally regarded as the second most important English dramatist of the Jacobean period, after William Shakespeare. His Protestant father, who had been imprisoned and deprived of his estate during the Catholic reign of Mary Tudor, died when he was young. His mother, left penniless and with no means of supporting her young son, was forced to marry a bricklayer.

Though his stepfather was a bricklayer, by good fortune the boy was able to attend Westminster School. The scholar Camden recognized Jonson's exceptional literary ability and took the young man under his wing. Though Jonson never received a formal university education, because of Camden's instruction Jonson became one of the most learned men of Elizabethan and Jacobean times, and eventually received honorary degrees from Oxford and Cambridge universities.

His formal education, however, ended early, and at first he followed his stepfather's trade, then fought with some success with the Protestant English forces in the Netherlands. The Orange Men were defending their religious and political freedom against Catholicism and Spanish rule. The fiery young poet proved to be a formidable soldier. In one particular incident, advancing before the English volunteers, he challenged a Spaniard to a single combat sword fight, killed him, and then, in an act straight out of Homer's *Odyssey*, stripped the corpse of its armor.

**SSENTIALS**

In 1596, his wife gave birth to a son whom Jonson called his "best piece of poetry." He was devastated when the boy died of the plague at age seven. Jonson plunged himself into the bohemian life of the city, drank a lot, and got into fights.

He returned to England in 1592, married a woman whom he would later describe as "a shrew, yet honest," and became an actor and playwright, though how good an actor was open to debate. (Good enough to play the leading role of Hieronimo in Kyd's *The Spanish Tragedie* it seems.) By 1597 he was writing plays for Philip Henslowe,

London's leading impresario. With one exception (*The Case Is Altered*), these early plays are known only by their titles.

## Rising Above

It was not until 1598 that he finally emerged from the crowd of unrecognized playwrights with *Every Man in His Humour*. Dedicated to Master Camden, *Every Man in His Humour* is a comedic masterpiece that paints a telling portrait of the Elizabethan age. Presented by the Lord Chamberlain's Men, legend has it that Shakespeare himself recommended his friend's play to them.

That same year Jonson got into a quarrel with the actor Gabriel Spencer and, in a duel, killed the man, though his blade was ten inches shorter than Spencer's. He was imprisoned and escaped capital punishment by pleading "benefit of clergy"—the ability to read from the Latin Bible. He was, however, branded on the thumb and his property confiscated.

**FACTS**

In 1606 Jonson and his wife were brought before the consistory court in London to explain why they failed to go to church. He denied that his wife was guilty but admitted that his own religious opinions held him aloof from attendance. The matter was resolved by his agreeing to debate learned men, who might persuade him if they could.

His release was celebrated by the performance of his new play *Every Man Out of His Humour* (1599). It was the longest play ever written for the Elizabethan public theater. The play, however, proved a disaster, and Jonson had to look elsewhere for a theater to present his work. The obvious place was a private theater, in which only young boys acted. The high price of admission they charged meant a select audience, and they were willing to try strong satire and formal experiment. Jonson wrote *Cynthia's Revels* (1600) and *Poetaster* (1601).

He made a mark second only to Shakespeare's in the public theater. His comedies *Volpone* or *The Foxe* (1606) and *The Alchemist*

(1610) were among the most popular and acclaimed plays of the period and are still performed today. Both plays are eloquent, compact, and satirical.

## Collaborations

Although constantly quarreling with his fellow playwrights, Jonson managed to collaborate with John Marston and George Chapman on *Eastward Ho!* (1605), a play that landed them all in prison. The play contained an unflattering reference to Scottish royalty and the new king, James I (formerly James VI of Scotland) took offense. Chapman and Marston were thrown into prison, and Jonson joined them there voluntarily, claiming equal responsibility for the play. In the end, they were spared—probably because of the newfound popularity Jonson was beginning to enjoy as a writer of masques for the court. Jonson also won royal attention with his *Entertainment at Althorpe*, presented to the new queen as she journeyed to England from Scotland in 1603.

The masque was a quasi-dramatic entertainment, primarily providing a pretense for a group of strangers to dance and sing before an audience of guests and attendants in a royal court or nobleman's house. During the reign of James I, it became an elaborate affair, partly because the architect Inigo Jones provided increasingly magnificent costumes and scenic effects for masques at court.

SSENTIALS

The Restoration dramatists' (post-1660) use of type names for their characters came directly from what was called "Jonsonian humour." In the late Jacobean and Caroline years, Jonson, Shakespeare, and Francis Beaumont and John Fletcher provided all the models. But it was Jonson, and Jonson alone, who gave the essential impulse to dramatic characterization in comedy of the Restoration and also into the eighteenth and nineteenth centuries.

It was Jonson, in collaboration with Jones, who gave the Jacobean masque its characteristic shape and style. That the two men should quarrel seemed inevitable, and the friction led to a complete break.

Jonson wrote the *Twelfth Night* masque for the court in 1625, but then had to wait five years before the court again asked for his services.

## Death

In 1628 he suffered what was apparently a stroke and, as a result, was confined to his room and chair, then ultimately to his bed. That same year he was made city chronologer and theoretically responsible for the city's pageants. In 1634 his salary for the post was made into a pension. Jonson died in 1637 and was buried in Westminster Abbey.

## John Marston

John Marston (1575–1634), one of the first Elizabethan satirists, was a playwright who helped pave the way for Jonson's later success. A good definition of a satire is a play where human faults and vices are exposed and made ridiculous. Marston came from a good family and was a gentleman.

In 1605, *Eastward Ho!* got him a jail sentence for insulting the new king, James I. He wrote one other play in 1606, after which he seems to have retired from the theater. Later in Marston's life, he joined the church and took orders. Marston was a great satirist of his time and was in constant competition with Ben Jonson, another of Shakespeare's rival playwrights.

## Beaumont and Fletcher

The names Francis Beaumont and John Fletcher go side by side in English literature, partly because of their collaborations and partly because they were asked to append introductory poems to Jonson's *Volpone*.

According to John Aubrey, the notorious seventeenth-century gossip and diarist, the two playwrights "lived together on the Banke side, not far from the Play-house, both batchelors. They lay together . . . had one wench in the house between them . . . the same cloathes and cloake, &c., betweene them."

Of the fifty-four plays with which their names or the names of their other collaborators are associated, one or two were written by Beaumont alone and only nine or ten were Beaumont and Fletcher collaborations. Beaumont's hand also probably appears in three other plays written together with Fletcher and Philip Massinger.

Attempts to disentangle the various shares of Beaumont and Fletcher in any given work are complicated by the fact that Beaumont sometimes revised Fletcher's scenes, and Fletcher edited some of Beaumont's work.

In the three masterpieces of the Beaumont and Fletcher collaboration, *The Maides Tragedy*, *Philaster*, and *A King and No King*, scholars assume that Beaumont had the controlling hand, since the plays manifest a firmer structure than Fletcher's single or collaborative efforts.

## John Fletcher

John Fletcher's (1579–1625) father, Richard Fletcher, was a successful clergyman who became the bishop successively of Bristol, Worcester, and London, gaining a measure of fame as a tormenting accuser in the trial of Mary, Queen of Scots, and as the chaplain sternly officiating at her execution.

When not quite twelve years old, Fletcher was accepted to Corpus Christi College, Cambridge, and two years later became a Bible clerk. From the time of his father's death (1596) until 1607 nothing is known of him, although the evidence of his later plays indicates that he did not inherit his father's religious bigotry.

After 1613, Fletcher collaborated with or had his plays revised by Philip Massinger, who succeeded him in 1625 as chief playwright of the King's Men. Other collaborators included Nathan Field and William Rowley. Throughout his career he also wrote plays unaided. In 1625, while the plague raged in London, he lingered in the city to be measured for a suit of clothes instead of making his escape to the country. He died along with some 40,000 others.

## Francis Beaumont

Francis Beaumont (1585–1616) was the son of Francis Beaumont, justice of common pleas in Charnwood Forest, Leicestershire. Beaumont entered Pembroke College, Oxford in 1597, but on the sudden death of his father left the university without a degree. In November 1600 he entered London's Inner Temple with the intention of picking up his legal studies, but instead began to frequent the Mermaid Tavern.

In 1602 he published a poem, *Salmacis and Hermaphroditus*, a lush rewriting of a poem by Ovid. By 1607 Beaumont and Fletcher began collaborating on plays for the Children of the Queen's Revels and its successor, and then from 1609 until Beaumont's retirement in 1613, mainly for the King's Men at the Globe and Blackfriars theaters.

FACTS

In 1613 Beaumont married an heiress, Ursula Isley of Sundridge in Kent, and retired from the theater. He died in London in 1616, a month before Shakespeare, and was buried in Westminster Abbey. As a playwright, Beaumont remains a shadowy figure whose contributions to drama are not as clear as Fletcher's.

## John Ford

Because of his disdain for orthodoxy and his sympathetic treatment of unorthodox love, John Ford (1586–1639) is often considered the most modern of Elizabethan and Jacobean dramatists. He first appeared in print with *Fame's Memorial* (1606), a long elegy on the death of the Earl of Devonshire, followed by other occasional pieces before he finally concentrated on drama. His first attempt was likely the writing or revising of *A Bad Beginning Makes a Good Ending*, which was acted by the King's Men at court in 1612, and which was one of the four unprinted plays of Ford that were accidentally destroyed.

His career as a playwright took off in 1621, when he coauthored *The Witch of Edmonton* with Thomas Dekker and William Rowley.

He collaborated with Dekker on several other plays and with Webster for at least one. After 1624, however, he worked alone, and his reputation rests chiefly upon his three tragedies of forbidden love, *'Tis Pity She's a Whore*, *The Broken Heart*, and *Love's Sacrifice*.

## Thomas Middleton

As a teenager, Thomas Middleton (1580–1627) published *The Wisdom of Solomon Paraphrased* (1597) and *Micro-Cynicon, Six Snarling Satires* (1599), but didn't graduate from Queen's College, Oxford, until 1598. There is no record of his connection with the theater until May 22, 1602, when Henslowe records in his diary a payment made to him together with Munday, Drayton, and Webster "in earnest of a book called *Caesar's Fall*."

While he sometimes wrote alone, more often he wrote in collaboration with other well-known dramatists, notably Dekker and Rowley. Two satirical tales, *The Black Book* and *Father Hubbard's Tale* (1604), show his early interest in the underside of London life, which he was to turn to good account in his comedies of manners written between 1604 and 1611.

**FACTS**

The temporary amalgamation of the companies of Princess Elizabeth and Prince Charles in 1614 or so brought Middleton and Rowley together, and their period of collaboration began shortly thereafter. *The Changeling*, the best of Middleton and Rowley's joint efforts, written in 1622 and performed at Whitehall in 1624, was not published until 1653.

Middleton's one unaided tragedy, *Women, Beware Women*, written around 1612, was followed in 1613 by his first masque, *The Triumphs of Truth*, and until his death he was in demand as a writer of this type of entertainment. Middleton possesses no great poetic gift, but his strengths were in his ability to structure drama and his well-honed dramatic sense.

## John Webster

John Webster (c. 1580–1625) was the last of the great Elizabethan playwrights. Like many of his contemporaries, little of certainty is known of him. A John Webster was admitted to the Middle Temple on August 1, 1598 to study law. If this is the dramatist Webster it would explain the legal bent of many of his plays, including trial scenes in *The White Devil*, *The Devil's Law Case*, and *Appius and Virginia*.

The earliest known records of Webster's employment as a playwright are found in the diary of impresario Philip Henslowe, who noted in 1602 payments to Webster, Anthony Munday, Thomas Middleton, Michael Drayton, "and the rest" for a play entitled *Caesar's Fall*. Over the next decade, Henslowe's records show Webster collaborating with Dekker and Heywood, writing a prologue to Marston's *Malcontent*, and composing two masterpieces, *The White Devil* and *The Duchess of Malfi*.

Webster's scope has been criticized as limited as he wrote mostly about anguish and evil. But his poetry is of a high standard and holds its own with the best of Marlowe and Shakespeare. T.S. Eliot described Webster as the poet who was "much possessed by death, and saw the skull beneath the skin."

After *The Duchess of Malfi*, Webster lapsed into mostly second-rate work. His death c.1625 marked the decline of the Elizabethan theater. The stage was filled with mediocre writers such as Glapthorne, Brome, Markham, Suckling, and D'Avenant, reputed to be Shakespeare's illegitimate son. Then in 1642, the Puritans closed the public theaters, and there was darkness.

## CHAPTER 5
# *How to Understand Elizabethan English*

The thought of dealing with Shakespeare's work can seem quite daunting and about as accessible as Japanese Noh theater. More than likely the misperceptions about Shakespeare's language cause the hang-ups—all those old time "thees" and "thous" and "prithees" and "folderols"—fol-de-what?

# Shakespeare's Language

Shakespeare was a poet, and he used words not only to explain the plot but also to create word images, lots of them, to tell us what the characters were really feeling. For example, he writes, "Now is the winter of our discontent, made glorious summer by this son of York . . ." (*King Richard III)* to describe the murderous bleakness of the Wars of the Roses—a civil war between two major contenders, the dukes of Lancaster and York, for the throne of England that went on for decades—as "winter." That one word conjures up cold, rain, snow, damp, bleakness, hardship, and so on. He then describes the winner of the war at the time of the play's beginning, the duke of York, as a "son of York" and his victory a "glorious summer" using "summer" to create images of warmth, peace, prosperity, etc., that contrasts directly with the "winter" it was about to replace.

**ESSENTIALS** If you're going to enjoy Shakespeare, it's important to see the plays or at least listen to audiotapes of them, not just read them on your own. Plays are tough things to read at the best of times, and while the poetry of Shakespeare will spring from the pages soon enough, it helps to have a visual aid.

And what's really great about Shakespeare is that he does in two lines, with two potent words, what it just took me several sentences to try to explain. Does reading Shakespeare take effort? Yes it does, but like every new accent or language that seems foreign at first, after a while, a certain familiarity allows you to make sense of what is being said.

## The Context of Language

We take very much for granted that English is fast becoming the universal global language, despite the fact that statistically many more people speak Chinese, for example. But have you stopped to think that the English you speak today would be hard for someone living in Wyoming in 1900 to follow? "After the move, I'm going to the mall to get a new modem for my computer. I'll probably pop into a cybercafé while

I'm there and check my e-mail because I'm expecting my travel agent to confirm my flight to London tonight."

Language is all about context. And Shakespeare's language has a context you need to be familiar with in order to make sense of what's going on and why people say and do the things they do in the plays. Good productions of the plays try to take care of this issue by drawing parallels with our own time. That's why Shakespeare is sometimes done in modern dress or set in particular periods of modern history. It's an aid to help us follow what's going on and what's being said.

## Shakespeare's English

Many people unfamiliar with the world of William Shakespeare think he wrote and spoke a form of Old English. But the English he wrote is remarkably close to the language we use today. In fact, he is credited with inventing words and phrases that are now part of our everyday speech, such as laughingstock, hot-blooded, ill-tempered, cold-blooded, puppy dog, eyesore, sea change, salad days, bated breath, and bag and baggage to mention but a handful.

It is true, though, that Shakespeare's syntax is not always the "subject-verb-object" sentence structure with which we are familiar. Some of the words he used are now archaic, and some have changed their meaning. The plays assume some sort of rudimentary knowledge of Elizabethan events and history, and they are filled with references to Renaissance learning: Greek and Roman mythology, astrology, alchemy, and the theory of "humours."

**FACTS**

Elizabethans believed that a person's physical and mental attributes were the result of a balance of four fluids or humors—blood, phlegm, choler, and bile. Imbalances in these fluids accounted for mood swings and personality traits (a "choleric" person, for example, was bad tempered).

Shakespeare was a writer who was very aware of words and their meanings, but some of the subtleties of his language are difficult for modern audiences to appreciate because the words have changed meaning. For example, naughty now means badly behaved, but in Shakespeare's time it meant wicked.

# The Evolution of the English Language

The English language evolved from a combination of sources. Before 1066 C.E., Britain was invaded and colonized mainly by Angles, Saxons, and Jutes from Denmark and Germany who overran the Celtic-speaking natives, many of whom fled either west to Wales and Ireland or north to Scotland. Anglo-Saxon was a Germanic-sounding language, and perhaps the most important piece written in it was the epic poem *Beowulf*.

When the Norman king, William the Conqueror, defeated King Harold at the battle of Hastings in 1066 and made himself king of England the language underwent a drastic change. While the natives continued to speak Anglo-Saxon, their new lords and masters spoke Norman French. By 1400, a melding of languages had taken place, and thousands of French and Latin words had become absorbed into the Germanic Anglo-Saxon to create a language that is called Middle English.

**ESSENTIALS**

By Shakespeare's time, thousands of new words were entering the language from the publication of Greek and Latin texts, as well as books in Italian, French, and Spanish. Of the approximately 25,000 different words that Shakespeare used in his plays, 2,000 of them were ones he either invented or recorded for the first time.

The major change was one of structure, however. The basis of all modern European romance tongues—French, Italian, and Spanish—is Latin. Word order is not very important in Latin (or Anglo-Saxon) because the words take their meaning from the differing endings or inflections they can have depending on the work they're supposed to do in a sentence.

Middle English became a language that more closely resembles our own in terms of sentence structure. The elements of a sentence (subject, verb, object, etc.), became more dependent on word order than word form. One of the masterpieces of this period was Geoffrey Chaucer's *The Canterbury Tales*. Two hundred years later, by the time Shakespeare was born, English men and women and were speaking Early Modern English. Later Modern English, which is essentially what we speak today, is considered to date from the middle of the seventeenth century when the concepts of grammar and spelling were codified and made uniform.

## Elizabethan English

Perhaps because English was still in flux, Elizabethans were fascinated with language, even the unschooled groundlings, and they delighted in puns. In *Romeo and Juliet* for example, as Mercutio dies he says, "Ask for me tomorrow, and you shall find me a grave man." The pun, of course, is a play on grave meaning serious and grave meaning dead. In *King Henry IV, Part II*, the Lord Chief Justice tells off the fat knight Sir John Falstaff, one-time drinking companion of Prince Harry, soon to be King Henry V:

> Lord Chief Justice: Your means are very slender, and your waste is great.
>> ("Waste" is a pun on the size of Falstaff's waist, that is, on his being fat. It is also a reference to the fact that he doesn't have much money because he's wasted it on drink, women, and gambling.)

> Sir John Falstaff: I would it were otherwise; I would my means were greater and my waist slenderer.
>> (Falstaff cleverly turns the word play around.)

So what did Elizabethan English sound like? In Shakespeare's day English was not the Received English of the upper and middle classes that we hear now in many plays and movies, nor the clipped cockney accent of London. Surprisingly, it was probably closer to the accents of northern England, Scotland, and Ireland, and some dialects of the rural eastern and southern parts of the United States. The renowned British director Peter Hall has proposed an American Shakespearean theater company partly to try and recreate the authenticity of the sound of the language. Language experts say that the inhabitants of Ocracoke Island, part of the Outer Banks of North Carolina, which was originally founded by Elizabethan sailors and their families, speak the closest to Elizabethan English to this day.

**FACTS**

As English developed from Middle English to Modern English, it underwent what is called the Great Vowel Shift. The pronunciation of vowels in modern-day Continental Romance languages (ah/eh/ee/oh/oo) changed to what is now considered the Received Pronunciation of the English middle and upper classes and American Standard (eh/ee/ah/oh/yew).

The reason Peter Hall and others want to try to recapture the original pronunciation as much as possible is that the lines sometimes make much more sense when spoken in the original dialect. For instance, if you can imagine an Irish accent speaking the following lines from *Julius Caesar* you would not hear Cassius say, "Upon what *meat* doth this our Caesar *feed*, that he hath grown so great." Instead, you might well hear, "Upon what *mate* doth this our Caesar *fade* . . ." and now we have a clever play on words (mate, also meaning friend; fade meaning of lessening importance).

## Playing with Words

In Shakespeare's day, the syntax of the language and grammar itself were still evolving, so some lines need more careful reading than others. Like many Elizabethans, Shakespeare loved to play with words. What's more, because there were no rules as to how to write English yet and Shakespeare felt the need for his lines to have the rhythm of poetry or scan, he used a rather stretched out sentence structure.

## New Words, New Meanings

Because of the changes in the structure of language as English developed from Middle English to Modern English, writers were able to invent new uses for words. Shakespeare often used nouns as verbs or adjectives as nouns, for example. But the massive flow of foreign words into the English language during the sixteenth century created a multitude of variations for nearly every word. Shakespeare used this expanded vocabulary to make his language both more precise and more evocative.

In *Love's Labour's Lost* Berowne's ingenious comment, "Light, seeking light, doth light of light beguile" plays upon four different senses of *light*—meaning in order: intellect, wisdom, eyesight, and daylight—so the sentence can be interpreted as reading: Wisdom can be as enticing to intellectuals as daylight to a sighted person.

ssENTIALS

A lot of words have disappeared from use. For example, who says *micher* meaning a petty thief or *slubber* meaning clumsy and messy? In Chaucer's time *nice* meant ignorant or licentious; by Shakespeare's time it meant precise, as in a "nice distinction," and today it means pleasant.

## Shakespearean Style

Shakespeare also wrote in blank verse, that is, the lines do not have to rhyme. When they do, it is usually to mark the end of a scene because there were no curtains, and the rhyme itself gave the clue to the audience that they were about to experience a scene change. The plays' language did have a rhythm, however, commonly called an iambic pentameter. This is a flashy way of saying that a typical line has five, two-syllable units, with the emphasis on the second syllable. It's considered one of the most successful ways to write poetry that has a natural spoken form.

But Shakespeare also wrote in prose, which he often ascribed to the lower classes and the low born, while his kings spoke verse. However, King Lear speaks in prose as he goes mad (*King Lear*), and *The Merry Wives of Windsor* is mainly in prose.

Shakespeare also used a lot of metaphors and similes. Everyone drew on the Bible, using such phrases as strong as Samson or wicked as Herod. Comparisons were also made to the widely known Robin Hood and King Arthur stories. Members of the upper-middle-class and nobles sprinkled their speech with references to the Greek and Roman classics, such as beauteous as Venus or bright as Phoebus Apollo. Shakespeare also personified inanimate objects, saying that trees blushed, or seas were angry.

## Elizabethan Pronunciation

Because pronunciation is tough, it's great to see and hear the plays before you read them, if you can. Perhaps the most obvious sound is that of the rolled *R* as in *mother*. Think a drawn-out pirate ARRGH. In general, try to think Irish, or southern United States. The following list of word pronunciations will give you a flavor of the language as it was spoken.

**Father**—the long *a* sounds like *a* in favor: F-ay-th-u-rrr.

**Want**—the *a* here sounds like the *a* in apple.

**Make**—the *a* sounds like *mek*.

**Head**—the *eh* sounds like someone from the deep south of the United States as in *haid*, or *daid* for dead.

**I**—pronounced (like a 1950s doo-wop singer) in two vowels, as in the *u* in cup and the *ee* in bee, thus *uh-ee*. This is the quintessential peasant sound. Die becomes "duh-ee," my becomes "muh-ee."

**Down**—another doo-wop sound, pronounced *uh-oo* with the *oo* as in soon. Think Canadian, as in *abuh-oot* for about.

**Mercy**—the *ur* sound is pronounced *mayor-cy*.

**Neither**—pronounced *neigh-ther*.

**Lord**—drawn out *oo* sound as in lured.

**Cup**—a short and rounded *o* as in coop.

**ESSENTIALS** Thee and thou were informal pronouns used to anyone who was your equal and intimate. One is the subject, the other the object of the sentence. For example, I prithee (a contraction of I pray thee) take a sip, and thou hast a fair face.

# Elizabethan Vocabulary

It helps to be familiar with several vocabulary words when reading or listening to Shakespeare. The following is a list of some of the more common Elizabethan words and their definitions.

**Anon**—until later

**Arise**—stand up or to get an erection

**Aroint**—away

**Aside**—a speech revealing the character's innermost thought, spoken directly to the audience

**Aye/yea**—yes

**Banns**—notice of intent to marry

**Beef**—meat or hooker

**Broadside**—a sheet of paper printed on one side often used for proclamations and ballads

**Bum**—buttocks

**Certes!**—certainly!

**Cod**—fish or male organ (hence, codpiece is a cup that covered the male genitals)

**Count**—numbers or a pun on female genitalia

**Cousin**—friend

**Dear**—significant or expensive

**Die**—pass on or have an orgasm

**E'en**—evening

**Enow**—enough

**Fare-thee-well**—goodbye

**Fie**—a curse

**Fond**—foolish

**Get**—to create or bring into existence

**Grammarcy**—thank you

**Green**—inexperienced or a color or virility

**Head**—army or source

**Hell**—Hades or female genitalia

**Hello!**—not a greeting, but an exclamation of surprise

**Jade**—jewel or prostitute

**Marry**—a mild curse contracted from "by the Virgin Mary"

**Mayhap/perchance/belike**—maybe

**Morrow**—day

**Nay**—no

**Ne'er**—never

**Nice**—trifling or silly

**Oft**—often

**Poppet**—a doll or child

**Prithee/pray**—please

**Privy, jakes, or ajax**—bathroom or john

**Rub**—to strike against something or an obstacle

**Sad**—serious

**Soliloquy**—a speech, somewhat like an aside, revealing a character's thoughts

**Sonnet**—a fourteen-line poem with an iambic pentameter

**Stay**—to wait

**Still**—always

**Sweeting**—a term of endearment

**Ta'en**—short form of taken or mistaken for

**Tell**—to count

**Thane**—a Scottish earl

**Thing**—an object or male genitalia

**Verily**—very or truly

**Wherefore**—why

**Will**—a name or sexual desire

## CHAPTER 6

# *Scenes from Elizabethan Life*

W hat follows are thumbnail sketches of everyday life in Shakespeare's England that will give you a better sense of what the world was like during his time. Knowing what coins were used, how beggars were treated, and so forth provides a context in which to appreciate Shakespeare's brilliance in finding the timeless universal elements in what would have been the familiar to contemporary audiences.

# Servants and Masters

Male servants in a large household were called grooms or serving men. Women were called serving maids or just maids. The term valet or manservant came into use in English about 1567. In *Romeo and Juliet*, for example, Benvolio refers to Romeo's ever-present servant as "his man."

As a noble, it was undignified to fetch and carry for yourself. As a noble's servant, it was undignified to let your master or mistress do their own fetching and carrying. Everyone knew their places in the special order and were comforted by its predictable elements. Servants intended to take advantage of the social hierarchy. They would use their wits to rise in the world, to create an even better place for their children. A pot boy, for example, might aspire to become a butler or steward in a great house.

Servants expected vails (tips) or douceurs (sweeteners) for services rendered. Taking a gratuity was only a problem if it created a clash of loyalties. A good master was paternalistic but stern. His superior station was God-given, and, ideally, he maintained it by honorable behavior, not debate.

## Rules of Working in a Great House

This list of "rules" comes from *A Book of Orders and Rules*, written by Sir Sibbald David Scott in 1595.

A servant must not be absent from morning or evening meals or prayers lest he be fined two pence for each time.

Any man waiting table without a trencher (i.e., small tray) in his hand, except for good excuse, will be fined one penny.

For each oath, a servant will be fined a penny.

Any man provoking another to strike or striking another will be liable to dismissal.

For a dirty shirt on Sunday or a missing button, the fine will be sixpence.

After 8:00 A.M. no bed must be found unmade and no fireplace or candle box left uncleaned, or the fine will be one penny.

The hall must be cleaned in an hour.

The whole house must be swept and dusted each Friday.

Any man leaving a door open that he found shut will be fined one penny unless he can show good cause.

## Patronage

As we've seen previously, young men sought patrons for their advancement. Nobles drew gentlemen like honey attracts flies, creating a feudal relationship based on personal loyalty, gifts, and favors. Some of the gentry put their sons into great homes for their education and advancement.

The lord also maintained retainers or personal attendants, some of whom were armed and dangerous—bodyguards by any other name. The noble put them in his livery and gave them nominal positions in the household, such as gentleman or yeoman usher.

**FACTS**

A noblewoman drew her cortege from relatives and the daughters of the gentry. Her gentlewomen joined her in sewing, minding the children, dispensing charity in the neighborhood, and taking charge of her clothing and jewelry. She would also help unmarried girls of good families find suitable marriages.

## Military Life

There was no standing army in England until the restoration of Charles II in 1660, so armies had to be raised when needed from the general population. When necessary, a recruiting officer would travel from town to town, enticing men to enlist and "take the Queen's shilling." The recruiting officer was responsible for making sure that recruits were fit for duty, and were not only sons (for reasons of inheritance) so that small businesses and farms could keep working. Sometimes he earned a bounty for every man he enlisted.

New soldiers received their first payment—"the Queen's shilling," which was sometimes sunk at the bottom of a tankard of ale. Once the recruit drank the ale, he was committed to serving and received a uniform (the cost of which was usually deducted from their pay), took an oath to the Queen, and then with little training went off to fight overseas. Life expectancy was short. Lord Mountjoy, Elizabeth's general in Ireland in 1601 commented that, "it has ever been seen that more than three parts of the four of these [men] do never return."

## Foreigners and Travel

During Elizabeth's reign, partly because of the many armed skirmishes taking place in Europe, England became wary of foreigners. As a result, unless they were in the armed forces, young people were discouraged from going abroad. The truth is, only the wealthy could afford to travel anyway. A poor person worked as a servant, or on the land, or became a bandit or beggar.

Yet, ironically, during the last twenty years of Elizabeth's reign in particular, the number of soldiers engaged in military service meant that more Englishmen traveled overseas than ever before.

**SSENTIALS** Italy, especially, was off limits—because the Pope, a powerful political figure at this time, lived there and because Catholicism was considered to be heretically infectious. Young men could lose their inheritance and social standing and come under serious official scrutiny just for traveling to Italy.

## Selected for Service

When recruits were urgently needed, however, men were conscripted, or "pressed," often against their will. In *King Henry IV, Part I*, Falstaff describes the tricks he used to get extra money from those he pressed:

> I press me none but good householders, yeomen's sons, inquire
> me out contracted bachelors, such as had been asked twice of
> the banns—such a commodity of warm slaves as had as lief hear
> the devil as a drum . . . and they have bought out their services.

In other words, he pressed only those who were willing to bribe him to let them go—ending up with the leftovers, a group of such "scarecrows" that he is ashamed to be seen with them.

All men between the ages of sixteen and sixty were eligible to serve and had to appear at musters in town squares, on village greens, and at other places, where unlucky individuals would be selected for service. Moreover, most of these men were used as "food for powder," according to Falstaff (*King Henry IV, Part I*). Only about 20 percent of the army was trained. The rest were simply given equipment and had to learn how to be a soldier while in the field.

**FACTS**

A soldier's rank often dictated whether or not he would live or die. The untrained common soldier often ended up as cannon fodder because the better-trained, more professional army was considered too valuable to send to a possible death overseas and was held back for England's defense.

## The Nature of Warfare

The medieval feudal system was breaking down, and the development of gunpowder ushered in a new era of warfare. The maces and lances of knights in armor and longbows and crossbows of archers gave way to the more accurate cannons and mortars and ranks of soldiers wielding fuse-lit muskets and small arms, which changed the nature of warfare.

Many experienced soldiers, however, were reluctant to give up their bows, partly because the technology of gunpowder weaponry was still in its infancy. Guns often exploded after being fired a few times because of poor metal working and the stress and heat of continued, compressed explosions inside the breech. For good reason, many soldiers took to turning away their heads while firing, thus missing their targets. It was much easier to train musketeers than bowmen, although a bow could be more accurate in the hands of an expert.

## Country Life

In Shakespeare's day, England was still very much an agrarian society. The comic image in *Monty Python and the Holy Grail* of peasants spending their days grubbing about in the mud and dung heaps is an exaggeration of what it was like to be poor in Elizabethan times, but it makes a point worth remembering. It was a hard life. People lived off land they didn't own and were considered virtual slaves of the wealthy landowners they rented their property from.

Peasants were totally at the whim and mercy of their betters. They "knew their place" in the social order and were grateful for what they had. Peasants were given a scrawny piece of land on which to build their one- or two-room shacks and to scratch out a subsistence level of living from their own crops and animals.

In exchange for having a place of their own, a peasant worked on the owner's land at least three days a week. An overseer made sure the peasant and his family did everything right. The rest of the time, the peasant worked on his own land banding together with other families to cope with big jobs such as bringing in the harvest and hay making. Women and children helped, though they often worked indoors cooking, cleaning, and taking care of babies.

**FACTS**

At harvest time, the owner received a portion of the peasant's crops. If the crops failed, everyone starved. If the peasant needed to grind his grain, he did it at the owner's mill, leaving behind a portion for the owner. If he needed to bake his bread, he could use the owner's ovens if he left behind a loaf of bread or two.

Peasants, like Bottom and his companions in *A Midsummer Night's Dream*, were at the bottom of the social ladder. They could not marry or travel without the landlord's permission and were expected to return home if they did travel. Of course they could leave the estate for good whenever they wanted, but how could they make a living without land? Besides, travel was dangerous. There were few roads, particularly through the forests that still covered much of the countryside, virtually no organized police force of any description, so if a thief stole their stuff or beat them, chances are nobody would help.

Except for Sundays and Holy Days, peasants worked long and hard in the fields, regardless of the weather. A lot of families didn't have enough food to feed themselves, so it shouldn't be a surprise to learn that average peasants lived only into their thirties. Diseases were many, and medicine was rudimentary and expensive. Babies and children often died.

Peasants had only two legitimate ways to gain their independence: save enough money to buy their own piece of land or marry a free person, but only with the landowner's permission, and there was no guarantee he would give it.

## Town Life

In exchange for an annual tax, townsfolk received a royal charter that allowed them to govern themselves. Once chartered, they were able to make their own laws, form trade guilds, and raise taxes. In most towns the people elected a mayor or bailiff and a local council to govern them.

The streets of the town, which were often noisy, chaotic places during the day, were filled with bustle and business. Tradesmen cried their wares at markets as they wandered through the streets. Here are some examples of town life, recorded in *Street Cries* by Orland Gibbons:

> "Buy any ink, will you buy any pens, very fine writing ink, will you buy any ink?"
>
> "I ha' ripe peascods, ripe. Ripe damsons, fine ripe damsons. Hard garlic, hard. Fine potatoes, fine."
>
> "What is't ye lack? Fine wrought shirts or smocks. Perfumed waistcoats, fine bone lace or edgings, sweet gloves, silk garters, very fine silk garters, fine combs or glasses. Old doublets, ha'ye any old doublets?"
>
> "Ha' ye any corns on your feet or toes? Will ye buy any starch for a clear complexion, mistress?"
>
> "Ha' ye any rats or mice to kill?"

## Merchants and Craftsmen

The growing middle class was composed of merchants and craftsmen who were freemen and generally had a more comfortable life than country peasants. Merchants tended to be either traders or factory owners (i.e., craftsmen). Merchants traded with other merchants both at home and abroad and often owned their own ships. Many hired mercenary soldiers to protect the goods that were being shipped.

**FACTS**

It was particularly important that the craftsmen douse any fires they used during the day, because houses were made from wood and plaster and were so packed together in narrow streets that if a house caught fire it was almost guaranteed that large parts of the town would burn, too.

Craftsmen deliberately set up shop in towns so that they could take advantage of the population's needs. Their houses were usually fair sized, sometimes two to three stories, and craftsmen often worked at windows that opened out onto the street, giving them the chance to show off their skills to passersby, as well as to get the best light to work by. Crafts included confectioner, blacksmith, shoemaker, button-maker, sadler, porter, box-maker, and soap-boiler.

Markets were held once or twice a week in the town square. They were always crowded, busy, noisy, smelly, and dirty with people shouting, pushing, and generally hustling "for a buck" among the wooden stalls and carts displaying wares. At sunset, town bells tolled a curfew. Everyone finished their business and went home.

## Entertainment

There was little in the way of entertainment besides drinking in pubs and alehouses and gambling, often at baiting or cockfights, or some other kind of blood sport. Town fairs were held once or twice a year and were filled with contests, sports, and games. Peasants needed their master's permission to attend. Guilds sometimes staged plays.

Merchants and craftsman came from far and wide to sell their goods at these fairs. Jugglers, dancers, acrobats, and minstrels would wander through the crowds or set up a booth somewhere. The minstrels, in particular, wandered from town to town strumming a guitar, lute, or a viol, singing ballads and telling stories such as the legend of Robin Hood, the outlaw of Sherwood Forest.

Towns also competed with each other on Sunday afternoons with games such as bladder ball (an early form of soccer), rounders (somewhat like baseball), archery, wrestling, and so forth. Nobles played real tennis, an indoor sport, battledores, and shuttlecocks (badminton), as well as fencing and horse riding.

## Guilds

Rather like the peasants during harvest in the countryside, town merchants and craftsmen decided they could improve their lot by working together rather than separately. They started banding together, forming clubs or unions, called guilds. If you were a member of a guild you were able to vote for the head of the guild, who would serve a limited term of office. Guilds were important in local economies, maintaining product quality and industry standards. They also formed the basis of political power, and potentially, a guild leader had a lot of power that could be abused.

ESSENTIALS

Apprentices were treated strictly, and punished if they stepped out of line. At a 1561 Christmas celebration, for example, a young apprentice was found strutting about in the clothes of "his betters" (i.e., someone of a higher social standing) and was fined for celebrating in ruffs and a silk hat.

Guilds were divided into hierarchies with masters at the top, journeymen in the middle, and apprentices at the bottom. A boy in his early teens would often be apprenticed to a master, who would be paid by the boy's family to care for him and educate him in his trade.

After seven or eight years the young man would rise to the rank of journeyman and receive a wage. After a journeyman acquired sufficient experience, he would create a "masterpiece," that was judged by other masters within his guild. If the piece won their approval, he joined the ranks of Guild Master.

Few guilds included women, although there was a guild of laundresses. In London, there was a law called the Widow's Law that stated if a guild member died, his widow could take his place as long as she employed a journeyman to do her husband's work and she split the profits with him.

## The Urban Poor

The number of urban poor had been increasing before Elizabeth's reign, and kept increasing during it. The trend toward the enclosure or private ownership of what was previously considered common farm land forced many people to turn to begging for their livelihood.

By Shakespeare's time, a large shifting population of landless unemployed men and women lived in London. "Masterless men" threatened the stability of society. They had no place in the social order and were the most likely to commit crimes to stay alive. Soldiers fortunate enough to return home from fighting overseas, but unlucky enough to be injured and unable to work, invariably became beggars on crutches.

**FACTS**

The rural poor consisted mainly of widows and children who did not have the means to support themselves and landless laborers, often unemployed in the winter once the harvests were done. Passing vagrants were likely to be ignored or persecuted for fear that they might squander the charity of the community or commit crime.

By the last decade of Elizabeth's reign the booming English economy was in decline and crime and vagrancy worsened. Poor harvests, outbreaks of the plague, and other ills caused agricultural prices to rise while wages plummeted. Nearly 80 percent of the English population fell below the subsistence level. Church and government aid was meager. Laws criminalized poverty, and the poor were punished brutally for the often desperate acts they committed to stay alive.

In the towns, the poor were considered a public nuisance, a potential threat to public welfare, and a burden on the greater community. Local authorities often tried to curb the practice of begging and discouraged the establishment of tenements—houses divided into many small suites to be rented to poor individuals or families.

# Coins and Money

The values of the many different types of coins changed depending on the value of the metal used to make them. When the coinage was "debased," that is, when the amount of gold or silver in the coin was reduced, the value of the coin itself was reduced.

Halfpennies (pronounced "hay-pennies") and farthings were made of brass, lead, and occasionally even leather. Some merchants issued tokens that were redeemable as payment for goods and services by themselves and other merchants, though certainly not by all.

## Value of the Coins

The following are some Elizabethan denominations with very rough current U.S. dollar equivalents. The translation of money values is a tricky subject, and while we can think of a penny then as being close to a dollar today, in truth it varied dramatically. At different times it could be worth only fifty cents or as much as $5 or more, depending on the variations of precious metals used to cast the coin (combinations of either brass, copper, silver, or gold), economic ups and downs, and a proportional value defined by the cost of goods and services against wages earned.

| Monetary Unit | Equivalent in U.S. Dollars |
| --- | --- |
| Farthing | $.40 |
| Halfpenny piece | $.80 |
| Three farthing piece | $1.20 |
| Penny | $1.66 |
| Half groat | $3.30 |
| Three penny piece | $5.00 |
| Groat | $6.60 |
| Sixpence | $10.00 |
| Shilling | $20.00 |
| Half Crown | $50.00 |
| Crown | $100.00 |
| Angel | $140.00 to $200.00 |
| Noble | $140.00 to $200.00 |
| Royal | $200.00 to $280.00 |
| £1 (pound) | $400.00 |
| Sovereign | $400.00 |

## The Cost of Living

A soldier's shopping list (based on a Tudor soldier's food allowance):

24 oz. wheat bread: 1 penny
$2/3$ gallon beer: 1 penny
2 lbs. beef or mutton (cod or herring on Fridays): 2 pence
   (tuppence)
$1/2$ lb. butter: $1 1/2$ pence (penny hay-penny)
1 lb. cheese: $1 1/2$ pence
Total: 7 pence
(Note the lack of vegetables and fruit.)

Average wages:

Skilled journeymen could earn sixpence a day (sometimes as much
   as a shilling), with food and drink included.
Actors were paid a shilling a day, but it is unlikely that they received food.

Apprentices received food, drink, and lodging.

Farm workers got maybe thruppence (three pennies) a day; women were paid less, and often supplemented their earnings by spinning thread.

Permanent servants were paid annually, with board and food included—often no more than six shillings a year, or sixpence a week.

## The Cost of the Theater

The average fees for attendance at a public theater were:

The lords' room: 1 shilling (12 pence)
The gentlemen's rooms: 6 pence
The galleries: 2 pence
The pit (for the groundlings): 1 penny

The cheapest seats in the private theaters were usually 6 pence, thus effectively excluding all but relatively wealthy patrons.

**SSENTIALS**   Playwright Philip Henslowe was paid £3 to 5 for a play; on a good day his gross gate for a performance of a new play would be over three pounds. On November 28, 1595, he took in £4 6s for the first performance of *Harey the V—The Famous Victories of King Henry V*.

## Outsiders

Unfortunately, Shakespeare's time wasn't lacking prejudice and injustice. Some ethnic and religious groups were mistreated due to their minority status. The following sections give a brief description of two minority groups—Jews and blacks—during Elizabethan times that were portrayed in Shakespeare's plays.

## Jews

In 1290, under Edward IV, the Jews in England were deported en masse to France. It was not until Oliver Cromwell's Commonwealth 430 years later (in 1656) that Jews were again allowed to establish communities in England.

In 1593, Dr. Rodrigo Lopez, a converted Jew and physician to Queen Elizabeth, was condemned to death for treason. Neither Queen Elizabeth nor Robert Cecil, Secretary of the Privy Council, believed that Lopez was guilty and he died proclaiming his innocence. However, the trial instigated a lot of anti-Semitism. Against this backdrop, Christopher Marlowe wrote *The Jew of Malta*. Interestingly, even Marlowe's villainous Jew was treated badly by the Christians in Malta—as was Shakespeare's Shylock.

Shylock is a challenging character for Elizabethans. Shylock has some wonderful speeches about the way that he is mistreated. He has given us one of the great statements that define humanity:

Hath not a Jew eyes?
Hath not a Jew hands, organs, dimensions, senses, affections, passions; fed with the same food, hurt with the same weapons, subject to the same diseases, healed by the same means, warmed and cooled by the same winter and summer as a Christian is? If you prick us do we not bleed? If you tickle us do we not laugh? If you poison us do we not die?

Meanwhile, Amsterdam and Venice flourished as centers of commerce, partly because they tolerated large, open communities of practicing Jews. Elsewhere in Europe, Jews were forced to pretend they had converted to Christianity to avoid persecution and deportation. The Jews in London were forced to worship in secret and attended Christian churches.

**FACTS**

Henry VIII passed a law allowing interest rates of up to 10 percent, but his son Edward VI repealed it. (More accurately, it was repealed by one of his regents because Edward was too young to make decisions for most of his short life.) The result was a black market of far higher rates.

Because Jews were banned from almost all kinds of work, they became moneylenders by default. But moneylending was a complicated profession. For centuries, usury (lending money and charging interest) was illegal and considered contrary to the law of God. But the vagaries of capitalism made banning the practice impractical.

## Blacks

Othello is called a Moor, which suggests someone of Arab descent. Yet his physical description suggests a black man from central Africa, rather than an Arab. (Rodrigo describes Othello as having "thick lips," for example.) Black people were living in London by Elizabeth's reign. By Shakespeare's time ships carrying black slaves passed through London. Many blacks stayed, working as "exotic" servants or in the brothels that sat cheek by jowl with the theaters, and gambling and baiting arenas. As foreigners, they were regarded with a mixture of curiosity and suspicion.

To be black was not just to be foreign, but also something of an oddity. There were too few blacks in London for prejudice in the modern sense, but the color black was traditionally associated with ugliness, savagery, and sin. (Caliban in *The Tempest* is a classic example.)

Shakespeare's first black character is Aaron in *Titus Andronicus*. While Aaron is as much a stereotype as everyone else in the play, a gore-splashed revenge tragedy, he is less brutal than those around him and is actually capable of affection, as witnessed by his feelings for his infant son.

It is remarkable that Shakespeare chose to make Othello, a black man, the protagonist of one of his great tragedies. Regardless of whether or not Othello is seen as noble or foolish, the play treats him sympathetically and explores the concept of how an outsider can be ill treated and demonized by society for no good reason.

CHAPTER 7

# *The Sonnets and Poems*

O ne of the definiting aspects of great writers is that they are also great philosophers, which is certainly true of Shakespeare. Four hundred years ago he was able to express profound thoughts and feelings in words of great beauty and power that still have meaning for us today.

## Becoming a Poet

Shakespeare's plays are as great as they are because, beyond his love of language, his humor, and his technical skills as a dramatist, Shakespeare was a poet. He was able to capture the speech of common men and the language of philosophers and distill it into his work to create some of the finest poetry that has ever been written in the English language.

The meter of his plays used the unrhymed iambic pentameter called blank verse, which was invented in Italy. English poets embraced it during the reign of Henry VIII. The University Wits, especially Christopher Marlowe, developed it into a dramatic verse form that Shakespeare perfected. In the company of John Milton, Shakespeare made it the greatest meter in English.

Although Shakespeare was established as a playwright and actor in London by 1592, these were not particularly respected professions. That year, the bubonic plague broke out again and the authorities in London closed all the theaters because of the risk of infection spreading among members of audiences. (A certain number of plague deaths in a given week automatically closed them.) Left without an income in London, Shakespeare had to consider what to do while the theaters were empty.

Poetry was considered far superior to mere public entertainment, even if that did happen to also be in verse. The writing of what was thought of as poetry proper was considered the highest form of literature. Edmund Spenser's unfinished allegorical poem *The Faerie Queene*, which was being published throughout the 1590s, was a prime example.

**FACTS**

It's clear that Shakespeare was interested in gaining social prestige, as the purchases of property in Stratford tell us. What's more, in 1596 he "became a gentleman" when his father John, after various reverses (probably due to him being a Roman Catholic) was finally granted a coat of arms.

The profession of poet, though by no means as lucrative as that of a playwright, could come close with some luck. If the poet was not a nobleman, then he (only a very few women were poets) required the patronage of a nobleman and all the gifts that went with it. Edmund Spenser, for example worked hard to gain the favor of Queen Elizabeth I.

Not only was nondramatic poetry considered a higher form of art, it also attracted social prestige. Being a playwright, just of itself, certainly did not. Most playwrights (Jonson, Chapman, Marston, Marlowe, but never, it seems, Shakespeare) spent periods in prison for annoying the authorities. The young Christopher Marlowe, the boldest, most gifted, and most recklessly subversive of them all was actually stabbed to death in an alehouse brawl in 1593.

In an attempt to bridge the gap in his sudden loss of income, and undoubtedly to get himself recognized as a legitimate poet, Shakespeare published a major lyric work, *Venus and Adonis*, in 1593. It had a somewhat obsequious dedication to Henry Wriothesley, Earl of Southampton and Baron of Titchfield (1573–1624) who was just nineteen years old at the time, but already a wealthy and influential patron of the arts. The poem described itself as "the first heir of my invention" while promising "some graver labour" to come.

## Rising to Fame

*Venus and Adonis*, a funny and erotic narrative poem loosely based on Ovid's *Metamorphosis*, was published by Richard Field, whom you may recall was a Stratford neighbor of Shakespeare's, probably a childhood friend, who was fast becoming one of London's leading bookseller/publishers.

A far more serious narrative poem, *The Rape of Lucrece*, published in May 1594, was based on an ancient legend recounted by the Roman poets Fasti and Livy among others. This poem was also dedicated to the Earl of Southampton, but the formal tone of the first poem's dedication was replaced by a certain warm familiarity.

One of the ironies of Shakespeare's life is that in his day he was famous, not as the creator of Lear, Othello, Prospero, or Hamlet, but as the playwright of *Titus Andronicus* and the author of *Venus and Adonis*. The poem was reprinted at least nine times during his lifetime and was the model for many imitators.

Both Venus and Adonis and The Rape of Lucrece are full of gorgeous imagery and pagan spirit and very obviously the work of an intense young man. The fame that these two poems brought

Shakespeare no doubt substantially raised his profile as a serious writer, and, when the theaters reopened in 1594, helped the by-now thirty-year-old actor/playwright join Richard Burbage's acting company, the Lord Chamberlain's Men.

**FACTS**

There is a story that the Earl of Southampton rewarded Shakespeare for his poetic labors with £1,000, a huge sum of money in those days. The biographer A. L. Rowse (*Shakespeare the Man*, 1973) is one of the few scholars who believes this story. Others seem to think it a bit fanciful.

Exactly what Shakespeare felt about a life in the theater is pure conjecture of course, and yet, there is some evidence that his ambition was to be known as a poet not a dramatist. Sonnet 111 says:

O for my sake doe you wish fortune chide,
The guiltie goddesse of my harmfull deeds,
That did not better for my life provide,
Then publick means which publick manners breeds.
Thence comes it that my name receives a brand,
And almost thence my nature is subdu'd
To what it works in, like the Dyer's hand.

Scholars generally agree that Shakespeare was being both sarcastic and ironic. But most scholars also agree that "harmful deeds" refers to his success in the theater, and the reference to his name receiving a "brand" (in the sense we would talk about a brand name today) because of his theatrical associations is unmistakable. The American scholar O. J. Campbell (*A Shakespeare Encyclopaedia*, 1966) said there was "little doubt for which achievement he wished to be remembered: the preservation of the plays is owed to the efforts of others [meaning the people who published the First Folio], the [two early narrative] poems Shakespeare seems to have seen through the press himself."

# *Venus and Adonis*

In short, *Venus and Adonis* describes the unrequited infatuation of Venus, the Roman goddess of love and beauty, for Adonis, a somewhat self-absorbed golden boy. All he wants to do is get on with his hunt, but Venus pursues him regardless. She pulls him off his horse, kisses him all over, aggressively chases him over hill and dale until the hunter has become the prey. She makes it pretty clear she has the "hots" for him, although he is not interested. "No, lady, no; my heart longs not to groan,/But soundly sleeps while now it sleeps alone," he says. He returns to his hunt and gets killed by a wild boar. In her grief, Venus puts a curse on love for all eternity:

> Sorrow on love hereafter shall attend.
> It shall be waited on with jealousy,
> Find sweet beginning, but unsavoury end . . .
> The strongest body shall it make most weak,
> Strike the wise dumb, and teach the fool to speak . . .
> It shall be raging-mad, and silly-mild;
> Make the young old, the old become a child.
> It shall suspect where is no cause of fear;
> It shall not fear where it should most mistrust . . .
> It shall be cause of war and dire events,
> And set dissension 'twixt the son and sire . . .
> Sith in his prime death doth my love destroy,
> They that love best their loves shall not enjoy.

She turns Adonis into a purple and white flower and vows to wear this nosegay day and night.

**QUESTIONS?**

**Are any of Shakespeare's poems especially famous?**
Perhaps one poem is more famous than the other 154 sonnets for the sheer number of times its lines have been quoted. Sonnet 18 begins, "Shall I compare thee to a summer's day? Thou art more lovely and more temperate: Rough winds do shake the darling buds of May, And Summer's lease hath all too short a date. . ."

## *The Rape of Lucrece*

*The Rape of Lucrece* is more serious. It tells the story of Lucretia, an aristocratic Roman matron who is raped by Tarquin, the son of the Roman king. He steals into her bedroom determined to have his way with her, and the first half of the poem is told from his point of view as she begs to be spared. Nothing moves him. He tells her:

> This night I must enjoy thee.
> If thou deny, then force must work my way
> For in thy bed I purpose to destroy thee.

The last half of the poem is told from her point of view, and focuses on the terrible experience she has just endured. Despite her distress she proclaims, "I am the mistress of my fate," and decides to tell everyone what has happened to her before she kills herself. She tells her husband, father, and his lords what has been done to her and demands vengeance. Then she stabs herself in the heart to allow her soul to escape and her bloody corpse is paraded through the streets of Rome. Tarquin is banished, and according to legend, the political fallout of the rape ended the rule by kings and led to the establishment of the Roman Republic.

## Lesser-Known Poems

In 1599 a volume of poetry entitled *The Passionate Pilgrim* was published and attributed to Shakespeare. However, only five of the poems are definitely considered his, two appearing in other versions in the sonnets and three in *Love's Labour's Lost*. A love elegy, *The Phoenix and the Turtle*, was published in 1601 though pretty much ignored, as was *A Lover's Complaint*, which was published along with the sonnets in 1609 to fill out the pages of the volume.

*A Lover's Complaint* is a monologue delivered to an old shepherd by a distraught young woman who has been betrayed by her lover. He was handsome and intelligent, but she realized by the number of illegitimate children he fathered that he was not the marrying kind. She should have known better, but she let him have her way with her anyway, and he dropped her for someone else soon after.

In the 1980s and 1990s many Elizabethan scholars concluded that *A Funeral Elegy*, a poem published in 1612 and signed "W.S." exhibits many Shakespearean characteristics, although it has yet to be included in the canon.

ESSENTIALS

The enigmatic lyric *The Phoenix and the Turtle* (published in *Love's Martyr*, 1601), leaves many scholars bewildered. Is it a joke, obscene, or deadly serious? What is the "bird of loudest lay"? There has been little agreement and, relatively little commentary about it.

# The Sonnets

Shakespeare's sonnets were first published in 1609, but there is no clear evidence of when they were written. Scholars generally date them from 1594 to about 1599 (though some say 1597). Francis Meres in *Palladis Tamia* (1598) mentions that "honytongued Shakespeare, witnes his *Venus and Adonis*, his *Lucrece*, his sugred Sonnets among his private frinds."

The sonnet is a formal rhyme scheme where each line is usually in iambic pentameter (meaning each line has ten syllables), denoting different thoughts, moods, or emotions, sometimes summed up in the last lines of the poem. The two main forms of the sonnet are the Petrarchan (Italian) and the Shakespearean (English).

## Italian Sonnet

While the Italians had been using the form for almost 200 years prior to Shakespeare's time, Sir Thomas Wyatt and Henry Howard, Earl of Surrey, were among the first to introduce the sonnet into England. William Shakespeare's first few years in London were spent writing in the Italian style.

There's no easy way to explain this, but here goes: The Italian sonnet form has an eight-line stanza (or octave) followed by a six-line stanza (or sestet). The octave has two quatrains, rhyming ABBA, ABBA, but avoiding a couplet. The first quatrain gives the theme, and the second develops it. The sestet is built on two or three different rhymes; the first three lines reflect on the theme, and the last three lines bring the whole poem to an end. Got that?

## English Sonnet

The English sonnet differs from the Italian in that it is divided into three quatrains, each rhymed differently, with an independently rhymed couplet at the end. The rhyme scheme of the English sonnet is ABAB, CDCD, EFEF, GG. Each quatrain takes a different appearance of the idea or develops a different image to express the theme. Except for a few early poems, all of Shakespeare's sonnets were in this form.

**SSENTIALS**

Are all these rhyme schemes confusing? Don't worry about it unless you're going to study this stuff seriously. It's easy enough to enjoy the sonnets as they are without having to delve into the technicalities.

## Personal Poetry

Sonnets were personal poetry and usually circulated among one's friends and close acquaintances. It was thought "bad form" to publish sonnets and undesirable to write them for the purpose of being published. They were private thoughts for a select few. William Wordsworth wrote, "With this key [the sonnet form], Shakespeare unlocked his heart."

Because there were no copyright laws in sixteenth century England, a printer named Thomas Thorpe somehow obtained copies of the sonnets and published them without Shakespeare's knowledge or consent. Some critics disagree; they suggest that given a *fait accompli*, Shakespeare may have decided to work with Thorpe.

## Are the Sonnets Autobiographical?

Shakespeare wrote 154 sonnets. Not much is known about Shakespeare's private life, so scholars have searched his plays and the sonnets in particular for hints, without much success. They have attracted more attention than anything else he wrote except *Hamlet*. As poetry, they are superb. However, people are just as interested in them because they may tell a story.

**FACTS**

Some scholars feel the sonnets are literary exercises without a personal theme. A middle view is that they explore personal relations in friendship and in love, and rehearse themes later dramatized in the plays. It's also not known if the order of the sonnets is what Shakespeare intended, although most scholars see little reason to question it.

The story is hinted at, rather than told and concerns Shakespeare's feelings toward a young nobleman who wronged him by stealing the affections of a sweetheart and by transferring his friendship to another poet. (Some think it might have been Kit Marlowe, though that is unlikely looking at the dates.) In the end the young nobleman is forgiven. Critics and scholars disagree about whether the sonnets are autobiographical.

The first 126 sonnets are addressed to a man with the initials W. H. Scholars conjecture that W. H. may be the inverted initials of Henry Wriothesley, third Earl of Southampton, to whom Shakespeare had dedicated his earlier poems, or they may stand for William Herbert, Earl of Pembroke, or for someone else entirely.

The remaining poems are addressed to the so-called dark lady of the sonnets, since it is made clear that she is dark in hair and complexion. Guesses have been made as to who she might be. Some think it was Mary Fitton, a maid of honor at court and mistress of William Herbert. A. L. Rowse believed her to be Aemelia Lanyer. Neither supposition has enough evidence to prove it.

## Recurring Themes

Only by analyzing the entire set of sonnets, some critics say, is it possible to fathom Shakespeare's intent. For example, a sonnet with a certain meaning may be followed immediately by a sonnet conveying the opposite message. The first cannot be discussed without discussing the second because the contradiction defines the nature of its meaning. The sonnets build on, cancel out, and are formed by each other. The meanings of the sonnets are all relative, but in general they are marked by the recurring themes of beauty, youthful beauty ravaged by time, and the ability of love and art to transcend time and even death.

In the first twenty-seven sonnets, Shakespeare proposes one method to outwit the passage of time. He urges the young man to have children so that his beauty will be preserved in posterity and therefore time will not have won the battle. The first two lines of the first sonnet present this theme:

From fairest creatures we desire increase,
That thereby beauty's rose might never die.

In Sonnet 11, Shakespeare tells the young man that when he grows old he will be young in his children and that:

Herein lives wisdom, beauty and increase;
Without this, folly, age and cold decay.

The poet goes on to explain to the young man that nature has given him a gift of beauty so that he may reproduce it. The couplet sums it up:

She [mother nature] carved thee for her seal, and meant thereby
Thou shouldst print more, not let that copy die.

Shakespeare's suggestions to the young man sometimes turn into accusations that he is hoarding the beauty which he was lent, and therefore abusing the lease. After Sonnet 17, when it becomes apparent the young man is unwilling to marry, Shakespeare presents another way in which to wage war against time.

He says that his poetry will always exist and be read and that through his poetry his love will be forever alive. In Sonnet 15, Shakespeare writes in the last four lines:

> Where wasteful time debateth with decay
> To change your [the young man's] day of youth into sullied night;
> And all in war with time for love of you,
> As he [time] takes from you, I engraft you new.

## Homosexuality or Platonic Love?

The rest of the sonnets discuss aspects of the love between Shakespeare and the young man, and the poet and his mistress. They describe a number of circumstances in the poet's relationship with these people. The final opponent of time is presented in Sonnet 116:

> Love is not love
> Which alters when it alteration finds,
> Or bends with the remover to remove.
> O no, it is an ever fixed mark
> That looks on tempests and is never shaken;
> It is the star to every wand'ring barque,
> Whose worth's unknown although his height be taken.
> Love's not time's fool, though rosy lips and cheeks
> Within his bending sickle's compass come;
> Love alters not with his brief hours and weeks,
> But bears it out even to the edge of doom.

Some scholars suggest that the sonnets betray homosexuality between Shakespeare and another. The Elizabethans made a distinction between homosexual love and sodomy, which was against the law. While it may or may not be true, such arguments don't really take into account the concept of platonic love that was prevalent in the Renaissance.

Hallet Smith, writing in *The Riverside Shakespeare*, commented that, "the attitude of the poet toward the friend [the handsome young man] is one of love and admiration, deference and possessiveness, but it is not at all a sexual passion. Sonnet 20 makes quite clear the difference between the platonic love of a man for a man, more often expressed in the sixteenth century than the twentieth, and any kind of homosexual attachment."

**FACTS**

William Shakespeare was the first writer to be commemorated at Westminster Abbey's poet's corner, where there is still a bust of him over a door.

Regardless of the uncertainty about the who, where, when, and why, when it comes to Shakespeare, scholars agree that several of these poems are among the most perfect ever written.

## CHAPTER 8

# *An Introduction to the Plays*

ince his death, Shakespeare's plays have been performed almost continually, in English as well as other languages, and he is quoted more than any other single author. The plays have been constantly examined by critics trying to explain their timeless appeal, each criticism a reflection of the era that the critic lived in.

# Shakespeare and Elizabethan Theater

Critics sometimes faulted Shakespeare's inconsistency in holding to any particular philosophy, religion, or ideology. For example, *A Midsummer Night's Dream* includes a burlesque of the kind of tragic love that he treats idealistically in *Romeo and Juliet* and somewhat cynically in *Troilus and Cressida.*

The strength of Shakespeare's plays lies in the wealth of complex characters and their eloquent, vivid, and lyrical speech. Shakespeare's characters are neither all good nor all bad, and it's their flawed, inconsistent nature that makes them so memorable. Hamlet fascinates us because of his ambivalence over whether or not to avenge his father's death and our uncertainty over how mad he really is. As well as being genial, openhearted, and witty, Falstaff is also boisterous and cowardly, but ultimately moving.

ESSENTIALS

One thing about the Elizabethan theater worth remembering is that it was a much more intimate experience than going to the theater nowadays. While the costumes were lavishly rich and colorful, the Elizabethan stage was bare, save for a couple of props, and relied heavily on the actors' ability to connect with the audience.

The limited use of settings and props made it easy to take a play on tour. But more important, it allowed the audience to focus on the play, not its trappings, and brought the actors in closer contact with the audience than a modern proscenium stage often does. An Elizabethan player would be almost able to touch the nearest of the spectators, whether it was from the "apron" that thrust into the audience, or because the play was performed in the cleared courtyard of an inn or in a great hall in a Tudor mansion with the chairs and heavy wooden dining table pushed to one side to make room. The actor played almost from the audience, not just to it from above. Today, this effect can be somewhat achieved by staging plays "in the round," that is, with the audience sitting 360 degrees around the action of the play, not just viewing it from in front of a stage.

# The Four Time Periods

Shakespeare's plays can be broadly divided into four time periods:

1. Pre-1594 (*King Richard III*, *The Comedy of Errors*, etc.)
2. 1594–1600 (*King Henry V*, *A Midsummer Night's Dream*, etc.)
3. 1600–1608 (*Macbeth*, *King Lear*, etc.)
4. Post-1608 (*Cymbeline*, *The Tempest*, etc.)

The first period (pre-1594) has its roots in Greek, Roman, and medieval drama—the plays show a certain obviousness, leaning toward cliché. It's possible that Shakespeare was influenced by Christopher Marlowe—now considered Shakespeare's greatest literary rival—whose writing was gaining recognition as Shakespeare's playwriting career began.

The second period (1594–1600) shows a clearly maturing author, and the plays are less labored and predictable. The histories of this period portray royalty in human terms rather than as ciphers to move along a plot, and he experiments with blending comedy and tragedy, considered a trademark of Shakespeare's that would become a stylistic signature.

The third period (1600–1608) marks the great tragedies. At this point he wrote the plays that would earn him his place in history. Lear, Hamlet, Macbeth, and Othello are classic tragic Greek theater characters in the best dramatic sense. The comedies, meanwhile, are moody and ambiguous.

**FACTS**

Scholars still debate whether these last plays show Shakespeare writing in a form of dramatic shorthand, or whether the plays reflect an evolving theatrical trend from Elizabethan tastes to Jacobean as James I's reign took hold.

The last period is one of cynical plays and symbolism. At the end of his career, and facing middle age, Shakespeare seemed preoccupied with stories of redemption. The plays show Shakespeare at his most symbolic.

# Chronological Order of Plays

Despite the above, dating and grouping Shakespeare's plays is problematic. In 1598 commentator Francis Meres created a kind of literary marker when he wrote that Shakespeare was "the greatest English playwright," and listed his plays to date. This list has helped scholars distinguish the earlier plays from the later ones.

Meres also lists a play named *Love's Labour's Won,* which may have been revised and turned into *All's Well That Ends Well.* A reasonable approximation of the order of the plays has been deduced from dates of publication, references in writings of the same time, allusions in the plays to then-current events, thematic relationships, and stylistic comparisons.

## The Early Plays (Pre-1594)

Some scholars consider the first plays to be the three parts of *King Henry VI*; it is uncertain whether *Part I* was written before or after Parts *II* and *III. King Richard III* is related to these plays and is usually grouped with them as the final part of a first quartet of historical plays. Others think *The Comedy of Errors* was his first play. Some evidence suggests it might have been *King Edward III*, a new play now being considered by many critics as part of the canon.

After the early Henrys come: *The Comedy of Errors, Titus Andronicus, The Taming of the Shrew, The Two Gentlemen of Verona, Love's Labour's Lost,* and *Romeo and Juliet.* Some of the comedies of this early period are parodies with strong elements of farce. The two tragedies, *Titus Andronicus* and *Romeo and Juliet*, were both popular in Shakespeare's own lifetime. *Romeo and Juliet* in particular, shows a departure from genre and cliché with substantial development of minor characters.

After these early plays, and before his great tragedies, Shakespeare wrote *King Richard II, A Midsummer Night's Dream, King John, The Merchant of Venice, King Henry IV Parts I* and *II, Much Ado About Nothing, King Henry V, Julius Caesar, As You Like It,* and *Twelfth Night. King Richard II*, each part of *King Henry IV*, and *King Henry V* form a second quartet of historical plays, although each can stand alone. *King*

*Henry IV* introduces the fat knight Falstaff, one of Shakespeare's classic creations who has enjoyed immense popularity from the beginning.

## The Great Tragedies (1600–1608)

Shakespeare's great tragedies and the "problem plays" (meaning they are hard to categorize and critique) date from 1600 with *Hamlet.* Following this are *The Merry Wives of Windsor* (written on the request of Queen Elizabeth I who wanted to see a play featuring Falstaff), *Troilus and Cressida, All's Well That Ends Well, Measure for Measure, Othello, King Lear, Macbeth, Antony and Cleopatra, Coriolanus,* and *Timon of Athens.*

**FACTS**

*Othello, King Lear,* and *Macbeth* deal with the conflict of order and chaos, good and evil, and spirituality and hedonism. *Pericles, Cymbeline, The Winter's Tale,* and *The Tempest* are considered tragicomedies. The main characters seem to encompass a tragic potential to rival Lear or Othello, but the plays can be considered comedies because they end happily, often through magical ends.

## The Lost Plays

Little is known about *Cardenio,* considered a lost play and possibly developed from an episode in Cervantes's *Don Quixote.* In fact, *The Norton Shakespeare* is the first edition of Shakespeare's works to include a separate description of it. We know that on May 20, 1613, John Henings, who ran the King's Men, was presented a sum of money for performing six plays, one of which was entitled *Cardenio.* In 1728, Lewis Theobald published a play called *Double Falsehood,* or *The Distressed Lovers,* based on the story of *Cardenio,* "revised and adapted" from the play "originally written by William Shakespeare."

The tail end of Shakespeare's "retirement" to Stratford was spent collaborating with John Fletcher, who essentially took Shakespeare's place as the primary playwright of the King's Men. Fletcher was known to be a great admirer of Cervantes, and probably read *Don Quixote* in its original Spanish.

Historian Charles Hamilton claims to have uncovered Shakespeare and Fletcher's *Cardenio,* in *Shakespeare with John Fletcher: Cardenio or The Second Maiden's Tragedy* (New York: Marlowe & Company, 1994). Two more plays, *King Henry VIII* and *The Two Noble Kinsmen,* may also be collaborations with John Fletcher (*Cardenio* is omitted), and the canon is now considered by some scholars to include *King Edward III,* which fits in the sequence of Wars of the Roses plays chronologically before *King Richard II.*

There are several pages of a play called *Sir Thomas More* that have what appears to be the only extant examples of Shakespeare's handwriting beyond legal documents. A brief summary of the play is included later in this book.

*King Edward III* was first published anonymously in 1596, but it was not until Edward Capell re-edited the play in his *Prolusions* (1760) that Shakespeare was said to be the author. The Arden Shakespeare series, the leading publisher of William Shakespeare's works, has taken the new play into its canon as has the Cambridge University Press and American Riverside Press, although Oxford scholars are still holding out.

## Appreciating Shakespeare's Greatness

As with any exceptionally popular author, Shakespeare's work was appreciated differently over time. In his own day, for example, according to Ben Jonson, *Titus Andronicus*, a bloodthirsty revenge melodrama now regarded as one of Shakespeare's least interesting plays, was particularly enjoyed. The poet John Dryden (1631–1700) in *Essay on Dramatic Poesy*, preferred *King Richard II*; and Samuel Johnson (1709–84), in his *Preface to Shakespeare* admired the comedies.

It makes sense that *Titus Andronicus* would have suited the more vulgar tastes of the groundlings in an age where bloody executions were popular spectacles. Dryden and Johnson both belonged to neoclassical periods and it's not surprising, given the taste of the time, that Shakespeare was criticized for mixing comedy and tragedy and failing to observe the unities of time and place prescribed by Aristotle's rules of classical drama. Dryden and Johnson were among the critics who claimed that he had corrupted the language with false wit, puns, and ambiguity. These views are in direct contrast to those of modern critics who have praised their use in later plays especially for adding depth and resonance of meaning. Johnson's good nature no doubt caused him to respond to the comedies.

It's also worth noting that that both Ben Jonson and Dryden were ahead of their time in being able and willing to promote Shakespeare's genius, despite the rigid insistence on how things should be done by the now forgotten arbiters of taste of their age who disagreed with them.

Besides A. C. Bradley's seminal text on *Shakespearean Tragedy*, published in 1904, the twentieth century has been the most prolific in appreciating and commenting on Shakespeare's greatness. Wilson Knight (*The Imperial Theme* and *The Crown of Life*), Harley Granville-Barker (*Preface to Shakespeare*), and others have contributed to our understanding of the plays and poetry.

The first collected edition of Shakespeare is the First Folio, published in 1623 and includes all the plays except *Pericles* and *The Two Noble Kinsmen*. Eighteen of the plays exist in earlier quarto editions, eight of which are extremely corrupt, probably reconstructed from an actor's memory. In 1709, Nicholas Rowe was the first to publish Shakespeare's plays divided into acts and scenes and with exits and entrances marked. Other important early editions include Alexander Pope's (1725), Lewis Theobald's (1733), and Samuel Johnson's (1765).

Among Shakespeare's most important sources, Raphael Holinshed's *Chronicles of England, Scotland, and Ireland* (1587) is significant for the English history plays, although Shakespeare did not hesitate to transform a character when it suited him. For his Roman tragedies he used Sir Thomas North's translation (1579) of *Plutarch's Lives*. He rewrote old plays and turned English prose romances into drama (*As You Like It* and *The Winter's Tale*). He also freely used the works of his contemporaries in Europe.

The following table shows how Shakespeare's plays are usually grouped:

| Comedy | History | Tragedy |
| --- | --- | --- |
| All's Well That Ends Well | King Edward III | Antony and Cleopatra |
| As You Like It | King Henry IV, Part I | Cardenio |
| The Comedy of Errors | King Henry IV, Part II | Coriolanus |
| Cymbeline | King Henry V | Hamlet, Prince of Denmark |
| Love's Labour's Lost | King Henry VI, Part I | Julius Caesar |
| Measure for Measure | King Henry VI, Part II | King Lear |
| The Merchant of Venice | King Henry VI, Part III | Macbeth |
| The Merry Wives of Windsor | King Henry VIII | Othello, Moor of Venice |
| A Midsummer Night's Dream | King John | Romeo and Juliet |
| Much Ado About Nothing | King Richard II | Timon of Athens |
| Pericles, Prince of Tyre | King Richard III | Titus Andronicus |
| The Taming of the Shrew | Sir Thomas More | |
| The Tempest | | |
| Troilus and Cressida | | |
| Twelfth Night | | |
| The Two Gentlemen of Verona | | |
| The Two Noble Kinsmen | | |
| The Winter's Tale | | |

# Shakespearean Comedy

What defines a Shakespearean comedy, broadly, is a light touch and a happy ending, though these plays also contain farce and slapstick. As he developed as a writer, Shakespeare seemed to deliberately shun categorization, writing comedies that could be farcical, bitter, magical, and sometimes tragic all at the same time. To Shakespeare, comedy meant that foolish humans were able to triumph over adversity, which implies a positive reading of human experience. Comedy to some experts means looking to the future, past the wedding that concludes the action on stage to the offstage sexual union that ensures life goes on. The end of the comedy is an occasion for jokes, smiles, and nudges with an elbow.

Yet the more complicated and sophisticated the comedy, the more likely the triumphant ending will be undermined by melancholy. The paradox of difficult characters in the comedies, such as Shylock or Malvolio, and the potentially tragic events that seem to be averted at the eleventh hour, according to some scholars, suggest that Shakespeare was deliberately calling attention to the theatricality of the occasion.

**QUESTIONS?**

**Was *Romeo and Juliet* based on a true story?**
*Romeo and Juliet* was based on the life of two real lovers who both died for each other and lived in Verona, Italy, in 1303. Both the Capulets and Montagues existed in Verona at this time, and Shakespeare is reckoned to have discovered this tragic love story in Arthur Brooke's 1562 poem entitled "The Tragical Historye of Romeus and Juliet."

He invites his audiences to enjoy a temporary perfection not found in the real world. Outside the magic circle of the theater, lost children are not returned, wicked brothers rarely repent, statues do not come to life, and if we leave a Shakespearean comedy with a tear in our eyes, it is only an acknowledgment that the enchantment of the theater has staved off this "mortal coil" for an hour or two, but now we must return to the bitterness that life can bring us.

## Shakespearean History

With the exceptions of *King John*, *Sir Thomas Moore*, and *King Henry VIII* (coauthored with John Fletcher), the histories or historical plays cover the Wars of the Roses, a series of violent civil wars fought over the English crown. (*King John* stands as an odd man out, but it is a play more about character than plot.)

## The Tudor Dynasty

The history starts with Edward III, whose army defeated the French at the Battle of Crécy in 1346, establishing England as a great military power, and picks up the story again in 1398, two years before Richard II is deposed. It then moves to 1485, when Henry VII defeated Richard III at the battle of Bosworth and established the Tudor dynasty.

Henry VII was Elizabeth I's grandfather, and he went to considerable effort to legitimize his right to the throne of England by force of arms. *Sir Thomas More* is an unfinished play about the main character's problems with King Henry VIII's divorce, and *King Henry VIII* itself is about the birth of Queen Elizabeth as a result of that divorce.

The plays cleave quite rigidly to the Tudor party line. Shakespeare was certainly no fool and was not about to upset his patron the queen, or suggest that she was somehow not the legitimate heir to the throne regardless of historical truth.

## The Rise and Fall of the Lancaster Dynasty

The plays were not written in chronological order. The *King Henry VI* trilogy and *King Richard III* were written close together near the start of his career (around 1589–1593). They cover the fall of the Lancaster dynasty—that is, events in English history between 1422 and 1485. Then, about three years later (around 1595–1599), came *King Richard II*, and after another couple of years *King Henry IV, Parts I* and *II*, and then finally *King Henry V*. This second series, written at the height of Shakespeare's powers, moves back in time to examine the rise of the Lancastrians, covering English history from 1398 to 1420.

SSENTIALS Shakespeare's audiences would be somewhat familiar with the characters and events he was describing, but in a broad scope. The battles among houses and the rise and fall of kings were woven into the fabric of English culture and are part of the country's patriotic legends and national mythology.

## Sources of Historical Material

Shakespeare drew on a number of different sources in writing his history plays. His primary source for historical material, however, is generally agreed to be Raphael Holinshed's massive work, *The Chronicles of England, Scotland and Ireland*, published in 1586–7. Holinshed's account provides the chronology of events that Shakespeare reproduces, alters, compresses, or conveniently avoids—whichever serves his dramatic purposes best. However, Holinshed's work was only one of an entire genre of historical chronicles that were popular during Shakespeare's time. He may well have used other sources. For *King Richard II*, for example, he may have used more than seven primary sources.

ESSENTIALS

As he matured as a playwright, Shakespeare focused more on building character and less on plot or historical events. He realized that Falstaff and the Boar's Head tavern where he used to drink with Prince Hal, were worth more dramatically than a phony recreation of battle.

One of the principle questions that preoccupies the characters in the history plays is the divine right of kings, that is, whether or not the king of England is appointed by God. This linchpin philosophy of social order was not challenged until the overthrow of Charles I during the English Civil War in 1642. If a king is divinely appointed then his overthrow or murder will come to haunt the king who gains the throne through such blasphemous means.

This ghost manifests itself in *Hamlet*, *Macbeth*, *Julius Caesar*, and *King Richard III*, and it hovers over *King Richard II* and its sequels. The murder of the former King Richard II will haunt King Henry IV for the rest of his life, and only his son Henry V can redeem the curse.

When Shakespeare next returned to history, it was not to Holinshed's England, but to the Rome of Plutarch and Ovid for *Julius Caesar* and *Antony and Cleopatra*. Rightly, they are considered tragedies rather than histories because they so firmly focus on character.

## The Wars of the Roses

To best follow the eight Shakespeare plays that trace the Wars of the Roses it's helpful to understand the historical events they recreate. For over 100 years, England's royal family was split into two struggling factions: the Lancaster family, symbolized by a red rose, and the York family, symbolized by a white rose.

The problems began in the late fourteenth century, with the death of King Edward III. Edward had seven sons, and the third and fourth sons became dynastic heads: John of Gaunt, Duke of Lancaster and his younger brother Edmund, Duke of York.

Edward III was succeeded by Richard II, who was descended from Edward's oldest son, and was neither a Yorkist nor a Lancastrian. Richard ruled for several years before he was overthrown by his cousin, Henry Bolingbroke, the son of John of Gaunt. Bolingbroke became Henry IV and founded the Lancastrian dynasty. Henry IV was in turn succeeded by his son, Henry V, who was succeeded by his son, Henry VI.

In the late fifteenth century, fighting broke out again, this time between Lancastrians and Yorkists. After a bloody struggle, the Yorkists Edward, Clarence, and their younger brother Richard murdered Henry VI (along with his son and destined heir, Edward, Prince of Wales).

The oldest of the York brothers took the throne as King Edward IV. After he died, his younger brother Richard III took the throne, and he remained there until he was defeated in battle by Henry, Duke of Richmond, who became Henry VII and established peace and the Tudor dynasty.

# Shakespearean Tragedy

While Holinshed's history of England proved a source for many early plays, it's probably no exaggeration to say that North's translation of Plutarch's *Lives of Noble Greeks and Romans* exerted a greater influence over Shakespeare than anything else he read (with the possible exception of Aristotle on the essence of drama, which we can only conjecture he may have read as a schoolboy or schoolmaster). For example, many scholars consider *Julius Caesar* to be the play that bridges the history and tragedy genres, with Brutus the first of Shakespeare's tragic heroes.

Though there are others, the four most famous Shakespearean tragedies are *King Lear*, *Hamlet*, *Othello*, and *Macbeth*. *Hamlet* is about an emotionally scarred young man trying to come to terms with his urge to avenge the murder of his father, the king, and his awareness of the resultant perdition should he follow that urge. Othello, a Moor and feted general in the army of Venice, is victimized as a result of his love for Desdemona, the daughter of a Venetian statesman. The villain of the play is Iago, Othello's trusted advisor, who plots revenge against Othello, Desdemona, and Cassio because Othello has promoted Cassio to a position Iago feels should be his. Macbeth is a noble warrior driven by his ambition and that of his ruthless wife to murder to attain power. *King Lear* is a tragic story of hubris—of an old man who makes a foolish mistake and pays for it with a descent into madness as his children betray and abandon him, and his world crumbles around him.

**FACTS**

In Shakespeare's plays, the tragic hero is a nobleman who has enjoyed status and prosperity, but possesses a moral weakness or flaw that ultimately leads to his downfall. External circumstances such as fate can also play a part in the hero's fall, and evil agents can cause him to make wrong decisions.

Shakespeare's tragedies can be considered meditations on the spiritual conflict in the soul of man (and woman), and as such, great heroes like Macbeth, Othello, and Hamlet will always fail because their tragedy is that while they are great men capable of great deeds, they cannot withstand the inevitability of the character flaw that will bring about their own destruction. They are tragic heroes, doomed by the perilous stuff within their own hearts.

# PART 2

# The Plays in Alphabetical Order

# 1 § *A Midsummer Night's Dream*

## Main Characters

**Theseus**—Duke of Athens. He represents tradition, authority, and wisdom. He is about to marry Hippolyta.

**Hippolyta**—An Amazon. Theseus won her as a bride by defeating her in a sword fight.

**Egeus**—Hermia's father.

**Philostrate**—Master of Revels.

**Hermia**—Daughter of Egeus.

**Lysander**—A young man in love with Hermia.

**Helena**—Hermia's friend. In love with Demetrius.

**Demetrius**—Another young man in love with Hermia.

**Oberon**—King of the fairies.

**Titania**—Queen of the fairies.

**Puck**—Otherwise known as Robin Goodfellow.

**Peaseblossom, Cobweb, Moth, and Mustardseed**—Fairy attendants to Titania.

**Bottom, Peter Quince, Francis Flute, Tom Snout, Snug, Robin Starveling**—Athenian tradesmen.

## Introduction

*A Midsummer Night's Dream* is one of Shakespeare's early comedies, probably composed in 1595 or 1596. Most scholars believe that Shakespeare wrote the play as a light entertainment for the marriage celebration of Elizabeth Carey, granddaughter of a patron of the Lord Chamberlain's Men, the theatrical troupe of which Shakespeare was a partner. Unlike the vast majority of his works, *A Midsummer Night's Dream* was not based on other primary source materials, making it one of the few original plays Shakespeare wrote.

## The Play

Helena loves Demetrius. Demetrius once slept with Helena, but now loves her friend, Hermia. Hermia loves Lysander, and Lysander returns her love. Egeus, Hermia's father, gets Theseus, the Duke of Athens, to make Demetrius marry Hermia. According to Athenian law, Hermia has four days to choose between Demetrius, life in a nunnery, or a death sentence. Hermia flees with Lysander into the surrounding forest.

**FACTS**

Throughout the twentieth century, *A Midsummer Night's Dream* proved to be one of Shakespeare's most popular plays and many versions were staged and filmed.

In the forest, Oberon and Titania, king and queen of fairies, are arguing over a boy Titania has adopted and Oberon wants as one of his retinue. Oberon instructs his servant Puck to sprinkle love drops in the Queen's eyes while she sleeps. On awakening, Titania will fall in love with the first creature she sees.

Helena and Demetrius chase after Lysander and Hermia. Oberon, overhearing Demetrius reject the lovesick Helena, takes pity upon her, and tells Puck to use the love drops on Demetrius as well, so that Demetrius will fall for Helena. Puck gets confused and puts the drops in Lysander's eyes instead. He wakes up to see Helena. Now Lysander wants Helena and rejects a stunned Hermia.

Ignorant of all these comings and goings, a group of Athenian craftsmen are rehearsing a production of a play, *Pyramus and Thisbe*, to be acted at the Duke's wedding. Puck casts a spell on Bottom giving him the head of a donkey, and then organizes things so that Bottom is the first creature Titania sees when she wakes up.

Bottom is unaware of his new head, but ends up being kept lavishly by the fairy queen. Oberon enjoys Titania's humiliation, but is not happy that Puck has botched the attempt to reunite Demetrius and Helena. Oberon himself puts the love potion in Demetrius's eyes and makes sure Helena is the first person he sees. Helena is unconvinced, and thinks both Demetrius and Lysander are mocking her because both now profess love for her.

Oberon decides it's time to sort things out. He puts the four lovers to sleep and gives Lysander the antidote for the love potion so that he will love Hermia again when they all wake up. Next, Oberon gives Titania the antidote, and the king and queen reconcile.

Theseus and Hippolyta discover Lysander, Hermia, Helena, and Demetrius asleep in the forest. All return to Athens to make sense of what they think is a strange dream. Bottom, believing that he dreamt he had the head of an ass, returns to his players, and they perform *Pyramus and Thisbe* at the wedding feast which becomes the weddings of three couples.

**FACTS**

Various versions of the play, mostly abridged, were performed until 1840, when Madame Vestris (who also insisted on playing Oberon) restored the text. It was staged at Covent Garden in London, with music by Felix Mendelssohn that included the famous "Wedding March," heard regularly all over the world as brides and grooms leave the church afer being married.

## Commentary

*A Midsummer Night's Dream* is full of paradoxes. The play is not only the poet's dream but also the audience's. It blends imaginative fancy with the stately traditions of Athenian aristocracy. The conflicts between youthful rebellion and authoritarianism and between the magical and the everyday, lend the play a timeless quality blurring the distinction between reality and imagination for both audience and characters.

The play has been an interesting indicator of the eras it has been produced in. Modern interpretations, for example, have cast the fairy world as a Freudian repository of repressions and erotic desires. It is a testament to Shakespeare's genius that the play can be reinvented in so many different ways; the universal concerns of the nature of love, reality, sexuality, imagination, and the status-quo social order give the play a timeless appeal. It's worth recalling that unlike other forms of literature, plays have live audiences—not passive readers—that are active participants in the theatrical experience.

## Famous Lines

"For aught that I could ever read,
Could ever hear by tale or history,
The course of true love never did run smooth" (Act I, Scene I).

"Love looks not with the eyes, but with the mind;
And therefore is winged Cupid painted blind" (Act I, Scene I).

"That would hang us, every mother's son" (Act I, Scene II).

"I'll put a girdle round about the earth
In forty minutes" (Act II, Scene I).

"I know a bank where the wild thyme blows,
Where oxlips and the nodding violet grows,
Quite over-canopied with luscious woodbine,
With sweet musk-roses and with eglantine"   (Act II, Scene I).

"Lord, what fools these mortals be!" (Act III, Scene II).

"I have had a dream, past the wit of man to say what dream it was"
     (Act IV, Scene I).

"The best in this kind are but shadows" (Act V, Scene I).

# 2 § All's Well That Ends Well

## Main Characters

**Helena**—The daughter of a great doctor, now the ward of the Countess of Rosillion. She loves the countess's son, Bertram, though he does not return her affections.

**Bertram**—The Count of Rosillion. Handsome and well-liked, he is an excellent soldier, but a jerk in his relationship with Helena, whom he marries unwillingly and then abandons.

**Countess**—Bertram's mother and Helena's guardian.

**King of France**—Deathly ill when the play begins, he is miraculously cured by Helena, who uses one of her father's medicines. As a reward for saving his life, he makes Bertram marry Helena.

**Parolles**—A liar and a braggart.

**Lafew**—An old French nobleman.

**Dumaine, First Lord**—A genial French nobleman.

**Dumaine, Second Lord**—The First Lord Dumaine's brother.

**Diana**—A young Florentine Bertram tries to seduce. She helps Helena trick Bertram.

**Widow**—Diana's mother.

**Mariana**—A woman of Florence.

**Duke of Florence**—The ruler of Florence.

**Clown**—An old servant of the countess who serves as a messenger.

**Steward**—Another servant of the countess.

## Introduction

The earliest copy of *All's Well That Ends Well* appears in the Folio of 1623, seven years after Shakespeare died. Some critics date it from 1598 or earlier and associate it with a "lost play" called *Love's Labour's Won*, which is listed in a 1598 catalogue of Shakespeare's plays. Some critics think that *All's Well That Ends Well* is a reworked version that Shakespeare published at a later date.

The most common dating puts it between 1601 and 1606, grouping it with *Troilus and Cressida* and *Measure for Measure* in what are typically referred to as Shakespeare's "problem plays." All three share a bitter humor and a cynical view of human relations that contrast sharply with earlier, sunnier comedies such as *Twelfth Night* and *As You Like It*. In fact, the title of this play is almost ironic.

**FACTS**

Throughout his career, Shakespeare explored the paradox of the evil in good people and goodness in bad people. The only truly unsympathetic figure in *All's Well That Ends Well* is Parolles, who is less a villain than a comically amoral rogue.

The source of the story is Boccaccio's *Decameron*, a classic of early Renaissance literature, written between 1348 and 1358. The *Decameron* (essentially a short story collection with a framework somewhat like *Canterbury Tales* or *1001 Arabian Nights*), was translated into English in the mid-sixteenth century by William Painter as *The Palace of Pleasure*, and it was this version that Shakespeare probably drew upon.

Shakespeare, of course, altered and reshaped the original story, adding characters such as Lafew, the countess, and Parolles, but kept the basic elements—the bed-trick and the war in Florence.

## The Play

When his father dies, Bertram becomes Count of Rosillion. Helena is the orphaned daughter of a great doctor and has lived in the Rosillion household under the guardianship of Bertram's mother, the countess.

Helena follows Bertram to Paris, where the king of France has been taken deathly ill. Helena bears one of her father's prescriptions and when she cures the king, in gratitude he tells her she can have her pick of the bachelors at his court. Over the years, Helena has developed a secret love for Bertram. Now she can act on this love.

She picks Bertram, who is distressed by the prospect, feeling that Helena is beneath him. Under protest, Bertram agrees to the marriage.

Helena returns to Rosillion and the countess, at first assuming that Bertram will be along directly. Bertram, however, slips off to fight in Tuscany with his cowardly friend, Parolles.

It becomes apparent that Bertram is not returning home, and Bertram sends word that Helena can't call him husband until she wears his ring (which he always wears) and bears his child—not a simple task considering that Bertram is in Italy and has no intention of ever sleeping with her.

Helena now sets out for Florence. She winds up lodging with a widow whose daughter Diana, ironically, is the object of Bertram's affections. With Diana's help, Helena designs a trap for Bertram.

**SSENTIALS**   Audiences and critics are almost always divided on how they feel about Helena ending up with Bertram. As a result, *All's Well That Ends Well* is not performed much these days.

Diana makes Bertram give her his ring before they share a bed. Helena then takes Diana's place in the dark. She exchanges rings with him, giving him one that the king had given her for Bertram.

She next spreads a rumor that she has died, and Bertram figures that he is in the clear. However, back in France, the king recognizes the ring Bertram bears as the one he gave Helena. When Bertram is caught in a series of lies, the king has him arrested (supposing that Bertram has murdered her). Diana and her widowed mother arrive demanding justice, and when Helena finally turns up bearing Bertram's ring, carrying his child, and revealing the truth to all, Bertram repents the error of his ways and swears his love for Helena.

## Commentary

*All's Well That Ends Well* is often described as a problem play, distinguished from the earlier, more cheerful comedies by a sophisticated bitterness toward human relations. These plays' happy endings are really nothing of the sort. It's hard for a modern audience to imagine Bertram and Helena enjoying a happy marriage.

For a play about love, *All's Well That Ends Well* is remarkably cynical. Helena's low opinion of men seems well founded. The successful central deception is the bedroom switch that enables Helena to become pregnant by Bertram, who had avoided marrying her, to trick him into living with her. It works, Shakespeare suggests, because in the dark all women look alike to men.

For modern audiences, the idea of great women picking men who are unworthy of them is disquieting. It's particularly tough with *All's Well That Ends Well* because Bertram turns out to be such a jerk. He abandons Helena, tries to seduce an innocent woman, and only repents because he has no choice. It's either marriage or jail.

**QUESTIONS?**

**Was Shakespeare commenting on what it meant to be a woman alone, with few prospects of earning a living in a male-dominated world?**
Given the cynicism of the story, one can't help but wonder if an unrecognized desperation plays some small part in Helena's determination to "nail" Bertram.

The resourceful Helena, meanwhile, while loved by everyone (except Bertram), also gives us pause for thought. She seems to be a classic example of "why good women make bad choices." Why does she so relentlessly pursue a man who is so demonstratively unworthy of her? Nothing stands in Helena's way as she "gets her man." While we may admire her, by the time she's triumphant, our opinion of her good taste is all but gone.

## Famous Lines

"All the learned and authentic fellows" (Act II, Scene III).

"A young man married is a man that's marr'd" (Act II, Scene III).

"Praising what is lost makes the remembrance dear"
(Act V, Scene III).

# 3 ✤ *Antony and Cleopatra*

## Main Characters

**Mark Antony**—Along with Octavius Caesar and Lepidus, he is a member of the triumvirate that rules the Roman Empire. Once a great general and powerful politician, Antony has abandoned Rome and his wife Fulvia in order to frolic in Egypt with Cleopatra.

**Cleopatra**—The queen of Egypt and Antony's lover. She once seduced Julius Caesar.

**Octavius Caesar**—Julius Caesar's nephew and adopted son; one of the triumvirate of Rome.

**Domitius Enobarbus**—Antony's loyal supporter.

**Marcus Aemilius Lepidus**—The weakest member of the triumvirate. He tries to keep the peace between Octavius and Antony.

**Sextus Pompeius**—Son of a great general who was one of Julius Caesar's partners in power.

**Octavia**—Caesar's sister. She marries Antony in order to cement the alliance of the two triumvirs.

**Charmian and Iras**—Cleopatra's attendants.

**The Soothsayer**—An Egyptian fortuneteller.

**Dolabella**—One of Octavius Caesar's men.

**Agrippa**—One of Octavius Caesar's officers.

**Canidius**—Antony's general.

**Ventidius**—A Roman soldier under Antony's command.

**Scarus**—A brave soldier.

**Proculeius**—One of Caesar's soldiers.

**Mardian, Alexas, and Diomedes**—Cleopatra's servants.

**Thidias, Gallus, and Maecenas**—Caesar's men.

**Demetrius and Philo**—Antony's soldiers in Egypt.

**Eros**—An attendant, serving Antony.

**Menas, Menecrates, and Varrius**—Soldiers under Pompey.

**Seleucus**—Cleopatra's treasurer.

**Clown**—An Egyptian who brings the poisonous snake to Cleopatra.

**Decretas**—One of Antony's soldiers.

# Introduction

*Antony and Cleopatra* was written about 1606 and is considered Shakespeare's last great tragedy. It is an epic of the Roman Empire and a tragedy of global proportions.

Shakespeare's primary source for *Antony and Cleopatra* was the "Life of Marcus Antonius" contained in Plutarch's *Lives of Noble Greeks and Romans*, which was translated into English by Sir Thomas North in 1579. Large sections of North's language found their way into the play with only a few changes.

**FACTS**

This play greatly compresses a decade's worth of events. Antony is clearly much older than in *Julius Caesar*, and his political instincts seem to be waning. Octavius Caesar was a minor character in the earlier play, but now comes into his own as the man who will rise to become the first Roman Emperor, Caesar Augustus.

The plot of the play also remains close to North's story, although characters such as Enobarbus and Cleopatra's attendants are largely Shakespearean creations. The action of the story takes place roughly two years after Shakespeare's earlier play, *Julius Caesar*.

Most of the events of the play are historically accurate. From the images we have of Cleopatra, it seems she was rather plain. Clearly, her seductive qualities must have come from her personality.

# The Play

Octavius Caesar, Antony, and Lepidus form the Roman triumvirate that rules the Western world. Lepidus decides to retire, leaving Caesar and Antony in charge. Antony, although married to Fulvia, lives in Egypt with his mistress Cleopatra, the queen of Egypt. Disgusted by Antony's lifestyle in Egypt and angry about wars caused by Antony's relatives, Caesar recalls Antony to Rome. Fulvia dies and Caesar and Antony try to make peace through Antony's marriage to Caesar's sister Octavia.

Antony quickly returns to Cleopatra. Caesar vows to wrest Egypt from Antony and Cleopatra. As defeat seems near, Antony's best friend Enobarbus deserts him and joins Caesar's army, then filled with guilt, kills himself near Caesar's headquarters. Facing certain defeat, Antony kills himself by falling on his sword. Cleopatra, in grief over Antony's death and determined never to be taken in chains to Rome as a prisoner, commits suicide by allowing poisonous asps (snakes) to bite her.

## Commentary

*Antony and Cleopatra*, Shakespeare's final tragedy, is an ambitious epic play with a vast cast and complex politics. The title characters are defined not by their intense interior life as seen in Hamlet or Othello, but by their awareness of themselves as public figures. "But what about me?" they seem to ask. "When is my duty done? When does my personal happiness come?"

**SSENTIALS**

Antony and Cleopatra may lose an empire to Octavius, but in the poetry of their final hours, as they realize their personal ambitions, if only briefly, we are led to feel that their suicides are a victory and they will be united beyond the grave.

The real struggle in the play is not between armies, but for Antony's soul, and Cleopatra's Egypt wins. Cleopatra is a complex character: deeply in love with Antony, yet willing to consider betraying him. She is a sexually mature seductress with a childlike understanding of war; and above all, a performer who is always "on," playing herself for the benefit of those around her. While other Shakespearean tragic heroes, such as Hamlet or Macbeth, die in alienation and despair, Cleopatra and her lover achieve what she calls their "immortal longings."

## Famous Lines

"There's beggary in the love that can be reckon'd" (Act I, Scene I).

"My salad days,
When I was green in judgment" (Act I, Scene V).

"The barge she sat in, like a burnish'd throne,
Burn'd on the water; the poop was beaten gold;
Purple the sails, and so perfumed that
The winds were lovesick with them; the oars were silver,
Which to the tune of flutes kept stroke, and made
The water which they beat to follow faster,
As amorous of their strokes. For her own person,
It beggar'd all description" (Act II, Scene II).

"Age cannot wither her, nor custom stale
Her infinite variety" (Act II, Scene II).

"He wears the rose
Of youth upon him" (Act III, Scene XIII).

"I am dying, Egypt, dying" (Act IV, Scene XV).

"I have
Immortal longings in me" (Act V, Scene II).

# 4 ᕫ *As You Like It*

## Main Characters

**Duke Senior**—Forced to live in exile in the Forest of Arden after his kingdom was usurped by his brother Duke Frederick. Father of Rosalind.

**Rosalind (Ganymede)**—Daughter of Duke Senior. Forced to flee to the forest of Arden disguised as a young man called Ganymede. In love with Orlando.

**Lord Amiens**—A faithful lord of Duke Senior in exile in the forest; an optimist.

**Lord Jaques**—A faithful lord of Duke Senior in exile in the forest; a pessimist.

**Duke Frederick**—Duke Senior's brother and usurper of Senior's throne. Celia's father.

**Celia (Aliena)**—Duke Frederick's daughter and Rosalind's best friend. She falls in love with Oliver at first sight.

**Charles**—A champion wrestler.

**Touchstone**—A court clown who accompanies Rosalind and Celia. He falls in love with Audrey, a goatherd.

**Oliver**—Oldest son of Sir Rowland De Bois, and Orlando's older brother. For some reason, unknown even to himself, Oliver hates Orlando.

**Orlando**—Younger brother of Oliver. Fearing for his life, he flees to the Forest of Arden. He's in love with Rosalind.

**Adam**—An old retainer of Sir Rowland De Bois.

**Silvius**—A young shepherd, in love with Phebe.

**Phebe**—A young shepherdess who falls in love with Ganymede (Rosalind).

**Corin**—A friend of Silvius.

**Audrey**—A goatherd, in love with Touchstone.

**William**—A young country boy in love with Audrey.

# Introduction

*As You Like It* was most likely written between the years 1598 and 1600. It belongs to a literary tradition known as pastoral, which began in the literature of Ancient Greece, flourished through Roman times most particularly in the work of Virgil, and continued into Shakespeare's time.

**QUESTIONS?**

**What is a pastoral?**
Typically, a pastoral story involves exiles from urban life who arrive in the countryside and try to live as common folk. Their conversations are often about the benefits of "country versus town." In effect, the pastoral comedy became a useful forum for social commentary at a time when such open criticism could be professionally problematic for a writer, not to mention dangerous on occasion.

# The Play

As the play opens, Duke Senior has taken refuge in the Forest of Arden with a band of loyal followers, while his daughter, Rosalind, stays behind at the court of Duke Frederick, who has usurped his brother's throne.

We meet another set of brothers at odds with each other; Orlando and Oliver hate each other. Since their father's death, Oliver has long mistreated his younger brother, Orlando. When Orlando enters a wrestling match sponsored by Duke Frederick, Oliver tells Orlando's opponent, Charles—a champion wrestler—to break Orlando's neck if he can. To everyone's surprise, Orlando wins the match and attracts Rosalind's attention.

Duke Frederick decides to banish Rosalind to Arden as he did her father, Duke Senior. Celia, Frederick's daughter and Rosalind's best friend, decides to travel with her. Rosalind disguises herself as a boy called Ganymede, and Celia becomes Ganymede's sister, Aliena. The clown Touchstone accompanies them.

Orlando wanders the forest leaving love poems on the branches of trees for Rosalind. She, meanwhile, sets out to lead a pastoral life. Before long, however, disguised as Ganymede, Rosalind promises to help

Orlando win his love's affection. Pretending to be Ganymede she tells Orlando she will "play" Rosalind and help him woo her.

Still disguised as Ganymede, Rosalind tries to make a match between Silvius and Phebe that goes awry; Phebe falls for Ganymede instead. Touchstone courts a country girl named Audrey, adding to the multiple romances.

Oliver enters the forest after Orlando. But Orlando saves him from a lion, and the two brothers reconcile. Oliver then falls in love with Celia; Duke Senior promises to marry them the next day. Rosalind makes Phebe promise to marry Silvius if she can't have Ganymede, then tells Orlando that Rosalind will marry him that day as well.

When all have gathered for the wedding, Rosalind reveals herself as the erstwhile Ganymede. She and Orlando are happily reunited, and Phebe agrees to marry Silvius. Touchstone also marries Audrey. In a final resolution, we learn that Duke Frederick has seen the error of his ways and opted for a monastic life, restoring Duke Senior's throne.

## Commentary

*As You Like It* is considered one of Shakespeare's best comedies. It pokes fun at the conventions of romantic love and explores the evils of primogeniture, a common English practice during Shakespeare's time in which the oldest son inherited everything, leaving younger siblings at their older brother's mercy.

**FACTS**

*As You Like It* delights in the ridiculousness of humans, constantly punching holes in the beliefs of one character through the analysis of other characters who are equally blind to the absurdity of their own value systems. This technique raises the play from simple entertainment to one that offers a social critique and stresses the complexity of things—the simultaneous pleasures and pains of being human.

The play manipulates the typical conventions of a pastoral in order to explore other issues. For instance, it was common in a pastoral for people to wear disguises. In *As You Like It*, Rosalind dresses as a man in order to make her journey into exile less dangerous. But Shakespeare pushes the tradition by having Rosalind, in disguise, encounter Orlando, and then role-play herself in order to teach Orlando how to woo her. In effect, the play raises questions about gender roles.

## Famous Lines

"One out of suits with fortune" (Act I, Scene II).

"My pride fell with my fortunes" (Act I, Scene II).

"Beauty provoketh thieves sooner than gold" (Act I, Scene III).

"True is it that we have seen better days" (Act II, Scene VII).

"All the world's a stage,
And all the men and women merely players.
They have their exits and their entrances;
And one man in his time plays many parts,
His acts being seven ages. At first the infant,
Mewling and puking in the nurse's arms.
And then the whining school-boy, with his satchel
And shining morning face, creeping like snail
Unwillingly to school. And then the lover,
Sighing like furnace, with a woful ballad
Made to his mistress' eyebrow. Then a soldier,
Full of strange oaths and bearded like the pard;
Jealous in honour, sudden and quick in quarrel,
Seeking the bubble reputation
Even in the cannon's mouth. And then the justice,
In fair round belly with good capon lined,
With eyes severe and beard of formal cut,
Full of wise saws and modern instances;

And so he plays his part. The sixth age shifts
Into the lean and slipper'd pantaloon,
With spectacles on nose and pouch on side;
His youthful hose, well saved, a world too wide
For his shrunk shank; and his big manly voice,
Turning again toward childish treble, pipes
And whistles in his sound. Last scene of all,
That ends this strange eventful history,
Is second childishness and mere oblivion,
Sans teeth, sans eyes, sans taste, sans everything" (Act II, Scene VII).

"Blow, blow, thou winter wind!
Thou art not so unkind
As man's ingratitude" (Act II, Scene VII).

"He that wants money, means, and content is without three good
    friends" (Act III, Scene II).

"With bag and baggage" (Act III, Scene II).

"Neither rhyme nor reason" (Act III, Scene II).

"I had rather have a fool to make me merry than experience to make
    me sad" (Act IV, Scene I).

"Can one desire too much of a good thing?" (Act IV, Scene I).

"For ever and a day" (Act IV, Scene I).

"It is meat and drink to me" (Act V, Scene I).

"The fool doth think he is wise, but the wise man knows himself to
    be a fool" (Act V, Scene I).

"How bitter a thing it is to look into happiness through another man's
    eyes!" (Act V, Scene II).

"An ill-favoured thing, sir, but mine own" (Act V, Scene IV).

# 5 § *Cardenio*

## Main Characters

**The Tyrant**—Usurped the king's throne.

**Govianus**—The king. In love with the Lady.

**The Lady**—Govianus's love, and pursued by the Tyrant.

**Helvetius**—The Lady's father.

**Memphonius, Sophonirus, and Bellarius**—Nobles of the court.

**The Wife**—The wife of Anselmus.

**Anselmus**—Brother-in-law of Govianus.

**Votarius**—Anselmus's best friend.

**Leonella**—The Wife's servant.

## Introduction

*Cardenio* is considered by some scholars to be a lost play by William Shakespeare, probably coauthored with John Fletcher, and written around 1613. Little evidence of *Cardenio* appeared until 1728, when Lewis Theobald published a play called *Double Falsehood*, or *The Distressed Lovers*, based on the story of Cardenio and Lucinda in Cervantes's *Don Quixote*, which first appeared in English around 1612. Theobald said that he had revised the play and "adapted [it] to the stage" from an old manuscript "originally written by Fletcher and Shakespeare." He did not include it in his edition of Shakespeare.

In fact, the most recent version of *The Norton Shakespeare* is the first edition of Shakespeare's works to include a separate description of it. We know that on May 20, 1613, John Heminges, who ran the King's Men, was presented a sum of money for performing six plays, one of which was entitled *Cardenio* and another, *Cardenna*.

In 1653, the printer Humphrey Moseley entered in the Stationers' Register several plays, including "*The History of Cardenio*, by Mr. Fletcher and Mr. Shakespeare." In 1612 or thereabouts, an untitled, anonymous, handwritten final draft of a play was delivered to Sir George Buc, the

Master of the Revels to King James I, as the final step prior to performance. Confused by the lack of a title, he referred to it as "this *Second Mayden's Tragedy*," presumably for its resemblance to *The Maid's Tragedy* by Beaumont and Fletcher.

According to court diaries, the King's Men gave two performances at court of a play called "*Cardenno* [sic], by Mr. Fletcher & Mr. Shakespeare." Scholars long assumed that the script for that play was lost. The original script that Sir George censored, however, still lacking a title page, floated around until it was purchased sometime after 1807 by the British Museum, where it still sits.

The script appears to have been a prompt book used by Shakespeare's company. Among other things, it has handwritten references to actors known to have been a part of the King's Men in 1611.

It is well known that John Fletcher was a great admirer of Cervantes, and he was probably able to read *Don Quixote* in its original Spanish. Could Shakespeare and Fletcher have written a play based on the Cardenio episodes in Volume I of *Don Quixote*?

The few scholars who examined the script concluded that it was the work of Thomas Middddleton—until 1994, that is. Historian Charles Hamilton published the script, along with 140 pages of testimony (*Shakespeare with John Fletcher: Cardenio, or The Second Maiden's Tragedy*. New York: Marlowe & Company, 1994) arguing that it is, in fact, the play *Cardenio* referred to in those old court diaries coauthored by Shakespeare and Fletcher. If true, it would be the first play added to the Shakespearean canon, even if coauthored, since the publication of the Fourth Folio more than 300 years ago.

## The Play

*Cardenio* has two distinct plots that are linked by the relationships of the main characters. One plays against the other in a scene-by-scene progression that neatly uses one plot to contrast with, and comment on, the other.

Act I opens in the midst of a coup, as Govianus, the rightful king, loses his throne to an obsessive Tyrant. Rubbing salt in an open wound (and recalling Richard III and Lady Anne), the Tyrant proceeds to woo Govianus's love, referred to in the play only as the Lady.

She remains steadfast in her devotion to Govianus, even in the face of her own father's appeals to make things easier for everyone by simply appeasing the Tyrant and giving him what he wants. Govianus and the Lady are imprisoned. Frustrated by the Lady, the Tyrant sends his soldiers to force her to submit to him. Rather than be "borne with violence to the Tyrant's bed," she begs Govianus to kill her.

He can't bring himself to do that, so she kills herself instead. Undeterred and angry that the Lady has managed to thwart him, the Tyrant steals her corpse from its tomb intent on making her his queen anyway. Govianus is released, finds his way to court, and avenges her death. Restored to the throne, Govianus returns her body to the tomb.

In the subplot, a jealous lord, Anselmus, brother-in-law to Govianus, convinces his best friend, Votarius, to seduce his wife as a test of her fidelity. Surprised by their unexpected passion for each other, Votarius and the Wife begin a clandestine affair. To divert her husband's suspicions, the Wife and Votarius plot to have Anselmus overhear a conversation in which the Wife will seemingly spurn Votarius' advances with a sword. the Wife's servant, however, has poisoned the sword's tip, and the Wife unwittingly kills her lover. As the various plots and deceptions are revealed, all are slain.

## Commentary

Those who want to pursue the authorship question should start with Charles Hamilton's *Cardenio, or The Second Maiden's Tragedy* (New York: Marlowe & Co, 1994), Anne Lancashire's (ed.) *The Second Maiden's Tragedy* (Oxford: Manchester University Press, 1978), and Harold L. Stenger, Jr.'s *The Second Maiden's Tragedy: A Modernized*

*Edition with an Introduction* (unpublished dissertation, University of Pennsylvania, 1954).

For those who consider the play a lost Shakespeare piece, the evidence is seen in the characterizations, particularly of the women, such as the Lady herself, who seems to continue the lineage of the spiritually powerful princesses of *Cymbeline, The Winter's Tale*, and *Pericles*. The language also seems to be Shakespeare's by its delight in new words and powerful imagery.

SSENTIALS

For each list of arguments that tries to link Shakespeare's and Fletcher's works to *The Second Maiden's Tragedy,* an equally persuasive list of comparisons can be made with the plays of Thomas Middleton.

However, proving a play's authorship is something of a detective game. Hamilton, for example, based part of his evidence on handwriting analysis. The manuscript contains stage directions, censor's cuts, and slips of paper with textual corrections in the same hand as the body of the text, leading some scholars to conclude that the manuscript was handwritten by the playwright, while others believe it is a copy, prepared by a professional scribe. Particularly puzzling, is that there is no character named Cardenio in *The Second Maiden's Tragedy*.

# 6 & *Coriolanus*

## Main Characters

**Caius Martius**—A Roman general who is given the name "Coriolanus" after he defeats the Volscians. He is brave but arrogant.

**Volumnia**—Coriolanus's mother. She dominates her son.

**Menenius**—A friend of Coriolanus.

**Brutus**—A Roman tribune.

**Sicinius**—Brutus's ally in the plot against Coriolanus.

**Tullus Aufidius**—A Volscian general.

**Cominius**—A friend of Coriolanus.

**Titus Lartius**—An old Roman nobleman.

**Virgilia**—Coriolanus's wife.

**Valeria**—A friend of Virgilia and Volumnia.

**Young Martius**—Coriolanus and Virgilia's son.

## Introduction

*Coriolanus* was probably written in 1607 or 1608 and first performed in 1609 at the Blackfriars Theatre in London, although these dates are uncertain. It is the penultimate tragedy written by Shakespeare and follows *Othello*, *King Lear*, *Macbeth*, and *Antony and Cleopatra*, all of which Shakespeare probably composed between 1604 and 1606.

**FACTS**

The plot of *Coriolanus* probably came from *The Life of Caius Martius Coriolanus*, written in the first century by Plutarch and translated into English in 1579 by Sir Thomas North. (Another source may have been Livy's *History of Rome*.)

As was *Antony and Cleopatra*, it is a Roman play, but *Coriolanus* takes place early in Rome's history, when it was just one Italian city among many, fighting for survival. The play takes place just after the fall of Tarquin, the last Roman king, and highlights the period when Rome moved from being a monarchy to a republic.

Renaissance scholars were fascinated with Roman history (no doubt in part because of North's rich translation). Poets, playwrights, politicians, and philosophers alike consistently turned to Greece and Rome for inspiration, so Shakespeare's interest in the period makes a lot of sense.

However, one of the attractions of this play may have been the parallels between the events of the play and politics under the new king, James I. Jacobean London was plagued with radical thought and there was a struggle brewing between King James and Parliament as the middle class demanded more say in the running of their lives. The struggle culminated in 1642 in the English Civil War and the execution of James's son Charles I by parliamentarians under Oliver Cromwell. For a brief period, England became a republic before the restoration of the monarchy in 1660.

## The Play

Caius Martius is a legendary Roman general who considers himself better than other men, though he prefers to be a power behind the throne. He defeats the Volscian defenders of the city of Corioli and nearly beats their general Aufidius in hand-to-hand combat. At the last moment Aufidius flees.

For his accomplishments Marcius is renamed Caius Martius Coriolanus. He returns to Rome, where the patricians want to make him a tribune of the common people (the plebeians). The tribunes Sicinius Velutus and Junius Brutus are afraid that Coriolanus may become too powerful. They convince the plebes to condemn Coriolanus to death and Coriolanus does nothing to help his cause with his arrogant attitude.

Outraged, Coriolanus flees Rome, abandoning his wife Virgilia and mother Volumnia. Coriolanus heads to the city of Antium to help Aufidius and the Volscians defeat the Roman Empire and seize Rome. With Coriolanus's help, the Volscians plunder the outlying Roman towns and pause at the gates of Rome. Friends and relatives try to dissuade Coriolanus from attacking his own people. Volumnia convinces him to make peace by using Coriolanus's son to play on Coriolanus's emotions.

Aufidius becomes infuriated that Coriolanus failed to sack Rome. He murders Coriolanus in front of the lords of Corioli. Aufidius, though pleased that Coriolanus is dead, orders that he be given a noble memorial.

# Commentary

*Coriolanus* is something of a potboiler, and is clearly not one of Shakespeare's best plays. It lacks depth, and its characters are somewhat two dimensional. It is perhaps Shakespeare's most overtly political play.

While Coriolanus's skill in battle would seem to make him an ideal hero for the masses, his contempt for the "blue-collar" mob allows him to be set up as an enemy of the people. While Coriolanus was in part responsible for the expulsion of Tarquin, the last Roman king, Coriolanus is a kingly figure born to command and unwilling to con his way to power. He clearly has no place in the republic that is taking command of his city.

Volumnia is not able to achieve power in her own right in the male-dominated Roman society, so her ambition drives her son's. She alone is able to convince Coriolanus to spare Rome, thus unwittingly sealing his doom.

While Coriolanus may be direct, he is surrounded by manipulative characters such as his friend, Menenius, and the two tribunes, Sicinius and Brutus. Their manipulation of the masses turns the people of Rome against Coriolanus and almost brings about the city's downfall.

The play has been adopted by both the political left and right with equal relish, and depending upon a director's philosophical inclinations the play's ambiguities continue to fuel discussion.

# Famous Lines

"Nature teaches beasts to know their friends" (Act II, Scene I).

"His nature is too noble for the world:
He would not flatter Neptune for his trident,
Or Jove for 's power to thunder" (Act III, Scene I).

# 7 ◊ *Cymbeline*

## Main Characters

**Cymbeline**—The king of Britain and Imogen's father.

**Imogen**—Cymbeline's daughter. She is in love with lowborn Posthumus rather than Cymbeline's stepson Cloten.

**Posthumus**—Cymbeline's protégé. He marries Imogen in secret, against her father's wishes.

**Queen**—Cymbeline's wife. A villainous woman.

**Cloten**—The queen's son; an arrogant idiot.

**Iachimo**—A scheming Frenchman living in Italy.

**Pisanio**—Posthumus's loyal servant.

**Belarius**—A British nobleman, unjustly banished by Cymbeline. He kidnapped Cymbeline's infant sons to revenge himself on the king, and disguised as a shepherd, raised them as his own.

**Guiderius**—Cymbeline's eldest son raised by Belarius as Polydore.

**Arviragus**—Cymbeline's younger son raised by Belarius as Cadwal.

**Philario**—An Italian gentleman.

**Caius Lucius**—The Roman ambassador to Britain.

**Cornelius**—A doctor.

**Soothsayer**—A Roman seer.

**Jupiter**—The king of Olympus in Roman mythology.

## Introduction

*Cymbeline* is one of Shakespeare's last plays and was written and performed around 1609–10, probably on the indoor Blackfriars stage rather than at the more famous Globe. It joins *Pericles*, *The Winter's Tale*, and *The Tempest* in a list of problem plays that are considered tragicomedies. Death and despair, while never victorious in the end, loom as ever-present shadows.

# The Play

Twenty years ago, Cymbeline, the king of Britain, lost his two boys Guiderius and Arviragus in a kidnapping, leaving his daughter Imogen as the only heir to the throne. Cymbeline remarries, gaining an arrogant idiot stepson Cloten. Cymbeline wants Imogen to marry her stepbrother, but Imogen is in love with her childhood friend Posthumus Leonatus and secretly marries him. When he finds out, Cymbeline banishes Posthumus and confines Imogen to the castle grounds.

Posthumus goes to Rome to stay with his friend, Philario. Iachimo, a mutual acquaintance, bets Posthumus that Iachimo can seduce Imogen. In Britain, Iachimo finds Imogen a tough nut to crack, so he sneaks into her bedroom, peers at her while she is sleeping, steals her bracelet, and returns to Rome to successfully convince Posthumus that he has succeeded.

**SSENTIALS**

*Cymbeline* seems to be an original play. Though the Iachimo plot, in which a seduction is attempted on a virtuous wife, may have its roots in Boccaccio's *Decameron*, and the scenes in the Welsh wilderness recall fairy tales like "Snow White," most of the plot and characters are likely directly from Shakespeare's imagination.

Posthumus is distraught that Imogen has cuckolded him and orders his servant Pisanio to kill Imogen. Pisanio can't bring himself to do the deed. Instead, he makes it look like Imogen is dead then takes her to Milford Haven where she disguises herself as a man named Fidele.

In Milford Haven, Imogen (as Fidele) meets her kidnapped brothers though she doesn't know who they really are, of course. Belarius kidnapped the boys as revenge for Cymbeline's unfairly banishing him.

Cloten follows Imogen to Milford Haven wearing Posthumus's clothes, in hopes of tricking her. He gets into a fight with Guiderius, and Guiderius cuts off Cloten's head.

Meanwhile, the queen tries to trick Pisanio by giving him medicine (which she thinks is poison), hoping he will give it to Imogen or Posthumus as a gift. The queen figures if Imogen is dead her son becomes Cymbeline's only heir, and if Posthumus dies, Imogen will be widowed and thus forced to marry Cloten.

In Milford Haven, Imogen falls sick and takes the medicine Pisanio gave her as a present. It is not poison as the queen believed. The medicine puts Imogen into a deep sleep, and Belarius and sons, believing her dead, lay her beside Cloten's body. When Imogen recovers, she sees the headless body dressed in Posthumus's clothes and thinks that he is dead.

Meanwhile, Caius Lucius demands that Britain pay tribute to Rome and Augustus Caesar. Cymbeline refuses and Lucius declares war on Britain. The queen gets sick and on her deathbed admits her crimes and sins, including hating Cymbeline. Caius Lucius's army invades Britain, and he comes across Imogen and rescues her from the wild. In the only battle of the war, Cymbeline is captured by the Romans, then rescued by Belarius, Guiderius, and Arviragus, with help from Posthumus on the inside. The Britons then capture Posthumus, thinking he is Roman, and take him to Cymbeline. Posthumus has a vision where he is visited by the god Jupiter.

 **ESSENTIALS**

In the last scene of the play, Imogen returns to her father, Iachimo confesses he tricked everyone, Cornelius explains the queen's "poison," Cloten's death is explained, Belarius admits to kidnapping the princes, Cymbeline allows Imogen and Posthumus to stay married, a soothsayer explains a prophecy in a book left in Posthumus's lap by the god Jupiter, and peace is made with the Romans. Cymbeline does not punish Iachimo or Belarius.

## Commentary

*Cymbeline* is Shakespeare's attempt to tell a fairy tale using the elements of tragedy and it really doesn't work that well. The language, while rich, is often clumsy, and the mediocrity of certain scenes (notably the appearance of Jupiter) have led a number of critics to suggest that

Shakespeare may well have collaborated with a less talented playwright. While the play includes the wonderful Imogen and the entertaining Iachimo, the title character, Cymbeline, is rather two-dimensional, as is a lot of the supporting cast.

Like Helena and Portia, Imogen is a woman whose man does not really deserve her. Posthumus disappears from the action for long periods of time, and the various subplots make the play hard to follow.

The aging Shakespeare seems to have revisited elements of his earlier plays, albeit in a less impressive form. *Cymbeline* feels like a pastiche, as if Hollywood were to make a film that takes the best bits of several successful movies and stitches them together in another framework.

The Imogen-Cymbeline relationship suggests Lear and Cordelia in *King Lear*, though Cymbeline is a failure compared to Lear, while Iachimo reminds one of Iago in *Othello*, though he hardly reaches the depths of Iago's villainy, and Posthumus is a poor revisiting of Othello. The sleeping potion and Imogen awakening next to her "husband's" dead body remind us of *Romeo and Juliet*, while Imogen's cross-dressing recalls *As You Like It*, but none of these elements combine into a coherent whole. *Cymbeline* may seem a tragedy, yet disaster never really strikes. Only the wicked characters die, and by the end everyone is reconciled.

The final scene, in which all the tangled strands of plot are tied together is cleverly constructed with everyone getting their just deserts. The villains die, Imogen and Posthumus are reunited, and King Cymbeline's abducted sons are restored to him; as Cymbeline declares, "Pardon's the word to all."

## Famous Lines

"Hath his bellyful of fighting" (Act II, Scene I).

"As chaste as unsunn'd snow" (Act II, Scene V).

"Some griefs are medicinable" (Act III, Scene II).

"The game is up" (Act III, Scene III).

"I have not slept one wink" (Act III, Scene IV).

# 8 ♿ *Hamlet, Prince of Denmark*

## Main Characters

**Hamlet**—The prince of Denmark. The son of the late King Hamlet and the nephew of the present King Claudius.

**Claudius**—The king of Denmark. Hamlet's uncle who murdered Hamlet's father to obtain the throne.

**Gertrude**—The queen of Denmark. Hamlet's mother. After the death of her husband (Hamlet's father), Gertrude married her brother-in-law, Claudius.

**Polonius**—The lord chamberlain and father to Laertes and Ophelia.

**Horatio**—Hamlet's friend.

**Ophelia**—Polonius's daughter.

**Laertes**—Polonius's son.

**Fortinbras**—The prince of Norway. His father was killed by Hamlet's father. He intends to attack Denmark to avenge his father's death.

**The Ghost**—Hamlet's recently murdered father.

**Rosencrantz and Guildenstern**—Former friends of Hamlet from Wittenberg.

**Osric, Voltemand, and Cornelius**—Courtiers.

**Marcellus and Barnardo**—The officers of the watch who report seeing the ghost.

**Francisco**—A soldier.

**Reynaldo**—Polonius's servant.

## Introduction

*Hamlet* may well be the most famous play ever written in the English language. Composed during the first part of the seventeenth century at the close of Queen Elizabeth's reign, *Hamlet* was probably first performed in July 1602. It was first published in 1603 and appeared in a longer edition in 1604.

*Hamlet* is the story of a Danish prince whose uncle murders his father and marries his mother. Shakespeare likely knew the story from an earlier German play, from *Hystorie of Hamblet,* an English translation of a French prose work (Francois de Belleforest's *Histoires Tragiques)*, and from an ancient history of Denmark written by Saxo Grammaticus in the thirteenth century.

The revenge tragedy was a staple of the Elizabethan theater and it may seem that *Hamlet* falls into this genre; however, it is clearly much more. It is a rumination on life and death and the reason for existence.

What Shakespeare did with this raw material may well have been transformed by the death of his young son Hamnet, several years before the play was written. Critics speculate that Shakespeare's continuing grief for his son is echoed in Hamlet's grief for his father (also called Hamlet).

## The Play

Hamlet, prince of Denmark, has a lot to be depressed about: The ghost of his father haunts Elsinore claiming he was murdered by his brother, Claudius; Claudius, meanwhile, has married Queen Gertrude, Hamlet's mother, and assumed the throne; and Fortinbras of Norway threatens to invade Denmark.

The ghost demands that Hamlet exact revenge for his murder. In order to carry this out, Hamlet feigns madness. As part of his insanity, he scorns the affections of Ophelia whom he has previously been courting.

Polonius grows concerned over Hamlet's growing insanity and discusses his concern with the king and queen. Meanwhile, Hamlet tries to come to terms with the idea that his uncle may have murdered his father and in an effort to "catch the conscience of the king," Hamlet convinces a traveling troupe of actors to act out a play whose action closely parallels the murder of his father. Claudius reacts badly at the murder scene, convincing Hamlet the ghost told him the truth. Still, he can't bring himself to slay his uncle because he feels it is a sin.

Hamlet starts to torment his mother, Gertrude, by insisting she is sleeping with her husband's killer. Polonius, who hides behind a tapestry in the queen's chamber to eavesdrop, panics and cries for help. Hamlet stabs him, thinking it is his uncle Claudius.

Claudius sends Hamlet to England with Rosencrantz and Guildenstern, two of Hamlet's childhood friends. He gets Hamlet to carry a letter to the king of England in which Claudius asks England to kill Hamlet (the bearer of the letter). Hamlet turns the tables on his friends and they are put to death instead.

**QUESTIONS?**

**Is *Hamlet* Shakespeare's greatest play?**
Whether *Hamlet* is Shakespeare's greatest play is debatable. It is certainly his most famous. *Hamlet* has been analyzed exhaustively for its aesthetic, moral, political, psychological, historical, allegorical, logical, religious, and philosophical aspects. There are thousands of works devoted to the play, and while there may be wrong ways to understand the tragedy, there is no single right way.

Driven to madness herself by Hamlet's condition and the death of her father Polonius, Ophelia drowns herself. Her brother, Laertes, returns from his studies and vows his vengeance upon Hamlet for what the prince has done to his family. Claudius plots with Laertes to kill Hamlet. At Ophelia's funeral Laertes and Hamlet confront one another and Laertes challenges Hamlet to a duel.

Claudius tells Laertes to select a sharp blade instead of a dull one for the duel and to poison the tip so that a wound will kill the prince. Claudius also decides to keep some poisoned wine for Hamlet to drink. But everything goes wrong.

Laertes is unable to wound Hamlet during the first pass of the duel. Between passes, Gertrude drinks from the poisoned wine before Claudius can stop her. In the heat of the fray, Laertes wounds Hamlet but loses the poisoned rapier to him, and Laertes is poisoned as well. Gertrude collapses. Laertes reveals the plot against Hamlet before he dies, telling him he has "not a half-hour's life" in him. Hamlet stabs Claudius with the poisoned foil, then forces him to drink from the poisoned wine that killed his mother.

Hamlet now collapses and dies in Horatio's arms as Fortinbras enters the castle. Fortinbras is left to rule as the entire Danish royal family is dead. He tells his men to give Hamlet and the rest proper funerals.

# Commentary

Hamlet is one of the most complex and compelling characters of English literature. His actions and thoughts have been analyzed over and over, and it is this seemingly bottomless well of possibilities that accounts for *Hamlet*'s enduring appeal.

*Hamlet* is concerned with the profound truths of human nature and our place in the universe, and it is not possible to responsibly reduce the play to a set of simple themes. Things to consider, however, include Shakespeare's questioning of the whole revenge play genre, and the nature of revenge itself and how it affects us. Hamlet's struggle over whether or not to murder Claudius, echoed by the Fortinbras and Laertes subplots, acts as a base from which Shakespeare explores the relationship between thought and action. It is human instinct to want revenge when wronged, but is it right to act on that instinct?

Hamlet is not a man of action deliberately, but a scholar, a man of thought and consideration and learning, and many critics feel the imbalance between his active and passive natures is a tragic flaw that makes his wretched fate inevitable.

**ESSENTIALS**

Hamlet is a kind of everyman, and his dilemmas echo those that we all face in some form. We can come to any number of reasonable conclusions about Hamlet, but arriving at a definitive one is very difficult.

Other important themes explored in *Hamlet* include the line between sanity and madness, the nature of political power, the connection between the well-being of the state and the moral condition of its leaders, and the moral questions of living a good life and committing suicide. Hamlet's ghostly father is in agony in Purgatory having died unconfessed and with his sins still heavy on his shoulders. Hamlet considers killing himself, but fears God's wrath in the afterlife. Ophelia, clearly an innocent, in a fit of madness does kill herself, but will she still suffer in the afterlife because of it? Other themes are the relationship between sons and fathers (Hamlet and the ghost, Laertes and Polonius, Fortinbras and the dead king of Norway), the nature of the family, the inevitability of death, and, against that inevitability, the question of what gives life meaning.

Hamlet's love of learning and reason is pulverized by a growing nihilism, as every truth that is supposed to comfort him (religion, society, philosophy, love) either fails him or proves false. Just how insane Hamlet was and how much he faked it is one of the most hotly contested critical controversies surrounding the play. The likely answer is that he decided to feign madness as a strategic way of covering his deep distress at what the ghost reveals to him without putting himself in danger. Yet there is little doubt that his mind is so troubled, confused, and desperate that his pretense assumes the intensity of real madness for a while as he deals with the enormity of what happened.

## Famous Lines

"For this relief much thanks: 't is bitter cold,
And I am sick at heart" (Act I, Scene I).

"A little more than kin, and less than kind" (Act I, Scene II).

"All that lives must die,
Passing through nature to eternity" (Act I, Scene II).

"But I have that within which passeth show;
These but the trappings and the suits of woe" (Act I, Scene II).

"He was a man, take him for all in all,
I shall not look upon his like again" (Act I, Scene II).

"Give thy thoughts no tongue" (Act I, Scene III).

"Neither a borrower nor a lender be;
For loan oft loses both itself and friend,

And borrowing dulls the edge of husbandry.
This above all: to thine own self be true,
And it must follow, as the night the day,
Thou canst not then be false to any man" (Act I, Scene III).

"But to my mind, though I am native here
And to the manner born, it is a custom
More honoured in the breach than the observance" (Act I, Scene IV).

"Something is rotten in the state of Denmark" (Act I, Scene IV).

"There are more things in heaven and earth, Horatio,
Than are dreamt of in your philosophy" (Act I, Scene V).

"Brevity is the soul of wit" (Act II, Scene II).

"Doubt thou the stars are fire;
Doubt that the sun doth move;
Doubt truth to be a liar;
But never doubt I love" (Act II, Scene II).

"Though this be madness, yet there is method in 't" (Act II, Scene II).

"There is nothing either good or bad, but thinking makes it so" (Act II, Scene II).

"A dream itself is but a shadow" (Act II, Scene II).

"What a piece of work is a man! how noble in reason! how infinite in faculty! in form and moving how express and admirable! in action how like an angel! in apprehension how like a god!" (Act II, Scene II).

"The devil hath power
To assume a pleasing shape" (Act II, Scene II).

"To be, or not to be: that is the question:
Whether 't is nobler in the mind to suffer
The slings and arrows of outrageous fortune,
Or to take arms against a sea of troubles,
And by opposing end them? To die: to sleep:

No more; and by a sleep to say we end
The heartache and the thousand natural shocks
That flesh is heir to,—'t is a consummation
Devoutly to be wish'd. To die, to sleep;
To sleep: perchance to dream: ay, there's the rub:
For in that sleep of death what dreams may come,
When we have shuffled off this mortal coil,
Must give us pause: there's the respect
That makes calamity of so long life;
For who would bear the whips and scorns of time,
The oppressor's wrong, the proud man's contumely,
The pangs of despised love, the law's delay,
The insolence of office and the spurns
That patient merit of the unworthy takes,
When he himself might his quietus make
With a bare bodkin? who would fardels bear,
To grunt and sweat under a weary life,
But that the dread of something after death,
The undiscover'd country from whose bourn
No traveller returns, puzzles the will
And makes us rather bear those ills we have
Than fly to others that we know not of?
Thus conscience does make cowards of us all;
And thus the native hue of resolution
Is sicklied o'er with the pale cast of thought,
And enterprises of great pith and moment
With this regard their currents turn awry,
And lose the name of action" (Act III, Scene I).

"Be thou as chaste as ice, as pure as snow, thou shalt not escape
calumny. Get thee to a nunnery, go" (Act III, Scene I).

"Suit the action to the word, the word to the action; with this special
observance, that you o'erstep not the modesty of nature" (Act III,
Scene II).

"I must be cruel, only to be kind:
Thus bad begins, and worse remains behind" (Act III, Scene IV).

"When sorrows come, they come not single spies,
But in battalions" (Act IV, Scene V).

"Alas, poor Yorick! I knew him, Horatio: a fellow of infinite jest, of
most excellent fancy. He hath borne me on his back a thousand
times; and now, how abhorred in my imagination it is! my gorge
rises at it. Here hung those lips that I have kissed I know not
how oft. Where be your gibes now; your gambols, your songs?
your flashes of merriment, that were wont to set the table on a
roar? Not one now, to mock your own grinning? Quite chap-fallen?
Now get you to my lady's chamber, and tell her, let her paint an
inch thick, to this favour she must come" (Act V, Scene I).

"The rest is silence" (Act V, Scene II).

# 9 ✑ *Julius Caesar*

## Main Characters

**Julius Caesar**—A great Roman general and senator.

**Brutus**—The tragic hero of the play. A Roman senator.

**Mark Antony**—Caesar's friend.

**Cassius**—Conspirator against Caesar.

**Octavius**—Caesar's adopted son and appointed successor.

**Calphurnia**—Caesar's wife.

**Portia**—Brutus's wife.

**Flavius and Murellus**—Civil servants.

**Decius**—A member of the conspiracy.

**Cicero**—A famous Roman orator.

**Cinna**—One of the conspirators.

**Cinna the Poet**—An innocent man killed by the mob because he has the same name as Cinna the conspirator.

**Casca, Metellus, Trebonius, and Ligarius**—Conspirators against Caesar.

**Lepidus**—The third member of the triumvirate with Antony and Octavius.

**Artemidorus**—He tries to warn Caesar of the conspiracy.

**Soothsayer**—He warns Caesar about the Ides of March, but Caesar ignores him.

**Lucilius, Titinius, Pindarus, and Messala**—Soldiers in Brutus's army.

**Varrus and Claudio**—Brutus's attendants.

## Introduction

*Julius Caesar* is Shakespeare's shortest play. It was written around 1599 and performed at the Globe Theatre, a playhouse owned by Shakespeare's increasingly successful company, the Lord Chamberlain's Men. However, the only authoritative text of the play is the 1623 First Folio edition. The stage directions suggest this text is based on the theater company's promptbook rather than Shakespeare's manuscript.

*Julius Caesar* was the earliest of Shakespeare's three Roman plays. As are *Antony and Cleopatra* (which is a sort of sequel) and *Coriolanus*,

*Julius Caesar* is a history in that it dramatizes real events. The play is clearly a tragedy because of the tragic character of Brutus, the noble Roman whose involvement in the conspiracy to save the state plunges both him and his country into chaos.

**FACTS**

Shakespeare drew on North's popular translation of Plutarch's *Lives*. Plutarch saw the role of the biographer and history as bound together, saying that history was the result of the achievements of great men. Shakespeare was clearly influenced by this philosophy. In this regard *Julius Caesar* is unlike *Coriolanus*, which dramatizes the conflicts between the classes.

Rome was sharply divided into the patrician citizens, senators, and the growing but underrepresented plebeians, or common folk. Citizens who favored republican democratic rule were afraid that Julius Caesar's power would lead to their enslavement. So a group of conspirators assassinated Caesar, and the civil war they hoped to avoid erupted anyway. The play follows events leading up to Caesar's death and the civil war.

Elizabethans would have been quick to pick up on the parallels between Ancient Rome becoming an imperial power, and Elizabeth's ability to consolidate the powers of the monarchy.

By 1599, Queen Elizabeth I had been queen for close to forty years and had enlarged her powers at the expense of the aristocracy and the House of Commons. At age sixty-six, particularly old for her time, and with no heirs or named successor, many feared her death would plunge England into the kind of chaos suffered during the fifteenth century. The story of Caesar's downfall provided a perspective on what might happen when accepted methods of distributing power were disrupted.

## The Play

Julius Caesar enters as a hero having defeated the Gauls, then Pompey's army. Mark Antony attempts three times to crown Caesar king; however, some senators take this as a threat to Rome. Cassius, in particular, has serious misgivings about Caesar's ambition and is clearly jealous of his achievements. To offset Caesar's popular support, Cassius approaches Marcus Brutus, a nobleman known for his integrity. If Brutus were to support a coup, it will be more acceptable to the citizens of Rome, and equally important, Brutus is also a close friend of Caesar.

**ESSENTIALS**

Brutus clearly emerges as the most complex character and the play's tragic hero. He is a powerful public figure, but is also a loving husband and dignified military leader. His rigid idealism becomes both his greatest virtue and his tragic flaw.

During a great storm, Brutus considers his options realizing that the conspirators may well have to assassinate Caesar. Caesar, already warned by a soothsayer and Calphurnia, his wife, ignores all advice to the contrary and pays a visit to the Senate. There he is stabbed to death by Brutus, Cassius, and the rest.

Brutus dissuades the conspirators from slaying Antony with Caesar, and after the assassination Antony asks to accompany Caesar's body and speak at his funeral. Brutus agrees, and at the funeral delivers a stirring oratory that explains the reasoning for the assassination. Antony follows with his famous "Friends, Romans, countrymen" speech, and through his masterful use of irony stirs the crowd to the point where they call for the blood of Cassius, Brutus, and anyone else associated with Caesar's death.

Antony then joins Octavius (Caesar's nephew) and Lepidus to wrest control of Rome by force of arms. Brutus and Cassius raise armies against them. In a final battle, with many of his coconspirators now dead, Cassius kills himself when facing defeat, and is quickly followed by Brutus who takes his own life rather than be taken captive. Upon discovering the body, Antony laments the tragic fall of Brutus, calling him the noblest of them all.

## Commentary

In a world of self-serving ambition, Brutus is truly "the noblest Roman of them all," but his commitment to principle repeatedly causes him to miscalculate. He ignores Cassius's suggestion to kill Antony as well as Caesar, and then, again against Cassius's advice, he allows Antony to speak a funeral oration over Caesar's body, plunging the city and the country into chaos.

Antony, however, is strong where Brutus is weak. He is impulsive and quick-witted, and he is able to save himself by convincing the conspirators he is on their side, then in enraging the mob against the conspirators. Brutus is noble, to be sure, but Antony proves himself the consummate politician.

Shakespeare explores several themes in *Julius Caesar*. The play raises questions about what in our lives is determined by fate and how much free will we have. Cassius, for example, says "The fault, dear Brutus, is not in our stars, But in ourselves, that we are underlings." On the other hand, Caesar tells his wife, "death, a necessary end, will come when it will come." The text explores public self versus private self and inflexibility versus compromise.

Brutus interprets his defeat as the work of Caesar's ghost—empowered by the people's devotion to Caesar—and the legacy of a man who somehow transcended fate. Both Brutus and Caesar are stubborn men who ultimately suffer fatally for it. It is the adaptable people, the ones who will compromise, who survive.

## Famous Lines

"The live-long day" (Act I, Scene I).

"Beware the ides of March" (Act I, Scene II).

"Let me have men about me that are fat,
Sleek-headed men, and such as sleep o' nights:
Yond Cassius has a lean and hungry look;
He thinks too much: such men are dangerous" (Act I, Scene II).

"A dish fit for the gods" (Act II, Scene I).

"Cowards die many times before their deaths;
The valiant never taste of death but once.
Of all the wonders that I yet have heard,
It seems to me most strange that men should fear;
Seeing that death, a necessary end,
Will come when it will come" (Act II, Scene II).

"Et tu, Brute!" (Act III, Scene I).

"O, pardon me, thou bleeding piece of earth,
That I am meek and gentle with these butchers!
Thou art the ruins of the noblest man
That ever lived in the tide of times" (Act III, Scene I).

"Cry 'Havoc,' and let slip the dogs of war" (Act III, Scene I).

"Friends, Romans, countrymen, lend me your ears;
I come to bury Cæsar, not to praise him.
The evil that men do lives after them;
The good is oft interred with their bones" (Act III, Scene II).

"If you have tears, prepare to shed them now" (Act III, Scene II).

"This was the most unkindest cut of all" (Act III, Scene II).

"Great Cæsar fell.
O, what a fall was there, my countrymen!
Then I, and you, and all of us fell down,
Whilst bloody treason flourish'd over us" (Act III, Scene II).

"There is a tide in the affairs of men
Which taken at the flood, leads on to fortune;
Omitted, all the voyage of their life
Is bound in shallows and in miseries" (Act IV, Scene III).

"His life was gentle, and the elements
So mix'd in him, that Nature might stand up
And say to all the world, 'This was a man!'" (Act V, Scene V).

# 10 § *King Edward III*

## Main Characters

King Edward III
Queen Philippa (de Hainault)
Prince Edward (Prince of Wales)
Earl of Salisbury
Countess of Salisbury
Earl of Warwick
Sir William Montague
Earl of Derby
Lord Audley
Lord Percy
John Copland
Lodowick
Robert of Artois
Lord Montfort
Gobin Agace

King John II (the Good)
Prince Charles (of Normandy)
Prince Philip
Duke of Lorraine
Lord Villiers
French captain (at Calais)
Another captain
A mariner
King of Bohemia
Polonian captain
The Scots
King David II of Scotland
Douglas
Scottish messenger

## Introduction

For over 400 years everyone but a handful of renegade critics have classified *King Edward III* as an anonymous play. First printed in 1596 by the London bookseller and publisher, Cuthbert Burby, the play's title page told Elizabethan readers that "it hath bin sundrie times plaied about the Citie of London," but Burby credited no author. The play was likely very successful at the time, for Burby published another edition in 1599, again without naming an author. Capell re-edited the play in his *Prolusions* (1760) and first put forward the claim that Shakespeare wrote the play.

Although Capell's assertions received some support in the nineteenth century, most significantly from the poet Tennyson, critics remained unconvinced and *King Edward III* seemed doomed to remain part of the Shakespeare apocrypha; that is, material reputed to be written by Shakespeare but unproven to be so.

**FACTS**

Three problems hindered the play's acceptance: it was not mentioned in Francis Meres's book *Palladis Tamia* (1598), a work that listed Shakespeare's early plays; John Heminge and Henry Condell did not include the play in the First Folio of 1623; and the play is considered by some scholars not to display Shakespeare's writing ability.

However, over the last few years critics have reassessed the play's merits and are beginning to argue that "hollow and insincere" passages are not reason enough to deny that Shakespeare wrote the drama. The writing in *King Edward III* measures up to Shakespeare's early work in the *King Henry VI* trilogy and *King John*.

In 1998, the Arden Shakespeare series (the leading publisher of William Shakespeare's works), the Cambridge University Press, and American Riverside Press included the play in their collected Shakespeare editions (Oxford scholars are holding out). The publishers used computer analysis of the play's text and language to verify its main source of authorship. *King Edward III* is a major addition to the Shakespearean canon, and while no one claims Shakespeare is the sole author, he is considered the author of a significant part of the play.

The question remains: Why, if Shakespeare wrote *King Edward III*, did it become a forgotten play and omitted from the First Folio? This is pure speculation, of course, but it is considered an early play, possibly even his first. It's possible Shakespeare shelved the play because he was unhappy with it, and decided to use parts of it for other plays. As a result it did not become part of the repertoire that Shakespeare revised and revived, and Heminges and Condell did not know the play was his.

*King Edward III* tells the story of the first campaigns of the Hundred Years' War and is likely one of Shakespeare's earliest works. Written in verse, the play opens with a scene similar to the first scene of *King*

*Henry V*. The preparations for King Edward's campaign in France quickly give way to the romance of the king and the countess of Salisbury.

# The Play

King Edward opens the play by rejecting his political obligations to the French king and claiming the French crown. The king instructs Prince Edward to prepare to invade France, while he himself repulses the Scots besieging the Roxborough castle in the north. The prince is eager to do the job right, and his youthful idealism is in contrast to his father's political opportunism.

## Distracted by a Woman

Edward's campaign against the Scots is put on hold when he meets the Countess of Salisbury. He knows she is the wife of one of his loyal lords, but he becomes besotted with her nevertheless. Edward never confronts the Scottish king, forsaking war for lustful adultery. He commissions a poem from Lodowick, the court secretary, who seems to deliberately misunderstand the situation. Edward tries wooing her, but the countess says she realizes he is only testing her honor.

**SSENTIALS**    The dramatic tension of *King Edward III* is built on the contrast between King Edward and his son Prince Edward, the Black Prince. The king is a somewhat passive, less-than-honorable father, while the prince is a genuinely honorable warrior son.

Edward exacted a thoughtless oath of loyalty from the countess's father, the Earl of Warwick, and now asks him to win over the countess to his adulterous desires. Warwick is reluctant to break his oath and discusses the matter with his daughter who, to his relief, rejects the king's proposition.

While Edward has been besieging the countess, the prince has assembled an army to invade France. However, he gets a message that the countess is against war with France, and Edward now sees the invasion of France as a sin worse than adultery. The countess demands that both her husband Salisbury and the queen be put to death. Edward says he can't do that because what she wants is "beyond our law," and the countess tartly replies, "So is your desire [for me]."

Edward reluctantly agrees, and the countess pulls out two daggers, gives one to the king, and proposes that they kill their spouses by killing themselves, since they both carry the images of their spouses in their hearts. The countess now adds that if he doesn't leave her alone, she'll kill herself right now. Edward realizes that while the countess's suicide would certainly embarrass him politically, the war in France is a much better bet. He claims she has shamed him awake and leaves her alone and goes off to battle the French.

## Returning to War

In France, Prince Edward becomes his father's steward in the battle. At one point the prince is surrounded and in trouble, but the king refuses to help him. If the prince can "redeem" himself he will "win a world of honour." If not, the king says, "we have more sons than one, to comfort our declining age." Happily, the prince enters in triumph. The French king, however, escapes to Poitiers, and King Edward sends the prince to pursue him. The king, meanwhile, decides to wait at Calais.

In Poitiers, Prince Edward is surrounded by the French and is in danger of being killed. King Edward, meanwhile, captures Calais by insisting that the six richest men in the city throw themselves on his mercy. How Edward will treat these merchants is a mystery, but things do not look good.

The old knight Audley tells the prince they are surrounded by four French armies. The prince, characteristically optimistic, replies, not so, we have one army; they have one army: "One to one is fair equality."

Against great odds, the prince faces death bravely. The Battle of Poitiers ends in defeat for France's John II, whose army is cut to ribbons by the English Prince Edward. Edward, a badly wounded Audley, and their captives set out for King Edward at Calais.

King Edward, meanwhile, tells his men to put all to sword "and make the spoil your own." The six wealthy men of Calais beg for peace and mercy. Edward decides to take possession of the city in peace, but decides to drag the six men around the walls of the city, "and after feel the stroke of quartering steel."

Edward's queen, Philippa, who has just arrived at Calais, talks him into being merciful. The king agrees, claiming, somewhat ironically, "that we as well can master our affections as conquer others by the dint of sword."

At this point Copeland enters with the Scottish King David as his captive. Salisbury enters to announce that the prince has (apparently) fallen at Poitiers. But then the prince enters triumphant, with the French king and his son in tow.

## Commentary

Ironically, King Edward goes north to relieve the siege of Roxborough, only to passively become the besieger of the countess of Salisbury and Calais. His son becomes the active warrior who wrests great victories from daunting odds at Crécy and Poitiers. The king acts for political gain; the prince acts for honor and national pride, and without the prince, there would be, in this play, no conquest of France.

Written in verse throughout, the play opens with a scene similar to the first scene of *King Henry V.* No sooner are the preparations for the invasion put underway than we get King Edward's romantic besieging of the countess of Salisbury. Finally, when the king conquers his adulterous passion, the military conquest takes place, with the honorable Prince of Wales as its hero.

# 11 ❧ *King Henry IV, Part I*

## Main Characters

**King Henry IV**—The ruling king of England. He feels guilty about the murder of Richard II. He's also irritated by the irresponsible antics of his eldest son, Prince Hal.

**Prince Hal, the Prince of Wales**—He will become King Henry V. He is sometimes called "Harry" or "Harry Monmouth." He is the heir to the throne of England, but spends all his time hanging around the bad side of London, wasting his time with highwaymen, robbers, and whores.

**Hotspur**—The son and heir of the earl of Northumberland. His real name is Henry Percy.

**Sir John Falstaff**—A fat old knight, a rogue and Prince Hal's closest friend.

**Earl of Westmerland**—Allied with King Henry.

**Prince John of Lancaster**—Son of King Henry.

**Sir Walter Blunt**—Serves as a messenger of King Henry.

**Thomas Percy**—The earl of Worcester. The mastermind behind the Percy rebellion.

**Henry Percy**—The earl of Northumberland. Hotspur's father.

**Edmund Mortimer**—The earl of March.

**Owen Glendower**—The leader of the Welsh rebels.

**Archibald, earl of Douglas**—Usually called "The Douglas" (a traditional way of referring to a Scottish clan chief). The leader of the large army of Scots allied with the Percys.

**Sir Richard Vernon**—Allied with the Percys.

**Richard Scroop**—The archbishop of York.

**Ned Poins, Peto, Bardolph, and Gadshill**—Criminals and highwaymen who drink with Falstaff and of Prince Hal in the Boar's Head Tavern.

**Mistress Quickly**—Hostess of the Boar's Head Tavern, a seedy dive in Eastcheap, London.

# Introduction

*King Henry IV, Part I,* is the second part of a four-part series that deals with the rise of the house of Lancaster. The play was probably composed during 1596–1597. Set around the years 1400–1403, the action of *King Henry IV, Part I* takes place two centuries before Shakespeare's own time.

In general, it follows real events and uses historical people, although Shakespeare significantly alters or invents history as it suits him. For instance, the historical Hotspur was not the same age as Prince Hal, and Shakespeare's Mortimer is a conflation of two different historical people.

# The Play

King Henry IV is tormented by guilt over the murder of Richard II and is beside himself at the antics of his older son Prince Hal, the heir to the throne. Hal spends most of his time in taverns in the seedy part of London, hanging around with highwaymen, prostitutes, and vagrants. His closest friend is a worldly, fat old knight named Falstaff, a substitute father figure, who steals and lies for a living. He also lives on his wits with great gusto.

 **SSENTIALS** Falstaff, Prince Hal's fat, aged, and criminally degenerate mentor and friend is one of Shakespeare's most famous creations. Falstaff has many historical precedents such as the figures of Vice and Gluttony from the medieval morality plays, but he is second only to Hamlet as an object of critical interest.

A discontented family of noblemen, the Percys feel they have not been adequately rewarded for helping the king come to power, so they plan a rebellion. Harry Percy, known as Hotspur, leads the Percy forces. Hotspur is about Prince Hal's age, and as much as Hal is scorned and despised for his idle tavern life, Hotspur is widely respected for his bravery in battle.

The Percys gather a formidable army of rebels from Scotland and Wales and from amongst English nobles and clergymen who have grievances against King Henry. The king has no choice but to go to war. Prince Hal decides it is time to reform and plans to defeat Hotspur in battle in order to reclaim his good name. Drafting his tavern friends to fight in the king's army, Hal accompanies his father to the battlefront.

At the battle of Shrewsbury, Prince Hal saves his father's life in battle, thus winning his father's approval and affection. Hal also defeats Hotspur in single combat. The king's forces win, and most of the leaders of the Percy family are put to death. Falstaff manages to survive the battle by avoiding any actual fighting. Powerful rebel forces remain in Britain, however, so by play's end the ultimate outcome of the war has not yet been resolved.

## Commentary

*King Henry IV, Part I* has been called Shakespeare's greatest history play. Its three-dimensional characters and overt politics have been the subjects of many books and critical essays. It is an epic play, paralleling two worlds— the world of King Henry IV and his advisors and that of the low-class reprobates who spend their days at the pub in Eastcheap. Bridging the worlds is Prince Hal, who is actually involved in an unorthodox plan to prepare for the throne by getting to know the people he will eventually rule.

**FACTS**

*King Henry IV, Part I* refers to its "prequel," *King Richard II*. Its source was primarily Raphael Holinshed's *Chronicles of England, Scotland, and Ireland*.

The play mixes history and comedy, moving from the realm of kings and political intrigue to the world of rogues who become "cannon fodder" in the battles and spend their days in taverns or thievery. The play is concerned with the nature of kingship, honor, and loyalty.

Although the play is named after Henry IV, he is really a minor character. King Henry is politically shrewd, unlike his predecessor,

Richard II. But because he came to the throne as a usurper responsible for the death of God's anointed king, Richard, Henry's ability to rule is diminished, and the country is inevitably plunged into chaos.

Shakespeare explores honor through the characters of Hotspur, Falstaff, and Prince Hal. Prince Hal must balance the two extremes of honor—Hotspur's obsession with it and Falstaff's apparent lack of it—in order to distill his own concept so that he may become an honorable king.

## Famous Lines

"He will give the devil his due" (Act I, Scene II).

"I know a trick worth two of that" (Act II, Scene I).

"Out of this nettle, danger, we pluck this flower, safety" (Act II, Scene III).

"O, monstrous! but one half-pennyworth of bread to this intolerable deal of sack!" (Act II, Scene IV).

"Exceedingly well read" (Act III, Scene I).

"Two stars keep not their motion in one sphere" (Act V, Scene IV).

"The better part of valour is discretion" (Act V, Scene IV).

# 12 § *King Henry IV, Part II*

## Main Characters

**King Henry IV**—The ruling king of England.

**Prince Hal**—Also called Prince Henry, Harry, Prince Harry, Harry Monmouth, the Prince of Wales, and, after his father's death, King Henry V.

**Princes John, duke of Lancaster; Humphrey, duke of Gloucester; and Thomas, duke of Clarence**—Prince Hal's younger brothers.

**The Lord Chief Justice**—The most powerful law official in England.

**Earl of Warwick, earl of Surrey, earl of Westmerland, Gower, Harcourt, and Sir John Blunt**—King Henry IV's allies and advisors.

**Sir John Falstaff**—Sometimes called Jack. Prince Hal's mentor and close friend.

**Page**—A boy who serves Falstaff.

**Poins, Peto, and Bardolph**—Friends of Falstaff and Prince Hal.

**Ancient Pistol**—A soldier (ancient meant "ensign" in Elizabethan English).

**Mouldy, Shadow, Wart, Feeble, and Bullcalf**—Army recruits.

**Archbishop of York**—A powerful clergyman who leads the rebellion against King Henry IV.

**Mowbray and Hastings**—Two lords who conspire with the archbishop of York.

**Henry Percy, earl of Northumberland**—Brother of Worcester and father to Hotspur who have recently been killed in battle against King Henry IV.

**Travers**—Northumberland's servant.

**Hotspur**—Northumberland's son and a leader of the rebellion against the king.

**Lord Bardolph**—An ally of Northumberland (not to be confused with Falstaff's friend Bardolph).

**Owen Glendower**—A Welsh rebel leader.

**Mistress Quickly (the Hostess)**—Proprietor of the seedy Boar's Head Tavern in Eastcheap, London.

**Doll Tearsheet**—Falstaff's favorite prostitute and a good friend of Mistress Quickly.

**Fang and Snare**—Incompetent policemen.

**Justice Shallow and Justice Silence**—Justices of the peace (minor judges).

**Davy**—Justice Shallow's servant.

# Introduction

*King Henry IV, Part II* is the third part of Shakespeare's four-part series dealing with the rise of the English royal house of Lancaster. (It is preceded by *King Richard II* and *King Henry IV, Part I* and followed by *King Henry V*.) The play was probably written around the year 1598.

**ESSENTIALS**

There are no good contemporary film versions of either of the Henry IV plays, but people who have read them might get a kick out of *My Own Private Idaho*, a 1992 film by Gus Van Sant based loosely on the Henry IV plays.

# The Play

The Earl of Northumberland (Henry Percy) learns that his son Hotspur has been killed in battle and that Richard Scroop, the Archbishop of York, is continuing the rebellion against Henry IV.

Back in London, the lord chief justice criticizes Falstaff for his wicked ways and tells the old knight that King Henry IV has decided to separate Falstaff from Prince Hal by sending Falstaff with Prince John of Lancaster (Hal's brother) to fight Scroop and Northumberland. Prince Hal returns from fighting the Welsh and meets with some of his friends to discuss his father's sickness and a pompous letter Falstaff has written to Hal complaining about being abandoned by his friend.

Northumberland's wife and his daughter-in-law convince him to flee to Scotland. The earl of Warwick (with the earl of Surrey and Sir Walter

Blunt) assure the king that Northumberland will be defeated, though Henry repeats Richard II's prediction that Northumberland, who helped Henry IV to the throne, would eventually revolt and defeat Henry.

On his way to battle, Sir John Falstaff arrives at Justice Shallow's home seeking old friends to be soldiers. Falstaff conscripts Mouldy, Shadow, Wart, Feeble, and Bullcalf, though Bullcalf and Mouldy bribe Bardolph (Falstaff's friend) to avoid having to fight.

At the battlefield, Scroop, Mowbray, and Hastings learn that Northumberland will not help them. Prince John yields to Scroop's demands, granting protection to the rebelling nobles, who quickly tell their armies to disperse. Westmerland and Prince John now betray Hastings, Scroop, and Mowbray and arrest them for treason. Falstaff stumbles on Sir John Coleville of the Dale (a rebel) and captures him without a fight.

Hal arrives while Henry IV is asleep and tries on his father's crown. Henry wakes and rebukes Hal for wishing him dead and taking the crown. Hal claims he thought his father was dead and wanted to protect the crown.

Back in London, Henry IV vows to go on a crusade to the Holy Land if the rebellion is suppressed. When it is, he is distressed that Hal is still associating with criminals. Henry IV advises Hal when he is king to wage foreign wars to occupy Britain's time and to increase Hal's popularity. Henry IV then dies. Hal becomes King Henry V and swears to be kind to all, even the chief justice who once jailed Prince Hal.

Falstaff returns to London, hoping to receive favors from King Henry V, his alehouse friend. However, during a coronation march, Falstaff and his gang are banned from approaching Henry V within ten miles, after which Falstaff is arrested for his crimes.

## Commentary

In contrast with the earlier *King Henry IV*, this sequel is concerned with justice, sickness, and betrayal. The play is sometimes described as the battle between vice and virtue for the soul of a king, and although Hal banishes Falstaff, Falstaff's philosophy offers an alternative view to the serious and the rational.

The play captures the entire English national life from the country to the town and from lowly drinking houses to the anguish and responsibilities of kings. It reflects Shakespeare's own experience—the country boy who came from Stratford, then lived in the taverns of London, then made a success of his life by writing plays that are presented to kings, queens, and nobility.

## Famous Lines

"I do now remember the poor creature, small beer" (Act II, Scene II).

"Uneasy lies the head that wears the crown" (Act III, Scene I).

"We have heard the chimes at midnight" (Act III, Scene II).

"A man can die but once" (Act III, Scene II).

# 13 ⚜ *King Henry V*

## Main Characters

**King Henry V**—The young, recently crowned king of England.

**Exeter, Westmerland, Salisbury, and Warwick**—Advisors to the king.

**Clarence, Bedford, and Gloucester**—Henry's younger brothers.

**The archbishop of Canterbury and the bishop of Ely**—Wealthy and powerful clergymen.

**Cambridge, Scroop, and Grey**—Three conspirators against King Henry.

**York and Suffolk**—Cousins who die at the Battle of Agincourt.

**Charles VI**—The king of France.

**Isabel**—The queen of France.

**The Dauphin**—The son of the king of France and heir to the throne.

**Katherine**—The king of France's daughter.

**The constable of France, the duke of Orleans, the duke of Britain, the duke of Bourbon, the earl of Grandpre, Lord Rambures, the duke of Burgundy, and the governor of Harfleur**—French noblemen and military leaders.

**Sir Thomas Erpingham**—A veteran soldier.

**Fluellen, Macmorris, Jamy, and Captain Gower**—Captains of Henry's troops.

**Pistol, Bardolph, and Nym**—Commoners from London who serve with King Henry's army.

**Boy**—Formerly in the service of Falstaff, the nameless Boy leaves London after his master's death and goes with Pistol, Nym, and Bardolph to the war in France.

**Michael Williams, John Bates, and Alexander Court**—Common soldiers with whom King Henry argues (while in disguise) the night before the Battle of Agincourt.

**Mistress Quickly**—The keeper of the Boar's Head Tavern in London; she is married to Pistol.

**Alice**—Princess Katherine's maid.

**Montjoy**—The French herald.

**Monsieur le Fer**—A French soldier.

**Chorus**—The character who narrates the play.

# Introduction

*King Henry V* is the last part of the four-part series that deals with the historical rise of the English royal house of Lancaster. *King Henry V* was probably composed in 1599 and is one of the most popular of Shakespeare's history plays. It is rife with colorful characters, noble speeches, battles, and a young king (Henry) who seems to be brave, modest, and fiercely focused, yet with a sense of humor.

**ESSENTIALS**

This is a stirring play, and when you watch it, it's useful to keep the paradoxes of morality and character in mind. The brilliance of Henry's speeches and his wit make him a Kennedy-esque kind of inspiring leader.

# The Play

Worried over impending legislation that would effectively rob the Church of England of its power and wealth, the Archbishop of Canterbury convinces Henry V to instead lay claim to France. When he does so, however, the Dauphin sends an insulting response, balls—a gift of tennis balls—that convinces Henry that the French want war. He puts together an army to invade France. But before he can leave, he must sort out the last of the rebels against his father and his house.

Lords Cambridge, Scroop, and Grey conspire to assassinate Henry (they are paid by the French). The plot is discovered and Henry arrests them personally and oversees their public execution. The army then lays siege to Harfleur, France, capturing it after heavy losses.

The night before a battle where the English face overwhelming odds, Henry disguises himself as a commoner in order to mingle with his troops. He talks candidly with his men and discovers that they may be unsure of their king but they are steadfast in their willingness to beat the French.

The morning of the Battle of Agincourt, St. Crispin's Day, Henry makes a stirring speech, knowing his army is outnumbered five to one. His expert archers help Henry rout the French who are forced to ask for peace, which Henry grants on his own terms, of course. He signs the Treaty of Troyes, marries Princess Katherine of France, and insists he is named heir to the French throne, thus uniting England and France in peace.

# Commentary

The play is harder to analyze than it seems. Henry seems a model hero but for all his patriotism—or land lust, depending on your point of view—he invades a nonaggressive country and slaughters thousands. He sentences former friends and prisoners of war to death, paying lip service to mercy; and he never accepts any responsibility for the bloodshed he has initiated.

*King Henry V* concludes the saga begun in *King Henry IV, Part I*—the making of a king. At the end of *Part I*, Hal seems to have evolved from profligate prince to mature heir to the throne. Yet in *Part II*, while Prince Hal has become Prince Harry, he still appears to shun the responsibilities of his father's court in favour of Falstaff's clearly defined and "honestly" declared licentiousness. Prince Harry, caught trying on the crown while his father lies dying, intuitively understands (and fights against) the knowledge that "uneasy lies the head that wears the crown." Falstaff's anarchic, irresponsible world is hard to resist, particularly when the alternative is a kingdom embraced by vicious politics and feuding strife.

It is only at his father's deathbed that Prince Harry finally resolves the doubts that have plagued him. He recognizes that the crown, though blemished on his father's head because it was illegally wrested from Richard II, will sit comfortably on his own, because he will inherit it lawfully.

Prince Harry becomes Henry V, transforming himself finally into the great king who will defeat the French at Agincourt and win for England her lost dominions. But before making the last leg of this great journey, he must reject the disreputable and dishonorable anarchy of Falstaff's world, which he does with a chilling firmness: "I know thee not, old man. Fall to thy prayers."

# Famous Lines

"Turn him to any cause of policy,
The Gordian knot of it he will unloose,
Familiar as his garter: that when he speaks,
The air, a chartered libertine, is still" (Act I, Scene I).

"Even at the turning o' the tide" (Act II, Scene III).

"Once more unto the breach, dear friends, once more,
Or close the wall up with our English dead!
In peace there's nothing so becomes a man
As modest stillness and humility;
But when the blast of war blows in our ears,
Then imitate the action of the tiger:
Stiffen the sinews, summon up the blood" (Act III, Scene I).

"I would give all my fame for a pot of ale and safety" (Act III, Scene II).

"Men of few words are the best men" (Act III, Scene II).

"This day is called the feast of Crispian:
He that outlives this day and comes safe home,
Will stand a tip-toe when this day is named,
And rouse him at the name of Crispian" (Act IV, Scene III).

"We few, we happy few, we band of brothers" (Act IV, Scene III).

# 14 ❧ *King Henry VI, Part I*

## Main Characters

**King Henry VI**—King of England and various regions in France. The son of Henry V.

**Charles**—The Dauphin of France.

**Gloucester**—Regent until Henry is old enough to rule. He and Winchester are in a feud.

**Winchester**—Head of the English church; Gloucester's nemesis.

**Richard Plantagenet**—Later known as York. His father once had a claim to the throne of England before Henry IV killed him.

**Talbot**—English general of the troops in France. Talbot is so feared by the French that, when he is captured, they have archers guard him while he sleeps.

**Joan**—Also known as Joan of Arc.

**Somerset**—An English lord who argues with Richard Plantagenet.

**Suffolk**—An English lord.

**Mortimer**—Richard Plantagenet's uncle.

**Burgundy**—A French lord.

**Bedford**—An English general.

**Alençon**—A French lord.

**René**—A French lord.

**Bastard of Orléans**—A French lord.

**Exeter**—An English lord. Exeter becomes a kind of chorus, remarking on the problems caused by internal dissension and strife in England and abroad.

**Warwick**—An English lord.

**Salisbury**—An English soldier.

**Gargrave**—An English soldier.

**Glansdale**—An English soldier.

**Vernon**—One of Somerset's men.

**Basset**—One of York's men.

**Sir William Lucy**—A messenger.

**John**—Talbot's son.

**Margaret**—René's daughter, captured by Suffolk.

**Countess of Auvergne**—A French woman.

**Sir John Fastolf**—A cowardly English soldier (not the same as Falstaff).

**Woodville**—The warden of the Tower of London.

**The Lord Mayor**—The lord mayor of London.

**Master Gunner**—A French soldier.

**Boy**—The master gunner's son.

**Governor**—The governor of Paris.

**General**—The general of Bordeaux.

**Shepherd**—Joan's father.

# Introduction

*King Henry VI, Part I* was probably written in 1592 and is one of Shakespeare's earliest plays. It picks up events some seven years after the Battle of Agincourt. Henry V has just died. This play covers the origins of the Wars of the Roses and the loss of Britain's territories in France.

**FACTS**

Some scholars have theorized that Thomas Nashe wrote parts of *King Henry VI, Part I*; some believe Shakespeare wrote only the scene in the Temple Garden and the battle scenes in which Talbot and his son meet their deaths. Other scholars believe Shakespeare wrote the whole play, adding that the playwright was unlikely to have collaborated with other authors so early in his career.

Shakespeare wrote two more plays about Henry VI, *King Henry VI, Part II* and *Part III*. Interestingly, the second two plays were published first, and some believe them to have been written first as well, though no one knows whether the order of publication of Shakespeare's plays reflects their order of composition.

The *King Henry VI* plays figure among Shakespeare's first attempts at history plays. They were followed by plays that traced the years after Henry VI's death and the ensuing civil wars over the succession. Only later in his career did Shakespeare look back to the events prior to Henry VI's kingship, including that of his father Henry V.

The history play held a particular fascination for the Elizabethan public and helped create a sense of a collective national memory. Patriotic sentiment was no doubt still running high after the defeat of the invading Spanish Armada in 1588. The history play drew upon such sentiments. *King Henry VI, Part I* in particular appears to reference the specific event of the English campaign in France, led by Queen Elizabeth's charismatic favorite Essex. The play's depiction of fifteenth-century noblemen attacking the city of Rouen would certainly have reminded audiences of Essex's 1592 efforts at Rouen to aid the French in quashing a Protestant uprising.

Shakespeare probably used chronicles of the fifteenth century about the struggles during those years between the houses of York and Lancaster in the Wars of the Roses. His primary source was probably Raphael Holinshed's *Chronicles of England, Scotland, and Ireland.*

## The Play

Henry V, king of England and parts of France, has died, and his young son Henry VI is on the throne. Charles, the Dauphin of France, is nurturing a rebellion across the channel, and rifts among the nobles in England are festering, notably between the houses of York and Lancaster (which will eventually become the Wars of the Roses). Emboldened by the exploits of Joan of Arc, the French attack Talbot at Orléans. Henry VI manages to retake Orléans by night in a surprise attack.

In England, Richard Plantagenet and the duke of Somerset have a disagreement concerning the letter of a law. The two men ask others to show their support for their respective positions: those supporting Richard pick a white rose, and those supporting Somerset pick a red one. After talking with his uncle, Edmund Mortimer, Richard is convinced that the throne more rightfully belongs to the house of York than young King Henry. Meanwhile, Winchester and Gloucester, guardians of the young king, continue a feud of their own.

Back in France, Joan drives the English from Rouen, but an English counterattack gets it back. Joan now convinces the duke of Burgundy to switch over to the French side. Talbot marches against him, and Henry orders Richard and the duke of Somerset to reinforce Talbot in the battle. Somerset and Richard continue to feud however, and while Talbot fights valiantly, he is slain in the combat when the reinforcements never arrive.

**ESSENTIALS**

Like that of many public depictions of women, Joan's identity slips between the two biblical polarities of Mary the "virgin" and Mary the "whore." Queen Elizabeth I also provoked reverence with her title of "The Virgin Queen," as well as malicious rumors of infertility or a sexual defect. Both Joan of Arc and Queen Elizabeth could thus be read as exceptional people or as perversions of nature.

Richard and Somerset set aside their differences long enough to capture Joan of Arc and burn her as a witch. In the meantime, Gloucester tries to set up a match between Henry and Margaret, the daughter of a French lord, in order to force a peace between France and England. The earl of Suffolk, however, introduces another Margaret (of Anjou) to Henry in an attempt to get him to marry her. Suffolk hopes to use her to control Henry, which leads to the action of *King Henry VI, Part II*.

## Commentary

*King Henry VI, Part I* depicts England's struggle to retain its military and political control over French territories gained by Henry V. The play compresses early events of the early reign of Henry VI, including the feuding of English lords and the eventual loss of half the French lands.

Nowadays, Shakespeare's histories are not as popular as his tragedies and comedies. Many people assume they are tedious textbook recreations. But while Shakespeare drew on historical records, he condensed dates and events, reordering things to create drama. For example, Henry VI was actually only nine months old when he became king, while in the play he is a teenager. What's more, one of the play's most striking scenes, in the Temple Garden, in which the followers of Richard Plantagenet and Somerset pick white and red roses as emblems of their opposing views, is complete fabrication. It does, however, explain the origin of the Wars of the Roses, an affair whose actual origins are boring and complicated.

Shakespeare gives equal voice to two predominant theories on the cause of fifteenth-century British turmoil: (1) history is the result of human choices and actions and (2) the violence of the fifteenth century was some sort of divine punishment for the murder of King Richard II.

The warrior culture of *King Henry V* is changing around Henry VI. After Henry V's death, lords abandon a unity for the sake of king and country, and return to plotting their own advancement. War loses its chivalrous quality. The death of Talbot and his son signals the death of "romantic" chivalry.

While *King Henry V* (which was written later) portrays a man who claims his birthright and lives up to the full potential of his masculinity, *King Henry VI, Part I* acknowledges the potential weaknesses of men. Sometimes, as in the case of Queen Elizabeth I, a woman must step up to the plate and take charge even if it means usurping a traditional male role.

**FACTS**

Thomas Nashe wrote a pamphlet on the importance of the history play as a genre, stating that they helped to preserve the memories of glorious English heroes such as the chivalrous Lord Talbot. Nashe added that the history play creates a collective memory of the nation's past for the masses, celebrating the realm's heroes and particularly patriotic moments in English history.

## Famous Lines

"Halcyon days" (Act I, Scene II).

"She's beautiful, and therefore to be wooed;
She is a woman, therefore to be won" (Act V, Scene III).

# 15 ◎ *King Henry VI, Part II*

## Main Characters

**Henry VI**—King of England.

**Gloucester**—Regent until Henry is old enough to rule.

**Somerset**—Somerset stands for the red rose, against York and those who wear the white rose.

**Buckingham**—A lord who joins Somerset, Suffolk, Beaufort, and Margaret to plot against Gloucester.

**Beaufort**—Head of the English church. In *King Henry VI, Part I* he was called Winchester.

**York**—Called Richard in the earlier play. He is heir to Edward III's third son, while Henry is heir to Edward III's fourth son.

**Suffolk**—A lord of the court.

**Salisbury**—A lord of the court. Salisbury supports York.

**Warwick**—A lord of the court. Warwick supports York.

**Margaret**—A French woman. Captured during the French wars by Suffolk.

**Duchess**—Wife of Gloucester.

**Hume**—A procurer of conjurers and witches.

**Peter**—A working man.

**Horner**—Accused by Peter of treason.

**Witch**—Hired by the duchess, the Witch helps raise a spirit.

**Bolingbroke**—A conjurer.

**Simpcox**—A poor man who pretends he has been blind since birth.

**Jack Cade**—Hired by York to cause trouble in England while York is away.

**Captain**—In charge of the ship that captures Suffolk at sea.

**Whitmore**—One of the Captain's men. Whitmore kills Suffolk.

**Rebels**—Common people led by Jack Cade.

**Butcher**—One of Jack Cade's men.

**Weaver**—Another of Jack Cade's men.

**The Staffords**—Two nobles of the court who challenge Jack Cade. Stafford and his brother die, and their bodies are dragged behind Cade's horse to London.

**Lord Saye**—Sought and killed by Jack Cade.

**Sergeant**—Husband of the woman the Butcher rapes.

**Clifford**—A lord of the court. Clifford convinces Jack Cade's troops to surrender.

**Alexander Iden**—A noble who kills Cade.

**Edward**—York's son. Edward will be the next king of England.

**Richard**—York's son. Richard will become Richard III.

## Introduction

Some editors think *King Henry VI, Part II* was written before *King Henry VI, Part I*, probably in 1591, making it one of Shakespeare's earliest plays. It takes place after the French wars, when the English lost and regained most of the lands originally won by Henry V. During the wars, depicted in *King Henry VI, Part I*, disagreements between Somerset and York led to the creation of two factions, those who supported the red rose and those who supported the white, setting the stage for the civil wars known as the Wars of the Roses.

SSENTIALS

Shakespeare probably used Raphael Holinshed's *Chronicles of England, Scotland, and Ireland* for details of Cade's rebellion, modeling it on the revolt by Wat Tyler in the Peasant's Rebellion of 1381 during the reign of Richard II.

*King Henry VI, Part II* concerns the continued power struggles between Gloucester and Beaufort, and York and Somerset. This infighting and the popular uprising by Jack Cade show what happens when a king is too weak to rule. The play charts the rise and fall of many lords and lesser figures within the kingdom.

A version of the play was first published in 1594, while a longer version appeared in the First Folio in 1623. The relationship between these two texts has been a long-debated point in Shakespeare scholarship.

Some scholars have suggested that the shorter version was a reconstruction of the play prepared by actors, who remembered as much of the play as they could for publication. Others think the 1594 version may have been an early draft, and the later published play a more polished version. Most editors agree that actors, scribes, publishers, and censors all had a hand in altering the play as it moved onto the stage. The Oxford editors decided to use the later, longer version of the play, but incorporated lengthy stage directions and lines from the earlier version.

## The Play

The action picks up from the end of *Part I*. Humphrey, duke of Gloucester is unhappy with Margaret's lack of dowry and with Henry's giving up territory in France. Suffolk, who introduced Margaret to Henry in the hopes of controlling her, and thus the king, sets plots into motion against Gloucester. He sets up Gloucester's wife to be arrested for witchcraft. Meanwhile, York bides his time, convinced of the legitimacy of his claim to the throne.

Gloucester is eventually arrested on trumped-up charges. During Gloucester's trial, York is sent to Ireland to put down a revolt. While in Ireland, York encourages Jack Cade to muster support among the common folk for York to depose Henry. If Cade succeeds, York has an army at his back to use against Henry when he returns from Ireland.

Gloucester is murdered at Suffolk's behest. Henry banishes Suffolk. En route to France, Suffolk is captured by pirates and summarily put to death.

Cade's rebellion gathers support, and he marches on London leaving brutality and havoc in his wake, with Henry retreating before him. Buckingham confronts his force with an army and extends pardons to all who abandon Cade. After a five-day flight without food, Cade is killed while foraging in a private garden. In the wake of Cade's failed uprising, York returns from Ireland and demands that the king arrest Somerset before York's men lay down their arms.

The king does so, but Margaret, now queen but Suffolk's lover, frees him almost immediately. York declares war on King Henry, determined to take the crown by force if necessary. At the Battle of St. Albans, Richard, son of York, slays Somerset. The Yorkists then set out in pursuit of the fleeing Henry and Margaret.

## Commentary

It is Henry's weakness as a king and leader that is the focus of the play. If Henry were stronger, he would not have agreed to the imprisonment of an innocent man. Yet Henry seems powerless to resist his nobles and his wife. Suffolk arrests Gloucester, Beaufort orders him taken away, and the others all accuse him. And though the nobles agree that they have no real proof of wrongdoing, they agree he should be killed immediately, without a trial. Similar to Cade's rampage through the countryside, the nobles play out their own version of mob rule, removing their enemies from office and killing them without reason.

# 16 &#9835; *King Henry VI, Part III*

## Main Characters

**York**—Richard, the Duke of York.

**Henry VI**—King of England.

**Edward**—York's eldest son, soon to be Edward IV.

**George**—Also known as Clarence. Edward's younger brother.

**Richard**—Soon to be Richard III. A younger brother of Edward and George. Most noted for his physical deformities, including a humpback, lame leg, and shriveled arm.

**Warwick**—One of York's allies, who switches his allegiance to Henry.

**Margaret**—Henry's French wife.

**Prince Edward**—Son of Margaret and Henry.

**Rutland**—York's youngest son, killed by Clifford.

**Clifford**—He kills York's young son Rutland, then York himself.

**Montague**—One of Warwick's relatives.

**Westmerland**—One of Henry's supporters.

**Exeter**—One of Henry's supporters.

**Norfolk**—One of Henry's supporters.

**Somerset**—One of Edward's supporters.

**Northumberland**—One of Henry's supporters.

**Lady Bona**—Sister of Louis, King of France.

**Lady Grey**—Edward propositions her, but she refuses. Then she agrees to become queen.

**Louis**—King of France.

**Oxford**—One of Henry's supporters.

**Rivers**—One of Edward's supporters, brother of Lady Gray.

**Hastings**—One of Edward's supporters.

**Montgomery**—One of Edward's supporters.

**Richmond**—The young Henry, earl of Richmond (soon to be Henry VII).

# Introduction

*King Henry VI, Part III* has attracted attention for its boldness in adapting a complex historical narrative to the requirements of the theater and is considered one of Shakespeare's earliest plays. It was first published in 1595 in an octavo volume under the title *The True Tragedy of Richard Duke of York and the Good King Henry the Sixth.*

Some scholars believe that the first version was an early draft of a later folio edition. Other editors believe that the octavo version was reconstructed from memory by actors and audience members, which explains its shorter length. Editors think the folio version is based on Shakespeare's own manuscript before he gave it to his players, while the octavo version may have been based on a prompt book for the actual production. Most editors use the longer folio version with occasional additions from the octavo.

**FACTS**

Shakespeare again likely referred to fifteenth-century histories as well as Raphael Holinshed's *Chronicles of England, Scotland, and Ireland* and Edward Hall's *Union of the Two Noble and Illustre Families of Lancaster and York* (1548) when researching the play.

*King Henry VI, Part III* is a continuation of the depiction of the Wars of the Roses, begun in *King Henry VI, Parts I* and *II,* which trace the struggles between the Lancastrians (red rose) and Yorkist (white rose) descendants of Edward III. The third part depicts some of the many significant battles fought during that civil war.

# The Play

*Part III* picks up from the end of *Part II.* Following his victory at St. Albans, York is now set to take the crown of England. Henry VI presents York an offer: Henry will rule England until his death, and then the crown will pass to the house of York.

York agrees, but Queen Margaret is irate because her son, the Prince of Wales, should be the next king. Margaret fights a battle that kills the duke of York and his youngest son, Rutland. The Yorkists rally, however, and Margaret and Henry have to flee the country. Edward, eldest son of York, now becomes king.

Henry secretly returns to England, but is captured by Edward and put in the Tower of London. Margaret petitions the king of France for help. However, Warwick tries to outmaneuver her by attempting to broker a marriage between Edward and the French king's sister-in-law, Bona. This plan falls apart when word comes that Edward has married Lady Grey.

Back in England, Warwick manages to capture Edward, temporarily restoring Henry to the throne. Richard, now duke of Gloucester, rescues Edward. Edward and the Yorkists then defeat and kill Warwick at the Battle of Tewksbury. Margaret and the Prince of Wales are captured and while the prince is killed, Edward grants Margaret mercy.

Richard pays a visit to the Tower of London to see Henry, who is a prisoner. When Henry foretells Richard's bloody future, Richard kills him. Edward now holds the throne as King Edward IV, but his brother Richard plots to usurp the crown for himself. The story picks up in *King Richard III*.

## Commentary

Some critics have seen *King Henry VI, Part III* as a flawed play, perhaps showing Shakespeare's weariness with the dramatization of the Wars of the Roses, or the difficulty of getting so much historical matter on the stage. Yet contemporary productions have been successful, particularly in depicting the ruthless Margaret and the increasingly alienated and enraged Richard, who emerges as the play's antihero.

## Famous Lines

"The smallest worm will turn, being trodden on" (Act II, Scene II).

"Didst thou never hear
That things ill got had ever bad success?
And happy always was it for that son
Whose father for his hoarding went to hell?" (Act II, Scene II).

# 17 ⚬ *King Henry VIII*

## Main Characters

**King Henry VIII**—King of England.

**Cardinal Wolsey**—The king's right-hand man.

**Queen Katharine**—Married to King Henry VIII's brother before marrying Henry.

**Buckingham**—A lord of the court. He is accused of plotting to gain the throne.

**Anne Boleyn**—Spelled "Anne Bullen" in the play. Henry's future wife. She dies giving birth to the child Elizabeth.

**Cranmer**—Archbishop of Canterbury.

**Cardinal Campeius**—An emissary from the Pope.

**Norfolk**—A lord of the court. At first he doesn't believe Buckingham's criticism of Cardinal Wolsey and urges Buckingham to hold his tongue.

**Suffolk**—A lord of the court.

**Lord Chamberlain**—A lord of the court.

**Lord Chancellor**—A lord of the court.

**Cromwell**—Friend of Cardinal Wolsey. Cromwell is devastated by Wolsey's demise. Yet Wolsey encourages him to go back to the king and continue serving the state.

**Sands**—A lord of the court.

**Lovell**—A lord of the court.

**Gardiner**—Cardinal Wolsey's former secretary.

**Guildford**—A lord of the court.

**Vaux**—A lord of the court.

**Surrey**—Buckingham's son-in-law.

**Abergavenny**—Buckingham's friend.

**Brandon**—Sergeant at arms.

**Denny**—A lord of the court.

**Butts**—The king's doctor.

**Surveyor**—Surveyor to Buckingham.

**Old Lady**—Anne Boleyn's attendant.

**Griffith**—Queen Katharine's attendant.

**Capucius**—An ambassador from the king of Spain.

**The Child**—Christened Elizabeth, she will later become Queen Elizabeth I.

**Prologue**—A character who introduces the play to the audience.

**Epilogue**—A character who ends the play for the audience.

**Gentlemen**—People in the streets.

# Introduction

*King Henry VIII* was written in 1613 and combines the genres of history play with tragicomic romance, a genre gaining new popularity in the early seventeenth century. The play focuses on the instabilities of the royal court from roughly 1530 to 1533 when Elizabeth is born. The king of England, when Shakespeare wrote the play, was James I (James VI of Scotland), who was the son of Mary, Queen of Scots, the daughter of Henry VIII's sister who married a Scottish king. James, though a Stuart, is a direct descendent of the Tudors. The play centers on Henry VIII's break with Rome and the Catholic Church.

**FACTS**

*King Henry VIII* was performed on June 29, 1613, the day the Globe Theatre burned to the ground. Eyewitness accounts of the fire disagree about what point in the play it happened, but several small cannons were fired during certain scenes, which ignited the thatch roof of the theater and led to the fire. No one was hurt, though a man's pants caught fire. The theater was destroyed.

In 1531, disappointed that his wife Catherine of Aragon (spelled "Katharine" in this play) had not given him a male heir, Henry decided to divorce her. His advisors argued that because she had been his brother's widow the marriage was invalid, but the Pope ruled against the divorce.

Henry nevertheless went forward with the divorce and married Anne Boleyn ("Anne Bullen" in the play) in 1533. The Pope excommunicated Henry, and Henry declared himself the head of the Church of England and dissolved the monasteries and seized their wealth.

The rest of Henry's reign was plagued by rebellions of groups who wanted to restore Catholicism or who were supporters of various religious reformation groups. The actual break with the Pope is not dramatized in the play, but we see Henry's advisors discuss ways to negotiate a legal divorce. We even see Cardinal Wolsey urge the Pope to refuse the divorce. But the actual break is only alluded to.

The years following Henry's death were wracked with religious disagreement and rebellions. When Queen Elizabeth finally came to the throne, she returned England to Protestant rule although the religious unrest continued. The frequent public executions that took place following Henry's break with Rome and during the reigns of Mary and Elizabeth are foreshadowed by the execution of Buckingham.

No one believed Henry's reason for wanting to divorce Katharine resulted from a flare-up of his conscience about the legality of his marriage. Everyone knew he wanted to marry Anne because she could give him a son and heir. Despite a compliment to King James at the end of the play, criticism of Henry as an inattentive ruler was probably also aimed at King James, who was known to neglect affairs of state.

## The Play

Cardinal Wolsey, a close advisor to King Henry VII, has arranged the arrest of the duke of Buckingham on charges of treason. Henry's wife, Queen Katharine, pleads on Buckingham's behalf with no success. Buckingham is tried and executed.

At a party hosted by Wolsey, Henry meets and is smitten with Anne Bullen, a lady-in-waiting to Queen Katharine. Henry decides he needs a new wife and seeks Wolsey's advice. Henry's argument is that Katharine is the widow of his brother, which makes the marriage one step removed from incest—never mind that Henry and Katharine have been wed for almost twenty years.

Wolsey has become despised for taxes he has levied in King Henry's name, as well as for his role in Buckingham's death. He is now further despised because Henry wishes a divorce. Wolsey agrees to have the

Pope send a representative to render a decision on the matter. Katharine, however, views her marriage as sacred.

*King Henry VIII* recounts the fall of the three main figures of King Henry VIII's early court, and the near fall of a fourth. The traditional Renaissance idea of a wheel of fortune is at work here: What rises must inevitably fall.

Wolsey endures a series of political stumblings that present him in an unflattering light to King Henry. Most damning is Wolsey's meddling in the king's divorce. Wolsey is disgraced, and Henry divorces Katharine and marries Anne in secret regardless of the Pope's opinion. Wolsey dies soon after, and Katharine (who is in poor health) follows him to the grave.

The new archbishop of Canterbury, Cranmer, becomes the focus of a plot by Gardiner, Wolsey's secretary. Cranmer is brought to trial in much the same manner as Buckingham, but enjoys the king's protection. Henry exonerates the archbishop and has him christen his and Anne Bullen's new daughter Elizabeth. At the christening, Cranmer prophecies a noble reign for Elizabeth and glory for England in her time.

## Commentary

The merging of romance and history suggests that fate somehow helped shape English history and the most important of these fateful events is the birth of Elizabeth, future queen of England, who had died by the time the play was produced. In order for the birth to take place, a complex set of events must be put into motion, and anyone who stands in the way must be gotten rid of.

Unlike other histories that dealt with the fate of kings, this play deals with the rise and fall of lesser court figures such as Buckingham, Katharine, Wolsey, and Cranmer. Each downfall—or near downfall—is played out in scenes of pageantry.

With the exception of Cranmer, each must go because he or she prevents Elizabeth's being born. Buckingham believes he has a claim to Henry's throne; Katharine is queen and can't give Henry a male heir; and Wolsey opposes Henry's marriage to Anne. If Elizabeth's birth is ensured, then so is the legitimacy of the succession of the king who was currently on the throne when Shakespeare wrote the play; James I, who was chosen by Elizabeth as her successor.

It's a mystery why Cranmer survives his trial. He suffers from the same kind of negative rumor mill that brings down the other characters. Yet the king clearly wants to save him. We can conjecture that the cycle of lords blaming each other had to stop somewhere or it threatened to spin out of control and into civil conflict. But history reveals that Cranmer was later executed anyway.

## Famous Lines

"Heat not a furnace for your foe so hot
That it do singe yourself" (Act I, Scene I).

"Press not a falling man too far!" (Act III, Scene II).

"Had I but served my God with half the zeal
I served my king, he would not in mine age
Have left me naked to mine enemies" (Act III, Scene II).

"To dance attendance on their lordships' pleasures" (Act V, Scene II).

# 18 ♦ *King John*

## Main Characters

**King John**—The king of England, the third son of Henry II. His older brother, Richard the Lionheart, was king before him.

**Eleanor**—John's mother.

**Philip**—The king of France. Arthur's champion.

**Arthur**—Son of Geoffrey, John's elder brother.

**The Bastard**—Philip, the illegitimate son of Richard the Lionheart and a chorus for the play.

**Louis**—Philip's son.

**Pandulph**—A messenger from the Pope.

**Hubert**—One of John's men.

**Constance**—Arthur's mother.

**Pembroke**—One of John's followers.

**Salisbury**—One of John's followers.

**Austria**—One of Philip's men, killed by the Bastard.

**Blanch**—John's niece. She marries Louis, thus cementing a bond between John and Philip.

**Essex**—One of John's followers.

**Bigot**—One of John's followers.

**Melun**—One of Louis's men.

**Faulconbridge**—The Bastard's younger (legitimate) brother.

**Lady Faulconbridge**—The Bastard's mother.

**Chatillon**—A messenger from France.

**Prince Henry**—John's son. He becomes King Henry III at John's death.

## Introduction

*King John* was written about 1596 or earlier, and stands as the odd play out in the early histories that trace the Wars of the Roses. It was published in the First Folio of 1623. Chronologically, it is the earliest of the history plays, covering the period of John's reign from 1199 to 1216.

While parallels oversimplify the facts, they nevertheless capture the themes Shakespeare wanted to emphasize in this play. John's claim to the throne is based on his older brother Richard the Lionheart's will. Elizabeth's father, Henry VIII, made Elizabeth his heir by will, despite disputes about the legality of appointing successors. Also, the Pope excommunicated both John and Elizabeth for disobedience.

**ESSENTIALS** Some critics believe an earlier anonymous play, *The Troublesome Reign of John, King of England* (1591), was a primary source for *King John.* Both plays relied on Raphael Holinshed's *Chronicles of England, Scotland, and Ireland.*

John's rival to the throne was Arthur, the son of Geoffrey, John's elder brother, in much the same way that Elizabeth's rival, Mary, was the daughter of Henry VIII's older sister who married into the Scottish line of kings. (Her son, James VI of Scotland, became James I of England on Elizabeth's death.) Because succession traditionally passed to the son of the oldest child, both John's and Elizabeth's claims to the throne were weak. Arthur's cause was championed by King Philip of France, while Mary's claims were supported by King Philip II of Spain.

John brought about Arthur's death, regrets his decision, and tries to distance himself from it, just as Elizabeth ordered Mary's execution and then distanced herself from it. Arthur's death provided an excuse for a French invasion; Mary's death provoked Philip II to launch the Spanish Armada. What's more, the invasion against John in England is wrecked by a storm that shipwrecks the French reinforcements, while a storm also saved England from the brunt of the Spanish Armada in 1588.

## The Play

King John's nephew, Arthur, believes he is the rightful heir to the throne of England and is backed by Philip of France in a rebellion. Refusing the king of France's demand that he surrender his throne, John sends an army to

France under the command of Philip Faulconbridge (also known as Philip the Bastard), illegitimate son of Richard I and Arthur's half-brother.

The English army clashes with the French at Angiers, but neither can claim a decisive victory. John proposes peace, ceding Philip some English territory in France and arranging for the Dauphin (the French King's son) to wed his niece, Blanch.

The Pope excommunicates John over a dispute concerning the appointment of the archbishop of Canterbury. Pandulph, the Pope's legate, orders the French to resume their war with King John. John's army beats back the French and captures Arthur. John wishes him executed. His chamberlain, Hubert, disobeys the order, but Arthur later plunges to his death while trying to escape. Ironically, the nobles suspect John of murder, his original intent, and desert him for the French. Meanwhile, John arranges peace with Pandulph, to whom he turns over the crown of England. He will receive it back, therefore becoming a vassal of the church.

Now that John is back in the fold of Mother Church, Pandulph tries to stop the war. The French won't play ball, and the armies clash at St. Edmundsbury. During the battle, a French noble named Melun warns the turncoat English noblemen that the king of France will have them executed as soon as John has been conquered. The nobles, seeing the winds of fortune shift, return their allegiance to King John.

Without his allies, the French king comes to terms with Pandulph and John. John is hardly able to enjoy his victory. While staying at Swinstead Abbey he is poisoned by one of the monks. His son will ascend the throne as King Henry III.

## Commentary

*King John* focuses on historical events, but the events in *King John* seem repeatedly to get in the way of intention and outcome—the characters are continually thwarted by historical accident and adversity. It is almost the antithesis of Cassius's famous speech in *Julius Caesar*, "The fault, dear Brutus, is not in our stars, But in ourselves, that we are underlings": in other words, we control what happens to us. In *King John,* it seems, we don't control things.

**FACTS**

*King John* treats history as an unpredictable unfolding of events. Decisive moments seem insignificant episodes in a haphazard universe. Elizabethan audiences would have picked up on *King John's* comment on the contemporary debate about Queen Elizabeth I's legitimacy to the throne, as opposed to that of Mary, Queen of Scots.

While John thinks he can secure his hold on the throne by killing Arthur, his lords turn against him, proving him wrong. Arthur is actually spared, only to screw up by panicking and killing himself by accident. John is again foiled by fate.

## Famous Lines

"I would that I were low laid in my grave:
I am not worth this coil that's made for me" (Act II, Scene I).

"Talks as familiarly of roaring lions
As maids of thirteen do of puppy-dogs!" (Act II, Scene I).

"Grief fills the room up of my absent child,
Lies in his bed, walks up and down with me,
Puts on his pretty looks, repeats his words,
Remembers me of all his gracious parts,
Stuffs out his vacant garments with his form" (Act III, Scene IV).

"Life is as tedious as a twice-told tale
Vexing the dull ear of a drowsy man" (Act III, Scene IV).

"Make haste; the better foot before" (Act IV, Scene II).

# 19    *King Lear*

## Main Characters

**King Lear**—The aging king of Britain.

**Goneril**—King Lear's ruthless oldest daughter. Married to the duke of Albany.

**Regan**—King Lear's second daughter, as ruthless as Goneril. Married to the duke of Cornwall.

**Cordelia**—King Lear's youngest daughter.

**Gloucester**—Father of Edgar and Edmund.

**Edgar**—Gloucester's oldest son. He disguises himself as a crazy beggar called Poor Tom.

**Edmund**—Gloucester's younger, illegitimate son.

**Kent**—A nobleman loyal to King Lear.

**Fool**—Lear's fool. He mysteriously disappears during Act III.

**Albany**—Goneril's husband.

**Cornwall**—Regan's husband.

**Oswald**—Goneril's steward.

## Introduction

*King Lear* is one of Shakespeare's most famous tragedies, and along with *Hamlet* one of his most challenging. Written about 1605, between *Othello* and *Macbeth,* it rivals *Hamlet* as Shakespeare's greatest play.

*King Lear* is performed less often partly because it explores madness, despair, chaos, aging, and death. It is a difficult and disturbing play whose dark psychology and symbolic ambiguity seems relentlessly nihilistic. The scenes in which the mad Lear rages naked on a stormy heath against his deceitful daughters and nature itself are considered by many scholars to be the finest example of tragic poetry in the English language.

If the philosophical questioning of *Hamlet* (written around 1601) arose in part because of the death of Shakespeare's young son some four years earlier, one wonders what dark personal event was in the forefront of the

Bard's thoughts when he composed *Lear*? The cynicism and bitterness that invades his later works seems to find its zenith in *Lear*.

The actual text of *King Lear* also presents special problems. The play exists in two very different editions—an early one printed in 1608, and a revised version printed in 1623. Today, editions of *King Lear* vary depending upon which version is used. Most often, the two editions of the play are woven together.

## The Play

King Lear, the aging king of Britain, decides to split his kingdom among his three daughters: Goneril, Regan, and Cordelia. Goneril and Regan pour flattery on him protesting their love for their father, while Cordelia, sincere in her love of her father, simply says she loves him the way a daughter should. Lear is upset by her response and disinherits her. The king of France says that he will marry her anyway. When Kent, one of Lear's nobles, tries to reason with him, Lear banishes him as well.

**FACTS**

Shakespeare adapted a folktale based on older oral stories for the play's storyline. Shakespeare's was the first version of the tale where the king goes mad, his "good" daughter dies, and there is no happy ending.

Meanwhile, Edmund, Gloucester's bastard son, decides to gain his father's inheritance by tricking him into thinking that Edgar, his legitimate son, is plotting to murder Gloucester. Edgar flees for his life, and disguised as a madman, goes into hiding.

## The King's Fall

Lear soon discovers how much Goneril and Regan actually love him. Both daughters demean him and try to take away from him the little dignity and power he has kept for himself. Lear is transformed from a powerful king to an impotent old man with only Kent—who has disguised himself and disobeyed Lear's decree of banishment—and his Fool for company.

In the middle of the play, Lear is driven mad by his grief at his foolishness and the betrayal of his children. On a lonely heath, he rages, naked, at a storm. They meet Edgar who is disguised as Poor Tom. Gloucester provides them shelter and guides them to Dover to meet Cordelia and the French king, who has landed an army in England to come to Lear's aid. For pitying Lear, Gloucester is betrayed by Edmund; and Cornwall puts out Gloucester's eyes. However, a servant is so distressed by the scene that he fatally stabs Cornwall before Regan kills him in turn.

Now blind, Gloucester meets up with Edgar disguised as Poor Tom. Edgar does not reveal himself but leads his father toward Dover. Meanwhile, Goneril's husband Albany has begun to speak up for Lear and Gloucester because his wife is calling him a coward. Both sisters independently start affairs with Edmund.

## Father and Daughter United in Death

The English and French armies battle and the English win. Lear and Cordelia are taken prisoner, and Edmund orders them hanged. Edgar tracks down his brother and in a duel stabs Edmund fatally. Goneril poisons Regan to win Edmund from her, then kills herself when she learns of Edmund's fate. Realizing he is about to die, Edmund repents his sins and reveals his plots, including the imminent deaths of Lear and Cordelia.

It is all too late: Lear enters carrying Cordelia's body. Overcome by grief and exhaustion Lear collapses and dies a broken old man beside the only daughter who loved him. Gloucester dies after reconciling with Edgar. Kent and Edgar retire, leaving Albany to rule Britain.

 SSENTIALS

*King Lear* is a tragedy of such power that audiences are left emotionally drained at its conclusion. We can only wonder at the meaninglessness of life after the physical and moral horrors at the play's end. Kent, on seeing Lear reduced to a mad, pathetic creature with the murdered Cordelia in his arms, murmurs, "Is this the promis'd end?"

# Commentary

While traditional critics of *King Lear* find a heroic pattern in the story, modern audiences see a nihilistic play about the frailty and futility of the human condition. Even the most powerful are humbled before the forces of fate and nature.

One of the important questions about Lear is whether he learns from his mistakes and becomes more personally aware. Does his humiliation and insanity strip away the hubris that caused his downfall? It seems that while he never completely regains his sanity, his values do change for the better by the end of the play. As he is made to realize his insignificance by the awesome natural forces that are unleashed on him, he becomes a humbled yet caring man, finally appreciating Cordelia for the jewel she is, though too late to save either himself or her.

**ESSENTIALS**

Edmund's change of heart is rare among Shakespeare's villains and can make us wonder if Lear is not in some ways a play about the power of love amid carnage. Goneril and Regan, for example, totally lack love until they meet Edmund. How is it possible that they are sisters to Cordelia?

The depth of Cordelia's love for Lear is a counterpoint to the height of the king's arrogance. By banishing her, he abandons his soul and plunges his kingdom into chaos and brutal anarchy. As we watch Goneril and Regan torment and plot against their father, deliberately pushing Lear toward madness, we pray that Cordelia will come back and rescue him from himself and his dreadful fate.

When at last they find each other, their reunion marks the restoration of peace and order in the kingdom and the triumph of love and forgiveness over hatred and spite. This fleeting moment of redemption makes the devastating finale of *King Lear* that much more cruel, as Cordelia, the personification of kindness and virtue, is sacrificed for nothing, depriving Lear's world of the meaning he thought he had found at last.

## Famous Lines

"Although the last, not least" (Act I, Scene I).

"Nothing will come of nothing" (Act I, Scene, I).

"How sharper than a serpent's tooth it is
To have a thankless child!" (Act I, Scene IV).

"Striving to better, oft we mar what's well" (Act I, Scene IV).

"Blow, winds, and crack your cheeks! rage! blow!" (Act III, Scene II).

"A poor, infirm, weak, and despised old man" (Act III, Scene II).

"I am a man
More sinn'd against than sinning" (Act III, Scene II).

"Oh, that way madness lies; let me shun that" (Act III, Scene IV).

"The worst is not
So long as we can say, 'This is the worst.'" (Act IV, Scene I).

"Pray you now, forget and forgive" (Act IV, Scene VII).

"Her voice was ever soft,
Gentle, and low,—an excellent thing in woman" (Act V, Scene III).

# 20 ♭ *King Richard II*

## Main Characters

**King Richard II**—The king of England.

**Henry Bolingbroke**—Duke of Herford. Occasionally referred to by his nickname, "Harry." King Richard's cousin and the son of Richard's uncle, John of Gaunt.

**John of Gaunt**—Duke of Lancaster. Called either "Gaunt" or "Lancaster."

**Edmund of Langley**—Duke of York. Called "York." Richard's uncle, and a brother of John of Gaunt.

**Duke of Aumerle**—Earl of Rutland. Also called "Rutland."

**Thomas Mowbray**—Duke of Norfolk. Called "Norfolk."

**Bushy, Bagot, and Greene**—Richard's friends and supporters.

**Henry Percy, earl of Northumberland; Lord Ross; and Lord Willoughby**—Noblemen who join Bolingbroke's rebel army to fight against King Richard.

**Duchess of York**—The wife of the duke of York and mother of the duke of Aumerle.

**Duchess of Gloucester**—Sister-in-law of John of Gaunt and the duke of York.

**Queen Isabel**—King Richard's wife.

**Lord Berkeley**—The ruler of Berkeley Castle in Gloucestershire.

**Lord Salisbury**—A lord loyal to King Richard.

**Bishop of Carlisle**—A clergyman loyal to Richard.

**Sir Stephen Scroop**—A nobleman loyal to Richard.

**Abbot of Westminster**—A clergyman loyal to Richard.

**Sir Piers Exton**—A nobleman who assassinates King Richard.

## Introduction

*King Richard II* was probably composed around 1595, and certainly no later than 1597. It is set around the year 1398, and documents the fall of the last Plantagenet king, Richard II, and the rise of the first Lancastrian king, Henry IV.

Richard came to the throne as a young man. He chose his counselors unwisely and was detached from the people, wasting too much time spending money on his close friends and raising taxes to fund his pet wars in Ireland and elsewhere.

**FACTS**

*King Richard II* is chronologically the first play in Shakespeare's second "history quartet," a series of four plays that dramatizes the Wars of the Roses, an English civil war between the houses of Lancashire and Yorkshire that lasted close to 100 years. (Its sequels, although written earlier, are *King Henry IV, Parts I* and *II,* and *King Henry V.*)

He "rented out" pieces of English land to wealthy noblemen, and seized the lands and money of the duke of Lancaster on his death (the father of Henry Bolingbroke who will take the throne from Richard) in order to raise funds for a war, which upset both commoners and nobles alike. Bolingbroke, in particular, is very upset to learn that Richard has stolen his inheritance.

## The Play

Henry Bolingbroke and the duke of Norfolk get ready to settle an argument through trial by combat. Bolingbroke feels that Norfolk is responsible for the murder of Richard's uncle, the duke of Gloucester. However, at the last moment, King Richard decrees that both men are to be banished. Soon after, Bolingbroke's father, the duke of Lancaster, dies. Richard seizes the estates in order to raise an army for a campaign in Ireland.

Bolingbroke returns to find that the earl of Northumberland has joined with other disaffected nobles against the duke of York, Richard's regent while the king is in Ireland. When Richard returns, he discovers that

Bolingbroke has not only reclaimed the lands stolen from him but also dispersed Richard's army and executed two of Richard's favorites.

Richard flees to Flint Castle for his own protection. Bolingbroke overtakes him and brings him back to London as a prisoner. Richard is made to confess crimes against the state and abdicate the crown to Bolingbroke, who becomes King Henry IV.

The duke of York's son, Aumerle, loyal to Richard, conspires against King Henry. Aumerle is granted clemency, but Richard is imprisoned in Pomfreet Castle. Sir Pierce of Exton murders Richard because he thinks King Henry wants him dead. Henry disavows the deed when he hears of it; however he promises a Crusade to atone for Richard's death.

## Commentary

Richard's poetic and metaphysical musings on the nature of kingship and identity mark a new direction for Shakespeare and his histories. Some scholars feel that *King Richard II* reads like a dry run for the more mature *Hamlet*.

*King Richard II* is stylized and in sharp contrast to the "Henry" plays that follow it (though they were written before *King Richard II*), and it contains virtually no prose. The play is replete with grand metaphors, such as the famous comparison of England to a garden, and of its reigning king to a lion or to the sun.

## Famous Lines

"In rage deaf as the sea, hasty as fire" (Act I, Scene I).

"The tongues of dying men
Enforce attention like deep harmony" (Act II, Scene I).

"This royal throne of kings, this sceptred isle,
This earth of majesty, this seat of Mars,
This other Eden, demi-paradise,
This fortress built by Nature for herself

Against infection and the hand of war,
This happy breed of men, this little world,
This precious stone set in the silver sea,
Which serves it in the office of a wall
Or as a moat defensive to a house,
Against the envy of less happier lands,—
This blessed plot, this earth, this realm, this England"
　　(Act II, Scene I).

"The ripest fruit first falls" (Act II, Scene I).

"Let's talk of graves, of worms, and epitaphs" (Act III, Scene II).

"And nothing can we call our own but death
And that small model of the barren earth
Which serves as paste and cover to our bones.
For God's sake, let us sit upon the ground
And tell sad stories of the death of kings" (Act III, Scene II).

"Comes at the last, and with a little pin
Bores through his castle wall—and farewell king!" (Act III, Scene II).

"As in a theatre, the eyes of men,
After a well-graced actor leaves the stage,
Are idly bent on him that enters next,
Thinking his prattle to be tedious" (Act V, Scene II).

# 21 ✿ *King Richard III*

## Main Characters

**Richard**—The duke of Gloucester. Deformed in body and twisted in mind.

**Buckingham**—The duke of Buckingham. Richard's right-hand man.

**Ratcliff and Catesby**—Two of Richard's supporters.

**Tyrrel**—A murderer whom Richard hires.

**King Edward IV**—Older brother of Richard and Clarence.

**Clarence**—The trusting middle brother of Edward and Richard.

**Queen Elizabeth**—The wife of King Edward IV.

**Dorset, Rivers, and Grey**—Kinsmen and allies of Elizabeth.

**Anne**—The young widow of Prince Edward, son of the former king, Henry VI.

**Duchess of York**—Widowed mother of Richard, Clarence, and King Edward IV. Not to be confused with Margaret.

**Margaret**—Widow of the dead King Henry VI. Mother of the slain Prince Edward.

**The Princes (in the Tower)**—The two young sons of King Edward IV, Prince Edward and the young duke of York.

**Elizabeth**—Daughter of the former Queen Elizabeth who was married to Edward IV.

**Richmond**—Challenges Richard for the throne and becomes Henry VII.

**Hastings**—A lord who supports the Yorkist cause.

**Stanley**—Lord Stanley, earl of Derby. Stepfather of Richmond.

**Lord Mayor of London**—A gullible and suggestible fellow.

**Vaughan**—A friend of Elizabeth, Dorset, Rivers, and Grey.

## Introduction

*King Richard III* is the last of the four plays in Shakespeare's first quartet of history plays. It concludes a dramatic chronicle started in *King Henry VI, Part I* and then moving through *King Henry VI, Part II*, and *King*

*Henry VI, Part III.* The entire four-play saga was composed early in Shakespeare's career, and most scholars date *King Richard III* to about 1591 or 1592.

*King Richard III* is a dramatization of historical events that concluded in 1485 with the defeat of King Richard III at the battle of Bosworth, when the Tudors replaced the Plantagenet family as rulers of England. Shakespeare often plays fast and loose with the facts, however, stretching and altering the timeline. The events of this civil war—including the murders of King Henry and Prince Edward by the York brothers, and the earlier killing of Rutland by Henry's family—are an important background to *King Richard III*.

Elizabethan audiences were certainly familiar with these events and were particularly fascinated with Richard III. Shakespeare's audiences could readily identify the various political factions and complex family relationships depicted in the play. In Shakespeare's version, both Henry and Edward leave widows: Margaret and Lady Anne. Although Anne mourns Henry VI's death she nevertheless becomes Richard's wife.

Richard III is a fascinating figure, in the same way that we are entranced by the charismatic malevolence of a Hannibal Lecter, and audiences for generations have found themselves seduced by Richard's eloquence and cunning emotional manipulation, even as they are repelled by his evil.

When *King Richard III* begins, Edward IV is growing old. His malicious and deformed younger brother, Richard, is plotting to get his hands on the throne. But a great many people stand between him and the kingship. When Edward dies, he leaves behind two sons who are in line for the throne before Richard. They are still children, though, and Richard has them murdered while they live in captivity in the Tower of London. Their young sister, Elizabeth, becomes an important pawn in bringing peace to the realm.

Richard's ambition is also blocked by his older brother and Clarence's two children, all of whom Richard must get rid of in order to seize the throne. Once on the throne, however, Richard soon finds himself besieged by his second cousin, Henry, the earl of Richmond, who has been gathering strength overseas. Henry believes he has a rightful claim to the throne, and in preparing to challenge Richard sets up the final conflict of the Wars of Roses.

## The Play

The play picks up from the end of *King Henry VI, Part III*. Richard's brother is now King Edward IV. In order to gain the crown himself and eliminate his brothers, Richard pits his older brother George, duke of Clarence, against Edward. He convinces Edward that George is guilty of treason and has him arrested. He also brazenly woos Anne, widow of the murdered Prince of Wales, in the midst of her husband's funeral procession.

Shakespearean audiences would have thought of the "wicked Italian" Machiavelli when watching this play, because Richard is the epitome of the amoral, power-hungry courtier made famous in the book *The Prince* (1532) by the Renaissance Italian writer Niccolo Machiavelli.

Edward IV, who is deathly ill at the beginning of the play, dies. Richard has already arranged for his brother George to be murdered while in prison, and now he becomes regent until Edward's son (also named Edward, Prince of Wales) comes of age.

In order to "protect" the Prince of Wales and his younger brother, Richard puts them in the Tower of London. He then executes Edward's loyalist lords Vaughan, Rivers, Hastings, and Grey. With the aid of Buckingham, Richard has Edward's sons declared illegitimate. Buckingham "offers" the throne of England to Richard, who pretends to be reluctant to accept. Few are fooled by his false modesty. Even his mother curses him as a bloody tyrant.

Richard hires a murderer to kill the princes in the tower because Buckingham has refused to help him. Having married Anne, who conveniently dies, Richard proposes marriage to Princess Elizabeth, King Edward's daughter. Her mother Elizabeth (Edward's widow) pretends to go along with the match, but actually arranges for her daughter to marry the earl of Richmond instead.

Richmond is raising an army in France to fight Richard. Buckingham, out of favor with Richard because he refused to go along with the murder of the young princes, gives his allegiance to Richmond. Buckingham is captured and Richard has him executed.

Richmond finally lands with his army and marches for London. The French and English armies get ready to fight near Bosworth Field. The night before the battle, Richard is visited by the ghosts of the people he has killed, and all prophesy his death.

During the battle Richard is thrown from his horse ("A horse! a horse! my kingdom for a horse!"). He and Richmond fight to death with Richmond prevailing. Richmond is crowned King Henry VII. The Battle of Bosworth is the final engagement of the Wars of the Roses and marks the founding of the Tudor dynasty of kings and queens.

## Commentary

*King Richard III* is a chronicle of bloody deeds and atrocities, and modern audiences can find it difficult to follow the complex political intrigue, family relationships, and personal vendettas. The play is as much melodrama as history, and Richard is a self-professed villain of monstrous proportions comparable only to Iago in *Othello*, or to a lesser extent Edmund in *King Lear*. Richard's ambition makes Macbeth look like an amateur by comparison. He is a totally Machiavellian creature, able to splinter and nearly destroy the forces opposing him, until he is finally defeated by Richmond.

Richard is clearly ambitious and sadistic, but no clear reason for his motivations or his hatred is given. It is as if he decides early on in life that he will be as bitter and twisted inside as he is out because that is the only joy he can ever really expect to have. Like the character the Devil from medieval morality pageants who represented evil, Richard does not even try to justify what he does.

Richard was probably no more murderous than the kings who came before or after him. He was more the rightful king of England when he died in battle than Richmond. History is written by the victors, however, and at the time Shakespeare was writing England was ruled by Queen Elizabeth—granddaughter of King Henry VII, the man who defeated Richard. The official "party line" was that Richard had been a monster who was not the legitimate king of England. To suggest anything else would have been thoroughly dangerous for Shakespeare.

**FACTS**

Modern historians are split on whether the real Richard murdered the young princes or whether he even had a humpback. History reports that Richard came to be known as Humpty, and historians say the nursery rhyme Humpty Dumpty is about Richard's defeat at the Battle of Bosworth.

## Famous Lines

"Now is the winter of our discontent
Made glorious summer by this sun of York,
And all the clouds that loured upon our house
In the deep bosom of the ocean buried.
Now are our brows bound with victorious wreaths,
Our bruised arms hung up for monuments,
Our stern alarums changed to merry meetings,
Our dreadful marches to delightful measures.
Grim-visaged war hath smoothed his wrinkled front;
And now, instead of mounting barbed steeds
To fright the souls of fearful adversaries,
He capers nimbly in a lady's chamber
To the lascivious pleasing of a lute.
But I, that am not shaped for sportive tricks,
Nor made to court an amorous looking-glass;
I, that am rudely stamped, and want love's majesty
To strut before a wanton ambling nymph;

I, that am curtailed of this fair proportion,
Cheated of feature by dissembling nature,
Deformed, unfinished, sent before my time
Into this breathing world, scarce half made up,
And that so lamely and unfashionable
That dogs bark at me as I halt by them,—
Why, I, in this weak piping time of peace,
Have no delight to pass away the time,
Unless to spy my shadow in the sun" (Act I, Scene I).

"O, I have passed a miserable night,
So full of ugly sights, of ghastly dreams,
That, as I am a Christian faithful man,
I would not spend another such a night,
Though 't were to buy a world of happy days" (Act I, Scene IV).

"Lord, Lord! methought, what pain it was to drown!
What dreadful noise of waters in mine ears!
What ugly sights of death within mine eyes!
Methought I saw a thousand fearful wrecks,
Ten thousand men that fishes gnawed upon,
Wedges of gold, great anchors, heaps of pearl,
Inestimable stones, unvalued jewels,
All scattered in the bottom of the sea:
Some lay in dead men's skulls; and in those holes
Where eyes did once inhabit, there were crept,
As 't were in scorn of eyes, reflecting gems" (Act I, Scene IV).

"Off with his head!" (Act III, Scene IV).

"An honest tale speeds best, being plainly told" (Act IV, Scene IV).

"I have set my life upon a cast,
And I will stand the hazard of the die:
I think there be six Richmonds in the field" (Act V, Scene IV).

"A horse! a horse! my kingdom for a horse!" (Act V, Scene IV).

# 22 ✦ *Love's Labour's Lost*

## Main Characters

**Ferdinand**—King of Navarre, a scholar.

**Berowne, Longaville, and Dumaine**—Three lords who have joined the king in his oath of scholarship. They fall in love with Rosaline, Maria, and Katherine, respectively.

**Princess of France**—A visitor to the king.

**Rosaline, Maria, and Katherine**—Three ladies attending the princess who catch the fancy of the king's lords.

**Boyet**—A lord attending the princess.

**Don Armado**—Described as "a fantastical Spaniard." He catches Costard and Jaquenetta in the forest and falls in love with Jaquenetta.

**Moth**—Don Armado's page.

**Costard**—A clown.

**Jaquenetta**—A country girl.

**Sir Nathaniel**—A curate.

**Holofernes**—A schoolmaster.

**Dull**—A constable.

## Introduction

*Love's Labour's Lost* is an early play, published in 1598 and probably written about 1595. It was included as a comedy in Shakespeare's First Folio and is a meditation on love, though without a marriage at the end, which is untypical of a Shakespearean comedy. This is one of the few plays where the source of the play is unknown, though some scholars guess it may have come from *L'Académie Françoise* (1577) by Pierre de la Primaudaye, about a society of scholars.

**ESSENTIALS**

*Love's Labour's Lost* was probably first performed in December of 1597, most likely as a Christmas entertainment for Queen Elizabeth I, and repeated about the same time of year for King James I in 1604.

# The Play

Ferdinand, king of Navarre, declares that for a year his court will, in effect, become a school, and to keep distractions to a minimum, no women will be allowed during that time. His nobles, Berowne, Longaville, and Dumaine agree to cloister themselves with the king, although Berowne has his reservations about how successful they will be. Berowne also points out that the king has forgotten an embassy will arrive that very day with the princess of France. Rather than receive her at court, the Navarrese set out to meet the princess. Meanwhile, Costard, the king's fool, is about to be punished for dallying with a country girl, Jaquenetta.

The princess and her entourage are not happy when Ferdinand denies them entrance into the court. In protest, she camps in front of the court, and she and her ladies make plans to get even with Ferdinand and his courtiers.

Armado, who is in love with Jaquenetta, tells Costard he can go free if Costard delivers a letter to Jaquenetta. Next, Berowne asks him to take a letter to Rosaline. Totally confused, Costard delivers the letter intended for Jaquenetta to the princess of France, and gives Rosaline's letter to Jaquenetta.

Ferdinand and his men eavesdrop on one another and overhear each other professing love for the princess and her gentlewomen. When the lords pay a visit to the ladies in disguise, however, the women are forewarned, disguise themselves, and make fun of the men. The men return as themselves, but the women continue to bait them, delighting in the men's confusion.

When things are finally being sorted out, and they are to be entertained by a play performed by some amateur actors, the princess learns that her father has died, and she must leave immediately. She tells Ferdinand that if he spends a year cloistered in a remote hermitage for breaking his own oath, she will marry him. Each of her ladies-in-waiting exact similar promises from the king's lords vowing that they will return to Navarre the following year and marry if their loves have proven true.

# Commentary

The play examines the idea that despite efforts to avoid passion, as human beings we can't get away from our emotions. At the end, we are reminded of this truth when, in the middle of blooming love, the pain of loss intrudes. Shakespeare seems to be suggesting that we often don't treasure what we have until we no longer have it, sounding a warning to lovers to appreciate the happiness that may be right in front of them.

**FACTS**

Shakespeare is famous for his puns, and this play has over 200 of them. It is something of a send-up of Elizabethan manners and personality types, and so it tends to go over the head of modern audiences. However, while the play might seem a dour, dreary affair, in the right hands it can actually be pretty funny.

# Famous Lines

"Light seeking light doth light of light beguile" (Act I, Scene I).

"Affliction may one day smile again; and till then, sit thee down, sorrow!" (Act I, Scene I).

"To sell a bargain well is as cunning as fast and loose" (Act III, Scene I).

"They have been at a great feast of languages, and stolen the scraps" (Act V, Scene I).

"A jest's prosperity lies in the ear
Of him that hears it, never in the tongue
Of him that makes it" (Act V, Scene II).

# 23 ᕙ *Macbeth*

## Main Characters

**Macbeth**—An ambitious Scottish general.

**Lady Macbeth**—Macbeth's wife. A deeply ambitious woman.

**Banquo**—A brave general.

**King Duncan**—The king of Scotland Macbeth murders.

**Malcolm**—A Scottish prince, the son of Duncan.

**Macduff**—A Scottish nobleman.

**The Three Witches**—Seers who prophesy Macbeth's fate.

**Hecate**—The goddess of witchcraft.

**Fleance**—Banquo's son.

**Lennox**—A Scottish nobleman.

**Ross**—A Scottish nobleman.

**Siward**—An English general.

**The Murderers**—Assassins hired by Macbeth to kill Banquo and his children.

## Introduction

With the possible exception of *Titus Andronicus*, which is considered a lesser play, *Macbeth* is Shakespeare's bloodiest tragedy. It traces the disintegration of a powerful man who longs for more power and will stoop to anything, even murder, to get it.

*Macbeth* was probably composed in late 1606 or early 1607, and is the last of Shakespeare's four great tragedies, the others being *Hamlet*, *King Lear*, and *Othello*. *Macbeth*'s supernatural element suggests that fate plays with us if we let it. Macbeth chooses to walk the bloody path of ambition in order to attain the glory promised him by the witches.

*Macbeth* is loosely based on a historic king of the same name who lived from 1005 to 1057. He launched a civil war in his efforts to seize the throne from his cousin Duncan. There is no evidence that the real

Macbeth was ever incited by his wife, Gruoch, or that his actions led to the turmoil dramatized in the play. The real Macbeth, in fact, reigned peacefully for fifteen years.

**SSENTIALS** In theater lore, no actor ever actually calls *Macbeth* by its given name. It is called instead, "The Scottish Play" because it has been associated with bad luck over the centuries. The curse began, it is said, with the first performance of the play when the boy actor playing Lady Macbeth collapsed, apparently from a fever, and died before the play had finished.

An integral part of this theme of ambition is the play's most memorable character, Lady Macbeth. Unlike her husband, who is enticed by supernatural evil (in the form of Hecate and the witches) into pursuing his bloody path, Lady Macbeth's lust for power leads her naturally into the nightmare realm of hallucinations and madness.

## The Play

During a thunderstorm on a Scottish moor in the midst of a battle between the Scots and the Norwegians, Macbeth kills the traitorous Scot, Macdonald, Thane (Earl) of Cawdor. The king hears of the death and promises to make Macbeth Thane of Cawdor as soon as he sees him.

On the heath near the battlefield, Macbeth and Banquo come upon three witches. They hail Macbeth as Thane of Cawdor, baffling Macbeth, who has not yet learned of his promotion. They also say he will be king one day. They then call Banquo "lesser than Macbeth, and greater," and "not so happy, yet much happier." They tell him that he will never be king, but that his children will sit upon the throne.

When Macbeth and Banquo reunite with King Duncan, Macbeth learns that he has been promoted to Thane of Cawdor in place of the man he killed in battle. Part one of the witches' prophecy has come to pass. Macbeth begins to consider the possibility that he might be king one day. However, Duncan announces Malcolm as his heir. Publicly, Macbeth declares his joy, but privately he admits his disappointment. Macbeth invites Duncan to dine at his castle that evening, and Duncan agrees.

## Lady Macbeth

At the castle, Lady Macbeth reads a letter from her husband, announcing his promotion and detailing the promises of the witches. Lady Macbeth fears he is too full of "the milk of human kindness" to do what it takes to become king. If only she were a man, she would do the deeds herself, she says. She tells her husband she has a plan.

Duncan and his retinue arrive. Macbeth ponders his plan to assassinate Duncan. On the one hand, he considers murder morally wrong and admires the king; on the other hand is his driving ambition. He tells Lady Macbeth he no longer intends to kill Duncan, who has been kind to him. Outraged, she calls him a coward, unmanly, and convinces him to reconsider.

That night Lady Macbeth puts her plan into action. A tolling bell is the signal that the king's servants are asleep. Macbeth emerges from Duncan's chamber steeped in gore. He is badly shaken and says that as he killed the king he thought he heard a voice cry out that Macbeth would never sleep again.

Lady Macbeth tries to steady him, but is angry when she notices he has forgotten to leave the daggers with the servants to frame them for the killing. Macbeth refuses to go back into the room. Lady Macbeth takes them herself, calling him a coward once again. When Lady Macbeth returns she tells Macbeth a little water will clear them both of the murder.

Macduff and Lennox arrive asking for the king. Lennox describes storms that have raged during the night. He says no one can remember a night like it. Macduff goes to wake the king, and then returns horrified crying murder. Chaos reigns. Macbeth goes in to see and returns mourning, declaring that in a grief-stricken rage he killed the servants who murdered Duncan.

## Descent into Murder and Madness

Later that evening, Macduff meets with Ross outside the castle and tells Ross that Macbeth has been made king. Macduff adds that, although the servants seem the most likely murderers, suspicion has now fallen on the king's sons, the princes, as well because they have fled the scene.

The witches lurk as the personification of evil; yet their mischief is due mainly to their ability to exploit the weaknesses of their victims. They play upon Macbeth's ambition like puppeteers, while Banquo resists them.

Banquo takes time to think about Macbeth's coronation and the prophecy of the witches who foretold not only that Macbeth would be king, but also that Banquo's sons would sit on the throne. Macbeth, elsewhere, is pondering the same topic. His old friend Banquo is the only man in Scotland he now fears. According to the witches' prophecy, Duncan's murder has simply cleared the way for Banquo's sons to become king. Two murderers now enter. Macbeth asks them if they have the stomach to kill Banquo and his children. The assassins hide in a wooded park outside the palace and ambush Banquo and his son Fleance as they ride in and dismount. Banquo is killed, but Fleance escapes.

At the coronation feast the murderers quietly tell Macbeth what has happened. As Macbeth walks among his guests and goes to sit at the head of the table, he finds Banquo's ghost sitting in his chair. Horror-struck, Macbeth speaks to the ghost, which is invisible to the rest of the company. Lady Macbeth makes excuses for her husband, saying that he occasionally has such "visions," and that the guests should simply ignore his behavior. Macbeth cannot control his "fits," and in the end she has to send the guests away.

Lennox walks with another lord and both confess that they suspect Macbeth in the murders of Duncan and Banquo. The lord tells Lennox that Malcolm and Macduff have fled to England to ask King Edward for aid. Their success has prompted Macbeth to begin preparing for war. Lennox and the lord quietly wish Malcolm and Macduff luck.

Macbeth tells Lady Macbeth that he will visit the witches again in the hopes of learning more. Entering a dark cavern, Macbeth asks the witches to reveal more details of their prophecy to him. They summon horrible apparitions: a floating head tells him to beware Macduff; a bloody child tells him that "none of woman born" can harm him; and a crowned child holding a tree tells him that he is safe until "Great Birnam Wood to high Dunsinane Hill shall come against him." Then a procession of eight crowned kings walks through, the last carrying a mirror. Banquo's ghost is at the end of the line. Macbeth demands to know the meaning of this final vision, but the witches cackle with glee and vanish.

## Death to the Macbeths

In Scotland, at night, in the king's palace at Dunsinane, Lady Macbeth enters in a trance bemoaning the murders of Lady Macduff and Banquo. She continually sees blood on her hands even though she has tried desperately to wash it off. She leaves, and the doctor and gentlewoman who are looking after her marvel at her descent into madness. Outside the castle, a group of Scottish lords discuss the military situation; the Scottish army will engage Malcolm's English army near Birnam Wood.

Macbeth boasts that he has nothing to fear from the English army or from Malcolm, since "none of woman born" can harm him. Malcolm and the English lord Siward decide that each soldier should cut down a bough of the forest and carry it in front of him as they march to the castle, thereby disguising their numbers.

While organizing defenses Macbeth is told the queen has killed herself. A messenger now enters with the astonishing news that the trees of Birnam Wood are advancing toward Dunsinane. The witches' prophecy is coming true. The battle commences. On the battlefield, Macbeth slaughters with vigor, reminded that "none of woman born" can harm him. Macduff fights his way toward him. They meet at last. As the fight gets underway Macduff tells Macbeth that he was not of woman born, but rather "from my mother's womb untimely ripp'd." (That is, he was born by Caesarian section.) He kills Macbeth.

Malcolm and Siward capture the castle. Macduff emerges with Macbeth's head in his hand and proclaims Malcolm king of Scotland.

Malcolm declares that all his thanes will be made earls, as is the English custom. They will be the first such lords in Scottish history. Cursing Macbeth and his "fiend-like" queen, he invites all to see him crowned at Scone.

# Commentary

*Macbeth* is often interpreted as an examination of what happens when ambition goes unchecked by moral constraints. Macbeth is a brave soldier who is tempted by the devil (Hecate) into becoming the king of Scotland. The bloodbath that results from trying to realize this destiny propels Macbeth and Lady Macbeth into a swift descent into arrogance, madness, and death.

It is not a particularly complicated play, but it is powerful, and is possibly Shakespeare's most emotionally intense. *Hamlet* and *Othello* explore the intellectual complications of their subjects, and *King Lear* deals with the inner chaos of a deranged mind, but *Macbeth* is like a scythe unerringly mowing down anything in its way, leaving corpse after corpse in its wake from the moment the witches appear. The play is a sharp, jagged sketch of theme and character, and, as such, it has shocked and fascinated audiences of stage and screen for nearly four hundred years.

**FACTS**

*Macbeth* is a powerful critique of political power as it ponders exactly what qualities make a good ruler, and the values or dangers of manliness. Whenever a discussion of manhood takes place during the play, it is swiftly followed by violence and death.

Macbeth starts the play as a noble, courageous warrior; he kills Duncan somewhat against his better judgment, but ends the play in a heat of frantic, boastful madness. Lady Macbeth, one of Shakespeare's most compelling female characters, mercilessly eggs on her husband's butchery without being able to imagine the awful price her ambition will cost both her and her husband.

The play also deals with the dangers of arrogant, testosterone-laden manliness. Lady Macbeth continually manipulates Macbeth by urging him to be a man, or asking him if he is a man. Macbeth encourages the murderers to kill Banquo and his children by questioning their manhood, and Malcolm consoles Macduff after the murders of his wife and children by encouraging him to take the news in "manly" fashion.

## Famous Lines

"When shall we three meet again
In thunder, lightning, or in rain?
When the hurlyburly's done,
When the battle's lost and won" (Act I, Scene I).

"What are these
So wither'd and so wild in their attire,
That look not like the inhabitants o' the earth,
And yet are on 't?" (Act I, Scene III).

"If you can look into the seeds of time,
And say which grain will grow and which will not" (Act I, Scene III).

"Nothing is
But what is not" (Act I, Scene III).

"Yet do I fear thy nature;
It is too full o' the milk of human kindness" (Act I, Scene V).

"I dare do all that may become a man;
Who dares do more is none" (Act I, Scene VII).

"Is this a dagger which I see before me,
The handle toward my hand? Come, let me clutch thee.
I have thee not, and yet I see thee still.
Art thou not, fatal vision, sensible
To feeling as to sight? or art thou but
A dagger of the mind, a false creation,
Proceeding from the heat-oppressed brain?" (Act II, Scene I).

"There's daggers in men's smiles" (Act II, Scene III).

"Stand not upon the order of your going,
But go at once" (Act III, Scene IV).

"Double, double toil and trouble;
Fire burn, and cauldron bubble" (Act IV, Scene I).

"By the pricking of my thumbs,
Something wicked this way comes.
Open, locks,
Whoever knocks!" (Act IV, Scene I).

"Out, damned spot! out, I say!" (Act V, Scene I).

"Fie, my lord, fie! a soldier, and afeard?" (Act V, Scene I).

"Yet who would have thought the old man to have had so much
   blood in him?" (Act V, Scene I).

"To-morrow, and to-morrow, and to-morrow,
Creeps in this petty pace from day to day
To the last syllable of recorded time,
And all our yesterdays have lighted fools
The way to dusty death. Out, out, brief candle!
Life 's but a walking shadow, a poor player
That struts and frets his hour upon the stage
And then is heard no more: it is a tale
Told by an idiot, full of sound and fury,
Signifying nothing" (Act V, Scene V).

# 24 ✤ *Measure for Measure*

## Main Characters

**Isabella**—A virtuous young woman, sister to Claudio.

**Vincentio**—The duke of Vienna. He spends most of his time disguised as a friar.

**Claudio**—Isabella's brother. Sentenced to death for impregnating an unmarried woman.

**Lord Angelo**—A hypocrite who rules strictly and without mercy.

**Escalus**—A wise lord who advises Angelo.

**Lucio**—A flamboyant bachelor.

**Mariana**—Angelo's fiancée.

**Mistress Overdone**—A madam.

**Pompey**—A clown who works for Mistress Overdone.

**Provost**—The jailer.

**Elbow**—A dimwitted constable.

**Barnadine**—A prisoner in the jail.

**Juliet**—Claudio's lover.

## Introduction

*Measure for Measure* takes its title from the gospel of Matthew: "with what measure ye mete, it shall be measured to you again" (Matthew 7:2), a passage from the Sermon on the Mount, one of Christ's most famous sermons.

While some documents indicate it was first performed at court at Whitehall on St. Stephen's Night (December 26), 1604, others suggest that it was written and first performed earlier that year. Lucio's allusion to a hoped-for peace may well refer to King James I's attempts in 1604 to negotiate a peace agreement with Spain; the proclamation to tear down the brothels may refer to King James's edict in 1603 to tear down houses affected by the plague (the plague and venereal disease were often related in Renaissance literature). A number of critics have noted similarities between the duke and King James's dislike of crowds, his use of disguise, and his aversion to slander.

**FACTS**

> Cinthio, an Italian writer and philosopher, first wrote this story as a 1565 novella called *Hecatommithi*, then as a play called *Epita* in 1583. Another dramatist, George Whetstone, wrote the story as a play in 1578 called *Promos and Cassandra*, and in 1581 Thomas Lupton wrote a play called *Too Good To Be True.*

The earliest, and thus most authoritative, text for the play is the First Folio, which was printed in 1623. The lack of stage directions suggests it is a prompt copy. Shakespeare took the source of the play from a real case in Italy. In 1547, a judge promised a murderer he would not be sentenced to death if the murderer's wife had sex with him. After he had enjoyed himself, the judge went back on his word and executed the man anyway.

## The Play

In order to find out why he is not a better ruler, Vincentio, Duke of Vienna, decides to take a sabbatical, appointing his deputy, Angelo, to rule in his place. The duke wants to enforce morality laws, and he empowers Angelo to do so, mainly because the duke doesn't want to seem a bad guy, and someone has to accept the unpopular task of being more strict. Because Angelo is a zealot the duke considers him perfect for the task. Meanwhile, the duke decides to keep an eye on things by remaining in town disguised as a monk.

### Claudio's Death Sentence

Angelo's harshness upsets a lot of people, particularly when Claudio is arrested for getting his fiancée, Juliet, pregnant before they are married. Angelo condemns him to death. While agreeing with his moral stance, Claudio's sister, Isabella, nevertheless pleads with Angelo for her brother's life.

Angelo won't budge at first. Gradually, Isabella's beauty and chaste virtue excite him. He propositions her: He will pardon Claudio if she sleeps with him. Isabella turns him down, vowing that her chastity and honor are her life.

When she tells Claudio what happened, he at first goes along, but soon tries to talk his sister into trading her virtue for his life. The duke (in disguise) overhears their conversation and sets into motion a plot to save both Claudio and Isabella from their predicament.

## The Duke Steps In

The duke knows Angelo was once engaged to Mariana, who still loves him. He persuades Isabella to feign acceptance of Angelo's offer and when the moment comes, Mariana will switch places in the dark with Isabella (the bed trick of *All's Well That Ends Well*). Mariana agrees, and events go as planned except that after getting his way, Angelo orders Claudio's execution anyway.

Luckily, the duke hears about this and persuades the jailer to substitute another condemned man for Claudio and to carry out the execution "as planned." Isabella is led to believe that Claudio has died; Angelo has betrayed her and she should seek justice from the duke who is expected to return soon.

Isabel and Mariana make their accusations against Angelo to the duke, who appears as himself. Angelo first says Isabella is lying and blames the "monk" for putting her up to this. When the duke reveals himself as the monk, Angelo is forced to throw himself on the mercy of the duke and Isabella. Claudio is revealed to be alive, Mariana pleads for Angelo's life, and the duke orders that Angelo should marry Mariana and Claudio should marry Juliet. The duke makes his own arrangements to be married to Isabella.

## Commentary

*Measure for Measure* has been criticized for having an unsatisfying resolution and plain gaps in plotting. For example, why does Isabella agree to the duke's plan? After all, the bed switch still makes Mariana commit the same crime that Claudio is condemned for, and Isabella is vocal in condemning her brother's actions. The irony is, she agrees with Angelo. She just disagrees on the punishment he intends to mete out.

At the beginning of the play Isabella was about to become a nun. At no time during the play does she profess love for the duke, or he for her. He's disguised as a monk for most of it anyway. Yet we are left with the distinct impression she will become his bride.

*Measure for Measure*'s themes of sexual harassment and women's rights had hardly been explored at the time the play was first performed, and they have made it a popular play. It touches on issues of sexuality, independence, and the objectification of women, and does so without one strong female character. In fact, the female characters in *Measure for Measure* are unusually weak for Shakespeare. They simply go along with what the men decide. Despite this, the play is considered a comedy, and the story is filled with amusing minor characters as well as broad sociological questions.

The play certainly raises important moral issues. Its structure revolves around secret identities: the duke disguises himself as a monk, and most of the problems are resolved when he reveals his identity. The duke solves Claudio and Isabella's problem with a plan involving mistaken identity. Mariana takes Isabella's place, and the head of a dead pirate is used to deceive Angelo.

The duke, in effect, functions as a kind of ringmaster. He may have placed a proxy ruler in power during his absence, but he is still pulling the puppet strings. He is an interesting paradox: a character who is wise, but unable to maintain order.

*Measure for Measure* is also a problem play because it does not follow through with the moral questions it raises. No one reconsiders his or her beliefs about freedom, justice, sexual relationships, or morality, and Isabella in particular never really has to deal with the consequences of having to commit a sin in order to save her brother.

## Famous Lines

"Our doubts are traitors,
And make us lose the good we oft might win
By fearing to attempt" (Act I, Scene IV).

"Some rise by sin, and some by virtue fall" (Act II, Scene I).

"Condemn the fault, and not the actor of it?" (Act II, Scene II).

"O, it is excellent
To have a giant's strength; but it is tyrannous
To use it like a giant" (Act II, Scene II).

"The miserable have no other medicine,
But only hope" (Act III, Scene I).

"O, what may man within him hide,
Though angel on the outward side!" (Act III, Scene II).

"They say, best men are moulded out of faults,
And, for the most, become much more the better
For being a little bad" (Act V, Scene I).

"What's mine is yours, and what is yours is mine" (Act V, Scene I).

# 25 ⚬ *Much Ado About Nothing*

## Main Characters

**Leonato**—The father of Hero and the uncle of Beatrice.

**Don Pedro**—Sometimes called "the Prince." A longtime friend of Leonato.

**Don John**—Sometimes called "the Bastard." The illegitimate brother of Don Pedro.

**Claudio**—A young soldier who falls in love with Hero.

**Hero**—The beautiful young daughter of Leonato and the cousin of Beatrice.

**Benedick**—A friend and soldier of Don Pedro.

**Beatrice**—Leonato's niece and Hero's cousin.

**Margaret**—Hero's maid.

**Ursula**—One of Hero's servingwomen.

**Borachio**—Don John's servant and Margaret's lover.

**Conrade**—One of Don John's servants.

**Dogberry**—The constable of Messina.

**Verges**—Dogberry's assistant.

**Antonio**—Leonato's older brother and uncle to Hero and Beatrice.

**Friar Francis**—A monk.

## Introduction

*Much Ado About Nothing* is generally considered one of Shakespeare's best comedies. It was probably written around 1598–9, as Shakespeare was approaching the middle of his career. Like *A Midsummer Night's Dream*, *As You Like It*, and *Twelfth Night*, it has few dark elements and provides a happy ending with no deaths.

The verbal sparring between Beatrice and Benedick may have been inspired by the fictional debates between a man and a woman created by the Italian writer Baldassare Castiglione in *The Book of the Courtier* (1528). Critics think the Hero-Claudio plot is based on *Orlando Furioso*

(1532), an Italian poem by Ludovico Ariosto. Shakespeare may have read a translation by Sir John Harrington published in 1591. The character of Dogberry, the comic policeman or constable, is reminiscent of Constable Dull in *Love's Labour's Lost* and is an original creation by Shakespeare.

**FACTS**

The play has been popular since it was first staged and it is a contemporary favorite. In 1862, Hector Berlioz used it as the basis for his opera *Beatrice and Benedict. What To Do About Nothing,* a 1998 play by Judy Sheehan, retells the story, using gossip and eavesdropping as key elements, and setting it against the backdrop of the McCarthy "red scare" in America of the early 1950s.

## The Play

Don Pedro, the prince of Arragon, and two of his officers, Benedick and Claudio, visit Don Pedro's old friend Leonato, the governor of Messina. Claudio quickly falls in love with Leonato's daughter, Hero. Benedick continues a battle of wits with Beatrice, the governor's niece.

Don Pedro, with Leonato, Claudio, and Hero's help, decides it's time Benedick and Beatrice stopped tormenting each other verbally, and admitted they were in love. To that end, both Benedick and Beatrice are made to think the other has secretly professed a great love for them.

Don John, who seems to be reconciled with his brother, Don Pedro, despises Claudio, and when he learns about his impending marriage to Hero, he decides to ruin it. He tells Claudio that Pedro wants Hero for himself. Then he gets his servant Borachio and Hero's maid Margaret to stage an episode that will make it seem as though Hero is a loose woman.

Claudio is so upset, he denounces Hero at the altar. Friar Francis hides her away and with Beatrice's help announces that Hero has died of grief. Borachio drunkenly boasts of his part in the plan—and the 1,000 ducats Don John paid him—and is arrested by Dogberry and the watch.

Hero is exonerated and Claudio is grief-stricken at what he has done, thinking Hero still dead. Leonato demands a public apology from Claudio, then tells him that he must marry one of his nieces in Hero's place. The niece turns out to be Hero, of course, miraculously brought back to life. Claudio and Hero are reunited, and Benedick and Beatrice realize they love each other and get married at the same time. The bastard Don John is apprehended and will be brought to justice for his mischief making.

## Commentary

Although *Much Ado About Nothing* is a light comedy, some critics are troubled by the anger, betrayal, hatred, grief, and despair that are at the center of the play. Like other Shakespearian comedies, for part of the time *Much Ado About Nothing* threatens to become a tragedy. The plot is an elaborate network of schemes and tricks, and it shares elements with *Romeo and Juliet*, *The Taming of the Shrew*, and even *Othello*, reminding us that comedy and tragedy are opposite ends of the same line.

Beatrice and Benedick's mature love affair can be compared in some ways to Antony and Cleopatra's, but is much happier and healthier. They are one of Shakespeare's most mature and nuanced of couples.

While Hero and Claudio are the engine of the plot, it is actually the courtship of the older and wiser Benedick and Beatrice that makes this play such fun. Their journey from an emotional defensiveness and withdrawal brought about by their ages, which they defend with great wit, to deep affection is developed with a rich humor and compassion.

## Famous Lines

"He wears his faith but as the fashion of his hat" (Act I, Scene I).

"What, my dear Lady Disdain! are you yet living?" (Act I, Scene I).

"Shall I never see a bachelor of threescore again?" (Act I, Scene I).

"As merry as the day is long" (Act II, Scene I).

"Speak low if you speak love" (Act II, Scene I).

"Friendship is constant in all other things
Save in the office and affairs of love:
Therefore all hearts in love use their own tongues;
Let every eye negotiate for itself
And trust no agent" (Act II, Scene I).

"Some Cupid kills with arrows, some with traps" (Act III, Scene I).

"Every one can master a grief but he that has it" (Act III, Scene II).

"Are you good men and true?" (Act III, Scene III).

"O, what men dare do! what men may do! what men daily do, not
    knowing what they do!" (Act IV, Scene I).

"For it so falls out
That what we have we prize not to the worth
Whiles we enjoy it, but being lack'd and lost,
Why, then we rack the value; then we find
The virtue that possession would not show us
Whiles it was ours" (Act IV, Scene I).

"Condemned into everlasting redemption" (Act IV, Scene II).

"For there was never yet philosopher
That could endure the toothache patiently" (Act V, Scene I).

"Done to death by slanderous tongues" (Act V, Scene III).

# 26 ◈ *Othello*

## Main Characters

**Othello**—A Moor commanding the armies of Venice.

**Desdemona**—The daughter of a Venetian senator, and Othello's bride.

**Iago**—Othello's ensign. Perhaps Shakespeare's greatest villain.

**Cassio**—Othello's lieutenant, promoted in place of Iago.

**Emilia**—Iago's wife and Desdemona's attendant.

**Roderigo**—A jealous suitor of Desdemona.

**Bianca**—A courtesan in Cyprus, and Cassio's mistress.

**Brabantio**—Desdemona's father, and a Senator in Venice.

**Lodovico**—Brabantio and Desdemona's kinsman.

**Gratiano**—Brabantio's brother.

**Clown**—Othello's servant.

**Montano**—The governor of Cyprus before Othello.

**The Duke of Venice**—The official authority in Venice.

## Introduction

*Othello* was likely written in early 1604, and first performed in front of King James I of England on November 1 of that year. The great Richard Burbage played Othello. In 1660, Margaret Hughes played Desdemona, and became the first woman allowed to perform on the English stage.

*Othello* is set against the backdrop of the wars between Venice and Turkey that raged in the latter part of the sixteenth century. Cyprus, which is the setting for most of the action, was a Venetian outpost attacked by the Turks in 1570 and conquered by the Ottomans the following year. Shakespeare's information probably comes from *The History of the Turks*, by Richard Knolles, which was published in England in autumn of 1603.

Shakespeare's choice of a black African as a hero was strikingly original. Blackness in Elizabethan England was a color associated with moral evil and death, and Moors in the theater, like Jews, were usually stereotyped as villains, such as Aaron the Moor in *Titus Andronicus,* an early play. Othello is a noble, towering figure whose good nature is the means to his downfall, making the play that much more tragic.

**E**SSENTIALS  Ira Aldridge (who died around 1867) was born a slave in the United States and moved to Europe, becoming an acclaimed Shakespearean actor. He is thought to be the first African American to play Othello.

Some scholars believe *Othello* is derived from an Italian prose tale written in 1565 by Giraldi Cinthio in his collection *Hecatommithi,* although there seems to have been no English translation at the time Shakespeare wrote *Othello* (prompting the thought that he may well have been able to read some Italian). The original story concerns a Moorish general who is deceived by his ensign into believing his wife is unfaithful.

# The Play

Othello, a celebrated Moorish general of Venice, has promoted Cassio as his lieutenant instead of Iago. Iago is incensed, and plots against Cassio and Othello to get his due. Othello and Desdemona, the beautiful daughter of Brabantio, fall in love, elope, and marry. Brabantio is deeply upset by the deceit and the marriage. When Othello is posted to Cyprus by the duke of Venice, Iago escorts Desdemona.

## Framing Cassio

Arriving in Cyprus, Iago immediately begins plotting. He tricks Cassio into getting drunk, then has Roderigo, a former suitor of Desdemona who is upset at her marriage, pick a fight with Cassio. Cassio ends up getting arrested and subsequently demoted. Iago then encourages Cassio to call on Desdemona, saying that if she speaks up for him with her husband, Othello may reinstate him.

Iago now goes to Othello, and as they watch Desdemona and Cassio talk, recalling her father's accusations of her betrayal of trust, Iago plants the seeds of jealousy in Othello. Iago suggests that Cassio and Desdemona are having an affair.

By chance, because his wife Emilia is Desdemona's maid, Iago gets hold of a handkerchief Othello gave Desdemona as a token of his love for her. Iago plants the handkerchief in Cassio's room, and then tells Othello that he saw Cassio with it. When Othello asks Desdemona about the handkerchief, she tells him that it was lost. Cassio, meanwhile, gives it to a courtesan with whom he is intimate. Iago then gets Othello to overhear a conversation whereby Othello thinks they are discussing Desdemona, when in fact they are talking about Bianca, the courtesan.

 **SSENTIALS**

Iago's evil is the antithesis of the love that Othello and Desdemona share. The purity of their passion is perhaps one of the strongest portrayals of romantic affection in any tragedy, including *Romeo and Juliet*. It is this deep love that Iago hates so much because he is incapable of it, and his awareness of his weakness provides him with the key to destroying Othello.

Based on this misinformation, Othello reacts. He tells Iago to kill Cassio and then angrily confronts Desdemona. Despite Desdemona's protests of innocence and Emilia's vouching for her, Othello is now convinced she is sleeping with Cassio.

## The Scheme Unravels

Iago gets Roderigo to murder Cassio. However, Roderigo only wounds him, and Iago kills Roderigo so Roderigo can't betray his machinations. Othello hears the commotion in the street, and thinks Iago has kept his part of their bargain. Now it is time to strangle Desdemona in her bed.

When Emilia discovers the crime, Desdemona, with her dying breath, refuses to accuse her husband. Emilia becomes distraught and accuses the Moor of being a murderous villain and refuses to believe that Iago has so evilly manipulated Othello. However, Iago's appearance and subsequent answers makes Emilia realize her husband is responsible for this tragedy.

Letters found on Roderigo's body confirm Iago's villainy. Faced with the shame of having murdered an innocent Desdemona, Othello stabs himself and dies on Desdemona's bed beside her.

# Commentary

*Othello* is an intense, fast-paced play with most of the action compressed into a twenty-four-hour period. Scenes begin in midconversation, and subplots are pretty inconsequential. Everything plays to the domestic tragedy, centering on the three principle characters manipulated by Iago. Indeed, in no other tragedy does a single figure have so much control over events.

The horror of the play is its inevitability. We know what Iago is planning, and we are forced to watch it unfold. The audience shares in the fate of Desdemona and Othello—caught in Iago's trap.

ESSENTIALS

We suffer with Iago's victims because he manages to use the purity of Othello and Desdemona's love against them. They, and we, are helpless against the chaos that Iago represents. Indeed, Othello says of Desdemona, "When I love thee not, Chaos is come again." And chaos, embodied in "honest Iago," seems to win the day.

The swiftness with which Iago manages to destroy Othello is stunning. He needs only two conversations and a missing handkerchief to convince the Moor that Desdemona has been unfaithful. Iago's "evidence" reminds Othello of her father's parting words: "Look to her, Moor, if thou hast eyes to see. She has deceived her father, and may thee."

Once Othello snaps, Shakespeare delays Desdemona's murder, and we can hope that she may be saved at the last moment. Instead, Iago tries to make Othello suffer even more. Once his plan has borne its bitter fruit, the play is ended.

# Famous Lines

"We cannot all be masters, nor all masters
Cannot be truly follow'd" (Act I, Scene I).

"I will wear my heart upon my sleeve
For daws to peck at" (Act I, Scene I).

"Reputation, reputation, reputation! Oh, I have lost my reputation! I
have lost the immortal part of myself, and what remains is bestial"
(Act II, Scene III).

"O God, that men should put an enemy in their mouths to steal away
their brains!" (Act II, Scene III).

"How poor are they that have not patience!" (Act II, Scene III).

"Good name in man and woman, dear my lord,
Is the immediate jewel of their souls:
Who steals my purse steals trash; 't is something, nothing;
'T was mine, 't is his, and has been slave to thousands;
But he that filches from me my good name
Robs me of that which not enriches him
And makes me poor indeed" (Act III, Scene III).

"O, beware, my lord, of jealousy!
It is the green-eyed monster which doth mock
The meat it feeds on" (Act III, Scene III).

"Trifles light as air
Are to the jealous confirmations strong
As proofs of holy writ" (Act III, Scene III).

"He that is robb'd, not wanting what is stolen,
Let him not know 't, and he's not robb'd at all" (Act III, Scene III).

"Take note, take note, O world,
To be direct and honest is not safe" (Act III, Scene III).

"'T is neither here nor there" (Act IV, Scene III).

"Put out the light, and then put out the light:
If I quench thee, thou flaming minister,
I can again thy former light restore
Should I repent me; but once put out thy light,
Thou cunning'st pattern of excelling nature,
I know not where is that Promethean heat
That can thy light relume" (Act V, Scene II).

"So sweet was ne'er so fatal" (Act V, Scene II).

"Then, must you speak
Of one that loved not wisely but too well;
Of one not easily jealous, but being wrought
Perplex'd in the extreme; of one whose hand,
Like the base Indian, threw a pearl away
Richer than all his tribe; of one whose subdued eyes,
Albeit unused to the melting mood,
Drop tears as fast as the Arabian trees
Their medicinal gum" (Act V, Scene II).

# 27 🔖 Pericles, Prince of Tyre

## Main Characters

**John Gower**—A chorus.

**Antiochus**—King of Antioch.

Antiochus's daughter.

**Thaliart**—A villain hired by Antiochus to kill Pericles.

**Pericles**—Husband of Thaisa and father of Marina.

**Helicanus**—One of Pericles's advisors in Tyre.

**Aeschines**—Another of Pericles's advisors.

**Cleon**—Governor of Tarsus, a city beset by famine.

**Dionyza**—Wife of Cleon.

**Simonides**—King of Pentapolis, father of Thaisa.

**Thaisa**—Daughter of Simonides, mother of Marina.

**Marina**—Daughter of Pericles and Thaisa.

**Leonine**—Murderer hired by Dionyza to kill Marina.

**Lychordia**—Thaisa's nurse, later Marina's nurse.

**Cerimon**—A kindly physician in Ephesus.

**Philomon**—Cerimon's assistant.

**Lysimachus**—Governor of Mytilene.

**Pander**—A brothel keeper.

**Bawd**—A madam who takes care of the prostitutes, probably
Pander's wife.

**Master**—The master of the fishermen who takes Pericles to the
jousting competition on Pentapolis.

**Knights**—Suitors for Thaisa's hand at the jousting competition in Pentapolis.

**Boult**—Servant to Pander and Bawd.

**Diana**—Goddess of chastity.

**Shipmaster**—Captain of the ship on which Thaisa allegedly dies.

## Introduction

*Pericles, Prince of Tyre* was probably written around 1607, came late in
Shakespeare's career. As in most of Shakespeare's plays (and those of his

contemporaries), Shakespeare drew on earlier authors and common stories as source material for the play. The fourteenth-century poet John Gower, who appears in the play as a kind of chorus, wrote the most important direct source for *Pericles*, a story about Apollonius of Tyre in his *Confessio Amantis*. The story probably dates back to fifth or sixth century Latin texts, and before that perhaps even a Greek romance influenced by Homer's *Odyssey*, which it cursorily resembles.

## Authorship

Scholars have long debated the actual authorship of *Pericles* without resolution. It is likely that another playwright named George Wilkins wrote the first nine scenes and Shakespeare wrote the remaining thirteen. Dual authorship is a good explanation for the stylistic differences between the two parts of the play. In the first part, the language closely reflects John Gower's fourteenth-century language rather than that of Shakespeare or his contemporaries.

Though both Wilkins and Shakespeare use iambic pentameter, Wilkins uses more rhyming couplets to end lines, while Shakespeare relies on his characteristic use of enjambment, where a phrase or idea doesn't end at the end of a line, but carries over to the next. Structurally, the dual-author theory works as well, since the actions of the first half of the play repeat themselves for the most part in the second half.

## Source Text

Another interesting problem about *Pericles* is the unreliability of its source text. Almost all of Shakespeare's other plays, first published in quarto form, draw directly on the author's manuscript or the actor's promptbooks. *Pericles*, however, was assembled out of reports from actors and spectators. Elizabethan citizens and actors lived in a world where far less printed text was available, so memorization was common. For this reason no authoritative text of *Pericles* exists.

Various editors have tackled this problem by making the greater or lesser efforts to increase the intelligibility of the play. Editors of the Oxford edition of the plays, for example, which many further adaptations draw from, decided to use a First Quarto version of this play, largely unchanged. Other editors have drawn on another of Wilkins's plays about *Pericles* to add more to the story. But if the First Quarto edition was already based on reported speech, then any edition that tries to further reconstruct what the original *Pericles* may have been probably strays even farther from any "original text."

It's important to remember that none of Shakespeare's texts are really word-for-word originals. Shakespeare worked in collaboration with a company of actors, and so his plays were constantly changing. Most likely what he first wrote changed substantially during rehearsals and again during performances.

## The Play

Pericles goes to Antioch to court the princess. He is given a riddle to solve, and correctly guesses that it reveals that Antiochus, the king, and his daughter are involved in an incestuous affair. Realizing that Pericles has guessed his secret, Antiochus determines to kill Pericles. His life in peril, Pericles runs for his life.

Antiochus is determined to nail Pericles. Knowing this, Pericles appoints his counselor Helicanus to rule as regent and then sails from Tyre for Tarsus, where he saves the people by bringing them much-needed supplies and wins the gratitude of the governor Cleon and his wife Dyoneza. He then sets sail for Pentapolis. On the way, the vessel is shipwrecked, and Pericles is the sole survivor.

At Pentapolis, Pericles participates in a tournament for the hand of Thaisa, daughter of Simonides. He wins the tournament, and Pericles and Thaisa marry. In the meantime, news arrives that Antiochus is dead and that the people of Tyre want their prince back. Pericles and Thaisa, who is now pregnant with their child, set sail for Tyre. During a storm, Marina, their daughter, is born. Thaisa is believed to have died in childbirth. She is sealed in a watertight coffin and buried at sea. The coffin washes up on the shores of Ephesus, where Cerimon manages to revive Thaisa who assumes that Pericles is lost at sea and promptly becomes a votaress (or "nun") in the Temple of Diana. Pericles leaves the baby Marina at Tarsus with Cleon and his wife Dionyza, and continues on to Tyre.

Sixteen years later, Dionyza becomes jealous of Marina and resolves to have her murdered. Dionyza's servant takes her to the shore, but cannot carry it out. As he stands there indecisively, pirates capture Marina. The servant reports back that Marina is dead, and Cleon mournfully raises a monument to her memory. Pericles encounters the tomb on a visit to Tarsus and falls into a deep despair.

Pericles sails into Mitylene still depressed about losing his daughter. He encounters Marina, and eventually recognizes her as his daughter. The two are happily reunited. Lysimachus, the governor, asks for Marina's hand, which Marina accepts. Then, Pericles is visited by a dream that instructs him to visit Ephesus. There he is reunited with Thaisa (who is now the head priestess of Diana), and the whole family is together again.

## Commentary

*Pericles* is not one of Shakespeare's best works. The style of the play is so uneven, scholars suspect it is not the work of a single author. Yet the play was very popular in its day and has been successfully performed since.

FACTS

Unlike many of Shakespeare's works, there is little connection made in this play between the nobility and peasants. The fishermen who help Pericles are forgotten, despite his promise to remember them. In the brothel in Mytilene, Marina constantly proves she is better than those who would lord it over her by virtue of her royal blood. Lower-class characters are caricatures.

Ben Jonson, one of Shakespeare's contemporaries, attributed the success to its use of "scraps out of every dish"—touches of fairy tales, the Bible, *The Tempest*, incest, a lost daughter and a wife presumed dead, several storms, several contests for the hand of a princess, and innumerable kingdoms ruled by men of greater or lesser stature.

Structurally, the play divides in two. In the first nine scenes, Pericles falls into unfortunate circumstances and his luck changes. In the final thirteen scenes, he repeats this pattern. One explanation for this repetition is that the authors shift after scene nine.

## Pericles's Sufferings

Pericles himself seems something of a cipher, largely because Shakespeare does not delve into the workings of his psyche as he did with characters in the tragic plays he wrote immediately before. Overall, the play suggests that, like Job, enduring miseries heaped one on another, Pericles ultimately gets his reward: his family reunited.

Pericles and his cohorts live in a pagan world, where even the goddess Diana becomes a character. Yet the complex plot is unwoven at the end to reveal a version of Christian providence, masquerading as the workings of the Greco-Roman gods. The trajectory from suffering to triumph is Christian in content.

## Redemption

The journey to self-knowledge from a place of unawareness is a repeating narrative for Shakespeare's characters. But Pericles leaves one kingdom in fear for his life because of a contest for the hand of the princess, only to enter an identical contest quite soon after. He loses his wife whom he barely knew, and then makes sure he won't know his daughter by leaving her in a different kingdom. At the end everyone is reunited, but Pericles divides the family again by sending Marina to Tyre and going to Pentapolis with Thaisa.

Meanwhile, most of Gower's monologues merely repeat the plot of scenes just past or narrate events that take place offstage. Only through Gower's conclusion are we given a sense of any kind of redemption in the plot. He explains to us, finally, that Antiochus and his daughter and Cleon and Dionyza are punished because they did evil, whereas Pericles and his family are rewarded. Gower also explains the role of the minor characters, who were living embodiments of their various virtues, such as loyalty (Helicanus) and charity (Cerimon).

# 28 ◊ *Romeo and Juliet*

## Main Characters

**Romeo**—A Montague. A teenager who falls in love with Juliet.

**Juliet**—A Capulet. Falls in love with Romeo.

**Friar Laurence**—A wise old priest.

**Nurse**—Juliet's second mother and confidant.

**Benvolio**—Romeo's cousin.

**Mercutio**—Romeo's best friend.

**Tybalt**—Juliet's hot-tempered cousin.

**Capulet**—Juliet's father.

**Lady Capulet**—Juliet's mother.

**Paris**—A nobleman. One of Juliet's suitors.

**Prince Escalus**—The ruler of Verona.

**Montague**—Romeo's father.

**Lady Montague**—Romeo's mother.

## Introduction

*Romeo and Juliet* was written early in Shakespeare's career, probably in 1594 or 1595 and was first published in 1597. It is his first nonhistorical tragedy, and despite its poetic naiveté, in many ways it holds the promise of the mature plays Shakespeare would come to write in a few years.

**FACTS**

The plot has become an archetypal love story for Western civilization. Scenes such as the balcony scene, for instance, are almost clichés now, and led to so many copies that a nineteenth-century French parody in Rostand's *Cyrano de Bergerac* was itself parodied in Steve Martin's film *Roxanne*.

The primary source was a poem entitled, *The Tragicall Historye of Romeus and Juliet* written in 1562 by Arthur Brooke. This, in turn, was a translation of a poem by a Frenchman, Pierre Boaistuau published in 1559. The French poem, it seems, was derived from a 1554 story by an Italian writer named Mateo Bandello, who in turn had gotten it from a version by Luigi Da Porto, published in 1530.

While the story of *Romeo and Juliet* was often told in the second half of the sixteenth century, Shakespeare's version has marked differences. His version has some of the greatest love poetry ever written in the English language, subtle and original characters (such as Mercutio and Tybalt, who are among some of Shakespeare's most memorable early characters), and a fast pace (the action was compressed into five days).

## The Play

In Verona, two feuding families, the Montagues and the Capulets, brawl constantly in the streets; the reason for the quarrel is never really made clear. In response to the constant fighting, the prince of Verona issues an edict imposing the death penalty on anyone caught dueling.

Romeo of the house of Montague has been infatuated with Rosaline, a niece of Capulet. He and his friends sneak into a masked ball at Capulet's house so that Romeo can see her. During the ball, Romeo catches sight of Juliet, Capulet's daughter, and quickly forgets about Rosaline.

That same night, Romeo creeps under Juliet's bedroom window and professes his love to Juliet, who is standing on her balcony above him and overhears his sighs of love. She confesses she returns his feelings. With the aid of Friar Laurence, Romeo makes plans with Juliet for them to be married in secret.

The phrase "Romeo, Romeo, wherefore art thou Romeo," is probably second only to Hamlet's "To be or not to be" as the most famous quotation from Shakespeare.

Tybalt, Juliet's cousin, discovers that Romeo attended the ball, and sets out to teach the young Montague a lesson. He challenges Romeo in the street. Romeo tries to avoid a duel because he is in love with Juliet. However, Romeo's best friend, Mercutio, takes up Tybalt's challenge and is killed by Tybalt. Before he realizes what he is doing, a distraught Romeo draws his sword and kills Tybalt in turn.

As a result of the bloodshed, despite the provocation, the prince of Verona banishes Romeo. Romeo has time to consummate his marriage to Juliet and bid her goodbye. He hopes that they will soon be reunited.

Juliet's parents, meanwhile, press her to marry Paris. With Friar Laurence's help, Juliet comes up with a desperate plan to avoid her parent's wishes. She obtains a drug that will make her seem dead for forty-two hours. While she is comatose, Friar Laurence will send word to Romeo so that he can rescue her from her family tomb.

Unfortunately, Friar Laurence's letter never gets to Romeo. Instead he hears that Juliet has died. Grief-stricken, Romeo buys some poison with the intention of killing himself. Friar Laurence discovers that Romeo never got his letter, and in horror rushes to Juliet's tomb.

Too late. At Juliet's tomb, Romeo encounters Paris, who is mourning for his Juliet. In grief for Juliet's loss, the two men fight and Romeo kills Paris. Entering the tomb, Romeo discovers the "dead" Juliet and swallowing the poison, commits suicide at her side. Friar Laurence arrives at the scene just as Juliet wakes up. She discovers the body of her beloved Romeo beside her and taking Romeo's dagger stabs herself in the heart.

The prince and the parents arrive, and Friar Laurence explains what has happened. Faced with the awful price their feud has cost them, the Montagues and Capulets swear to end the bitterness between the two families.

## Commentary

This is an early play (1594), written by a young poet with terrific talent. Despite its story, it is really quite optimistic, especially when compared to the latter tragedies and dark comedies. In modern times, critics have tended to disparage the play in favor of his great tragedies (*Hamlet*, *King Lear*, *Macbeth*, and *Othello*). Certainly, when compared to these plays, *Romeo and Juliet* lacks psychological depth and structural complexity.

More recently, however, scholars have reconsidered their opinion, opting to judge *Romeo and Juliet* in its own right. Viewed in this light, the tragedy of the star-crossed teenagers is an extraordinary experimental play, featuring radical departures from long-standing conventions too complex to go into here.

## Romeo

In Juliet, Romeo finds that rare gift, a soulmate—a lover of such purity and passion that when he learns she has died he cannot endure life without her. At first blush this may seem an immature reaction. In fact, it can also be seen as a tragic sign of maturity. Romeo is the romantic in this couple. He grows up through "the love of a good woman," grounding his romantic notions, but it is Juliet who is the level-headed one of the pair. She inspires Romeo to utter some of the most beautiful and intense love poetry ever written.

**ESSENTIALS**

The ardor and romantic intensity of *Romeo and Juliet*, as well as its theme of young lovers struggling against the oppressive values of their parents, make it an extremely youthful play. It is a young playwright's first gropings toward the profound philosophical tragedies of *Hamlet*, *King Lear*, and *Othello*.

At the beginning of the play, Romeo pines for Rosaline, proclaiming her the paragon of women and despairing of her indifference toward him. His histrionics seem frankly juvenile, and he gets the teasing he deserves from his friends and relatives. Sure enough, Rosaline evaporates from Romeo's thoughts the first time he sees Juliet. But Juliet is not just another infatuation.

As Romeo's love matures from shallow desire to a profound passion, he also matures as a person. Against great provocation, he tries his best to avoid fighting with Tybalt, and only when Tybalt manages to include him in the death of his best friend Mercutio does Romeo "lose it." If only Romeo had restrained himself from killing Tybalt, or waited even a few hours before killing himself after seeing Juliet lying in her tomb, matters might have ended happily. But the same soaring passions that made his love for Juliet so powerful, condemned him to respond as he does in both cases.

## Juliet

Juliet is a fascinating character. While Romeo is the romantic, Juliet is determined, strong, and down-to-earth. Her growing love for Romeo propels her toward adulthood with the velocity of a rocket. She learns how to manage the adults on their own terms. She promises her mother, for example, that she will consider Paris as a possible husband with an outward show of obedience that is clearly meant to handle her mother.

**FACTS**

*Romeo and Juliet* has been interpreted and adapted thousands of times in opera, ballet, novels, on stage, screen, and television, and even so, the passage of time and changing cultural context does not seem to have diminished the play's innate innocence, youthful rebelliousness, or capacity to shock, delight, and move audiences.

Though profoundly in love with Romeo, Juliet is able to see and criticize Romeo's impetuosity and his tendency to romanticize things. After Romeo is banished, she does not follow him blindly to Mantua, but calmly and rationally decides what the course of action should be for the two of them. She then cuts herself loose from her Nurse and her parents in order to reunite with her husband.

When she wakes up in the tomb to find Romeo dead beside her, she decides to kill herself out of the same intensity of love that overwhelmed Romeo. Juliet's suicide actually requires more nerve, as befits her character: While he swallows poison, she stabs herself through the heart with a dagger. Juliet's development from a wide-eyed teenager to a self-assured, loyal, and capable woman is one of Shakespeare's early triumphs of characterization and marks one of his most confident and rounded treatments of a female character.

## Famous Lines

"The weakest goes to the wall" (Act I, Scene I).

"He that is strucken blind cannot forget
The precious treasure of his eyesight lost" (Act I, Scene I).

"True, I talk of dreams,
Which are the children of an idle brain,
Begot of nothing but vain fantasy" (Act I, Scene IV).

"But, soft! what light through yonder window breaks?
It is the east, and Juliet is the sun" (Act II, Scene II).

"See, how she leans her cheek upon her hand!
O that I were a glove upon that hand,
That I might touch that cheek!" (Act II, Scene II).

"O Romeo, Romeo! wherefore art thou Romeo?" (Act II, Scene II).

"What's in a name? That which we call a rose
By any other name would smell as sweet" (Act II, Scene II).

"This bud of love, by summer's ripening breath,
May prove a beauteous flower when next we meet" (Act II, Scene II).

"Good night, good night! parting is such sweet sorrow,
That I shall say good night till it be morrow" (Act II, Scene II).

"These violent delights have violent ends" (Act II, Scene VI).

"Taking the measure of an unmade grave" (Act III, Scene III).

"Not stepping o'er the bounds of modesty" (Act IV, Scene II).

"Eyes, look your last!
Arms, take your last embrace!" (Act V, Scene III).

"Too swift arrives as tardy as too slow" (Act II, Scene VI).

"A plague o' both your houses!" (Act III, Scene I).

# 29 🔖 *Sir Thomas More*

## Introduction

Anthony Munday wrote the original script of *Sir Thomas More* between 1592 and 1595. However, the Master of Revels prevented its performance because scenes showing Londoners rioting might set a bad example. Years before, plays that in the opinion of government authorities disparaged the established religion or the government were banned. Other writers later revised the play, making it less politically provocative and among those writers, according to strong evidence, was William Shakespeare.

Sir Thomas More (1478–1535) was a leading Renaissance scholar and his opposition to Henry VIII's divorce from Catherine of Aragon and his subsequent refusal to swear that the king's authority superseded the Pope's led to his execution in 1535.

Before clashing with Henry, More was a religious man of great principle. He was also the sheriff of London, a position he assumed in 1510. After attracting Henry's attention, More rose further in the political ranks, serving as a diplomat, speaker of the House of Commons, an adviser to the king, and finally lord chancellor of England. However, More's opposition to Henry's divorce effectively ended his career.

Two years after he resigned as chancellor, the king imprisoned him, held a mock trial, and ordered his beheading. More was canonized a saint by the Roman Catholic Church in 1935.

## Commentary

The play is sympathetic to Sir Thomas More, and presents him as a wise and worthy English citizen and public servant who exhibited honesty, right thinking, and courage. He paid with his head for sticking to his principles and opposing Henry VIII's marriage to Anne Boleyn.

Shakespeare's participation in the production of the play has added weight to the belief of some scholars that, like his mother, Shakespeare was a practicing Roman Catholic, and not a member of the Church of England.

# 30 ❧ *The Comedy of Errors*

## Main Characters

**Antipholus of Syracuse**—The twin brother of Antipholus of Ephesus and the son of Egeon.

**Antipholus of Ephesus**—The twin brother of Antipholus of Syracuse and the son of Egeon. A well-respected merchant in Ephesus and Adriana's husband.

**Dromio of Syracuse**—The slave of Antipholus of Syracuse and the twin brother of Dromio of Ephesus.

**Dromio of Ephesus**—The slave of Antipholus of Ephesus and the twin brother of Dromio of Syracuse.

**Adriana**—The wife of Antipholus of Ephesus.

**Luciana**—Adriana's unmarried sister.

**Solinus**—The duke of Ephesus.

**Egeon**—Husband of the Abbess (Emilia); father of the two Antipholuses. He is searching for the missing half of his family.

**Abbess**—Emilia, the long-lost wife of Egeon and the mother of both the Antipholuses.

**Balthasar**—A merchant in Syracuse.

**Angelo**—A goldsmith in Syracuse.

**Merchant**—A friend of Antipholus of Syracuse.

**Second Merchant**—A tradesman to whom Angelo is in debt.

**Doctor Pinch**—A schoolteacher and would-be exorcist.

**Luce/Nell**—Dromio of Ephesus's wife.

**Courtesan**—An expensive prostitute.

## Introduction

*The Comedy of Errors* is an early play (some scholars think Shakespeare's first) with an emphasis on slapstick. It was first performed on December 28, 1594, at the Gray's Inn Christmas Revels, to an audience largely composed of lawyers and law students.

Shakespeare drew on the Roman comedy *Menaechmi* by Plautus (c.254–184 B.C.E.) for his plot. Shakespeare had a grammar school education, and was possibly a schoolteacher background prior to moving to London, so he may well have read the play in its original Latin. However, in 1594 an English translation was printed, though it had probably been floating around in manuscript form some time before that.

**FACTS**

As usual, Shakespeare made a number of changes to the original story: a second set of identical twins (the Dromios), the expansion of Adriana's character, a new character Luciana, and the subplot of Egeon and Emilia. The style of the comedy is modeled on the commedia dell'arte that developed in northern Italy from about 1550 onward.

*The Comedy of Errors* is driven by coincidence and slapstick, its events confined within a single day. Characters are mistaken for one another, but do not pretend to be other than they are—there are no disguises here.

Typical of Shakespeare, there are also hints of tragedy—the story hinges on a threat of execution, and includes broken families, troubled marriages, slavery, beatings, and a beheading.

## The Play

The play is concerned with the separation and ultimate reunion of Egeon and his wife Emilia, and their twin sons, Antipholus of Ephesus (Antipholus E.) and Antipholus of Syracuse (Antipholus S.). The family is separated at sea during a storm, thirty-three years before the action of the play.

Egeon, Antipholus S., and Dromio S. survive the shipwreck together and grow up in Syracuse. Seven years before the action starts they decide to search, separately, for their lost family. Emilia survives with Antipholus E. and Dromio E., only to have a "rude" fisherman steal the boys from her. In sorrow, she becomes a nun. Eventually, Antipholus E.

and Dromio E. move to Ephesus, though they don't know their mother Emilia is living there as well. Antipholus E. marries Adriana.

Ignoring a law that strangers can be put to death, Egeon comes to the city looking for Antipholus E. and his servant Dromio E. He is arrested and sentenced to death for entering enemy territory. Soon after, Antipholus S. and his servant, Dromio S., enter the city on business. The identical twins are easily confused by the citizens of Ephesus who think the Antipholus and Dromio they know have gone mad. Doctor Pinch, a psychiatrist, even tries to exorcise the devil from Antipholus E.

As Egeon's execution draws near, Egeon recognizes his son Antipholus E., though Antipholus E. doesn't recognize his father. Simultaneously, Emilia appears from the convent with Antipholus S. and Dromio S., who have taken refuge there, and the family reunites. The duke (Solinus) pardons Egeon for entering the city, Antipholus S. begins to court Luciana (Adriana's sister), and Emilia holds a feast to celebrate the family's reunion.

## Commentary

*The Comedy of Errors* is a comedy, so all the characters' confusion is cleared up at the end. The darker issues of imminent execution, cuckoldry, and a broken marriage are easily resolved. Duke Solinus begins the play as almost a tyrant, but ends it as a forgiving father figure. The broken halves of Egeon's family, separated for more than thirty years, get put back together, and husband and wife reconcile as if time were unimportant. Even the poor abused slaves, the Dromios, quickly forget their beatings and embrace, emphasizing the play's main theme: Love will triumph over all.

## Famous Lines

"The pleasing punishment that women bear" (Act I, Scene I).

"A wretched soul, bruised with adversity" (Act III, Scene I).

"Every why hath a wherefore" (Act II, Scene II).

"Let's go hand in hand, not one before another" (Act V, Scene I).

# 31 § *The Merchant of Venice*

## Main Characters

**Portia**—A wealthy heiress from Belmont.

**Shylock**—A Jewish moneylender in Venice.

**Antonio**—A merchant and friend to Bassanio.

**Bassanio**—Antonio's friend, a gentleman of Venice.

**Gratiano**—A friend of Bassanio who is fiercely anti-Semitic.

**Lorenzo**—A friend of Bassanio and Antonio. In love with Jessica.

**Jessica**—Shylock's daughter. In love with Lorenzo.

**Nerissa**—Portia's lady-in-waiting.

**Salerio and Solanio**—Venetian gentlemen.

**Launcelot Gobbo**—Shylock's servant.

**Old Gobbo**—Launcelot's father.

**The Prince of Morocco**—One of Portia's suitors.

**The Prince of Arragon**—One of Portia's suitors.

**Tubal**—A Jew, one of Shylock's friends.

## Introduction

Many people forget that *The Merchant of Venice* is a comedy because the character of Shylock and the theme of anti-Semitism are so serious, and somewhat treated as such in the play. It was written around 1596.

FACTS

*The Merchant of Venice* weaves together two ancient folktales; one involving a vengeful, greedy creditor trying to exact a pound of flesh, the other involving a suitor's choice among three chests to thereby win his mate.

The characters of the merchant, the suitor, the lady, and the villainous Jew can be found in several contemporary Italian story collections. The cross-dressing heroine and the Italian location make *The Merchant of*

*Venice* similar to earlier comedies. Portia is considered by many scholars to be Shakespeare's first great heroine, and Shylock's complex and not altogether unsympathetic villain make the play one of Shakespeare's best.

While Shylock is clearly a stereotypical caricature of a money-obsessed, vicious medieval Jew, a case can be made that Shakespeare wanted to make anti-Semites peer into a mirror and see their own reflection. By merging the two stories, Shakespeare makes one a metaphor for the other.

Shylock is one of the most interesting Shakespearean characters for modern audiences. England had excluded communities of Jews for centuries though there were Portuguese Jews in London about this time, so all the moneylenders in London would have been Christians. Anti-Semitism was common in the sixteenth century throughout most of Europe, where Catholics and Protestants were busy finding excuses to slaughter one another; Jews were often comic villains in Elizabethan theater.

## The Play

Antonio, a wealthy merchant, is feeling depressed, while his friend, Bassanio, needs his financial help so that he can court a wealthy woman, Portia, and win her hand in marriage. Antonio agrees to help Bassanio.

Portia complains to her servant, Nerissa, about the provisions of her father's will. The suitor who correctly chooses one of three chests (gold, silver, and lead) may marry Portia and get her money. If they fail, they must never marry. Portia doesn't like any of her suitors, except Bassanio, and prays that he chooses in time and correctly.

Back in Venice, Bassanio convinces Shylock the Jew to lend him 3,000 ducats. Antonio becomes his guarantor, putting up "a pound of flesh" as the bond. Shylock hates Antonio, and lends the money hoping Antonio will default on the loan. Antonio is certain one of his ships will arrive before the three-month deadline is up.

Shylock's servant, Launcelot Gobbo, tells his father, old Gobbo, that he wants to leave Shylock and work for Bassanio. Shylock's daughter, Jessica, meanwhile, has fallen in love with Antonio's friend Lorenzo and intends to convert to Christianity in order to marry him.

Gratiano, Salerio, and Lorenzo help Jessica elope with Lorenzo. They all head off to meet Bassanio. Solanio and Salerio gossip about Antonio's ship sinking and make fun of Shylock's losing his daughter.

**ESSENTIALS**

Bassanio correctly chooses the lead casket and wins Portia's hand and fortune in marriage. To seal the deal, Portia gives Bassanio a ring, warning him never to lose it, or he'll risk losing her love. Gratiano then announces his intention to wed Nerissa.

Salerio, Lorenzo, and Jessica arrive and tell Bassanio that Antonio has lost his ships. What's more, Shylock is determined Antonio should forfeit his bond. Bassanio immediately leaves for Venice to repay the loan. Meanwhile, Shylock has Antonio arrested for failure to repay the loan in time. Portia and Nerissa decide to disguise themselves as a lawyer and his clerk and follow Bassiano to Venice.

## Shylock's Petition

The duke presides over Shylock's petition to cut "a pound of flesh from Antonio's breast" since that was the terms of the bond, even though Bassanio offers him 6,000 ducats (rather than the 3,000 he originally lent) for repayment. Nerissa and Portia, disguised as a court clerk and doctor of civil law, arrive at the court and join Gratiano, Bassanio, and the duke, in trying to dissuade Shylock, to no avail. He will have his bond, no more no less, that is what the law allows. Shylock seems to be victorious.

Then Portia points out that he's correct in that the law does indeed let him collect his pound of flesh, but he must be careful: no blood must be shed and exactly one pound must be taken. Shylock realizes this is impossible. He tries to change his mind and take the money instead. Portia pounds home another nail: Shylock is himself guilty of conspiring to kill Antonio, a fellow citizen. As punishment, the duke and Antonio decide that Shylock must give half his possessions to the court and promise to give the rest to his daughter and new son-in-law (Lorenzo) upon his death. What's more, he must become a Christian. Defeated, Shylock is forced to agree.

## A Happy Ending

Still disguised as the lawyer, Portia asks Bassanio for his wedding ring. Despite his vow, and after some prodding by Antonio, Bassiano reluctantly hands it over. Nerissa (disguised as Portia's clerk) gets her husband (Gratiano) to do the same thing with his wedding ring.

Back at Portia's house, Bassanio and Portia, and Gratiano and Nerissa reunite. After quarreling over the loss of rings, the women admit their ruse and return the rings to their husbands. Antonio also discovers that three of his ships have come to port full of merchandise, and Jessica and Lorenzo learn they will get Shylock's possessions on his death.

Shylock is, first and foremost, an anti-Semitic creation for an Elizabethan audience accustomed to seeing Jews as comic foils for Christian heroes. However, Shylock's eloquence is so great modern productions elevate him to the level of tragic hero. But, the play is ultimately a comedy, as Shylock's elimination at the end of Act IV and the happy ending in Act V shows.

## Commentary

The play is really two fairy tales that come together at the trial scene. Until this point, Shylock's story takes center stage and Portia's courtships are something of a subplot. By the trial, Shylock has had enough. He has become a vengeful figure, blinded to humanity and compassion by the chance to finally exact revenge against those who have wronged him: "I'll have my bond," he gloats, ignoring pleas for mercy from all around him.

Portia sets up Shylock, offering him a chance to escape with the money. If he is merciful it is a win-win situation for everyone. When Shylock refuses, she is justified in crushing him. But he threatens to turn the play into something other than it is, and he must be gotten rid of once and for all so that the happy ending can take place.

Shylock seems almost too vivid for the rest of the characters in *The Merchant of Venice*. However, his determination to extract his pound of flesh at any cost is clearly the work of a comic villain whose downfall we will applaud. The good-humored intrigue of the rings that ends the play is something of an anticlimax: love, mercy, and compassion have conquered all.

## Famous Lines

"I hold the world but as the world, Gratiano,—
A stage, where every man must play a part;
And mine a sad one" (Act I, Scene I).

"In my school-days, when I had lost one shaft,
I shot his fellow of the selfsame flight
The selfsame way, with more advised watch,
To find the other forth; and by adventuring both,
I oft found both" (Act I, Scene I).

"God made him, and therefore let him pass for a man"
(Act I, Scene II).

"I will buy with you, sell with you, talk with you, walk with you, and
so following; but I will not eat with you, drink with you, nor pray
with you. What news on the Rialto?" (Act I, Scene III).

"The devil can cite Scripture for his purpose" (Act I, Scene III).

"You call me misbeliever, cut-throat dog,
And spit upon my Jewish gaberdine" (Act I, Scene III).

"Mislike me not for my complexion,
The shadow'd livery of the burnish'd sun" (Act II, Scene I).

"It is a wise father that knows his own child" (Act II, Scene II).

"Truth will come to sight; murder cannot be hid long"
(Act II, Scene II).

"In the twinkling of an eye" (Act II, Scene II).

"But love is blind, and lovers cannot see
The pretty follies that themselves commit" (Act II, Scene VI).

"All that glisters is not gold" (Act II, Scene VI).

"I am a Jew. Hath not a Jew eyes? Hath not a Jew hands, organs,
dimensions, senses, affections, passions?" (Act III, Scene I).

"The villany you teach me I will execute, and it shall go hard, but I
will better the instruction" (Act III, Scene I).

"Tell me where is fancy bred,
Or in the heart or in the head?
How begot, how nourished?
Reply, reply" (Act III, Scene II).

"There is no vice so simple but assumes
Some mark of virtue in his outward parts" (Act III, Scene II).

"You take my house when you do take the prop
That doth sustain my house; you take my life
When you do take the means whereby I live" (Act IV, Scene I).

# 32 ❦ *The Merry Wives of Windsor*

## Main Characters

**Mistress Ford**—Married to Ford and a friend of Mistress Page.

**Mistress Page**—A friend of Mistress Ford. She and her husband disagree about who should marry their daughter, Anne.

**Falstaff**—A knight and a scoundrel.

**Ford**—Husband of Mistress Ford. Calls himself Brooke.

**Page**—Husband of Mistress Page.

**Sir Hugh Evans**—The local clergyman. He is Welsh.

**Caius**—The local doctor. He is French.

**Anne Page**—Daughter of Page and Mistress Page.

**Fenton**—A suitor for Anne Page's hand.

**Slender**—A suitor for Anne Page's hand.

**Shallow**—A figure of the law, who is foolish.

**Mistress Quickly**—Caius's servant.

**Bardolph, Pistol, and Nim**—Falstaff's men.

**Host**—Host of the Garter Inn.

**William Page**—Anne's brother and Page's son.

**Simple**—Slender's servant.

## Introduction

*The Merry Wives of Windsor* was probably written around 1597. It is Shakespeare's most middle-class play in setting, subject matter, and outlook. It's also one of his most farcical, using physical gags and linguistic jokes to establish a comic tone that influences the play's ultimate spirit of reconciliation. It is concerned with phenomena of an emerging merchant/guild middle class filling the gap between agrarian peasant and landed gentry.

According to theatrical legend, Elizabeth saw *King Henry IV, Part I* and liked the character of Falstaff so much she asked Shakespeare to write another play about him, allegedly giving him only fourteen days.

It's thought that Shakespeare may have put aside *King Henry IV, Part II* to complete *The Merry Wives of Windsor*, and he included several characters who appear in both plays, including Pistol, Nim, Bardolph, Mistress Quickly, and Shallow. Falstaff and his entourage were supposedly good friends with Prince Hal, later Henry V, which lends a royal flavor to the archetypal suburban events of *The Merry Wives of Windsor*. Windsor, its castle still used as a residence by royalty today, has always been considered a royal town.

**FACTS**

*The Merry Wives of Windsor* captures life in an English provincial town in the late sixteenth century and refers to other, older plays. The main plot closely resembles *Il Pecorone*, a 1558 Italian play by Ser Giovanni Fiorentino, which in turn draws on ancient Roman comedy.

Scholars concur that the first performance was on April 23, 1597 at a feast of the Order of the Garter, which Queen Elizabeth I attended. There are two different versions: the First Quarto (1602) and the First Folio (1623). The Quarto is most likely a reconstruction from memory by actors and others. It is half the length of the Folio version, and is likely poorly remembered, or trimmed for provincial performances. The Folio version is printed from a manuscript that was based on either a playhouse promptbook or an authorial manuscript, and has a close connection with the first performance of the play.

## The Play

Sir John Falstaff, a rogue who is "financially challenged," hatches a scheme to raise funds by seducing Mistresses Ford and Page at the same time in an attempt to get at their husbands' money. Falstaff, however, has overestimated his charm and his ingenuity. The two women are friends, and discovering his plot, decide to make him suffer for his impertinence. They send him letters encouraging his advances.

Mistresses Ford and Page enjoy their fun. Falstaff is in danger of being discovered and hides in a basket of dirty laundry, which is then tossed into the River Thames. He is later dressed as a woman and beaten. Finally, the women tell their husbands what's going on, and all plot one final humiliation for the old knight.

Meanwhile, Page's daughter, Anne, is being courted by two suitors favored by her parents, but she is in love with Fenton. It is decided that Sir Hugh Evans will lead Anne and the town's children dressed as fairies in a late night attack on the knight as he waits in the woods for Mistresses Page and Ford. Anne's father, Page, tells Slender, one of Anne's suitors, that he should elope with his daughter after the prank. Mistress Page pulls her favorite suitor, Doctor Caius, aside and tells him the same thing. Because she will be in disguise, the two men will recognize Anne by the color of her dress. Anne, meanwhile, makes plans of her own to elope with Fenton.

**FACTS**

*The Merry Wives of Windsor* was a great favorite of Friedrich Engels, coauthor with Karl Marx of the *Communist Manifesto*. No doubt he enjoyed the way Shakespeare made fun of the emerging bourgeoisie. With the exception of *The Comedy of Errors*, it is probably Shakespeare's most overtly farcical play.

Falstaff is convinced to dress up as the god Herne (complete with antlers). While he waits in anticipation for the women to come to him, he is suddenly set upon and tormented by Anne and the children, dressed as fairies. The wives and husbands eventually reveal themselves to Falstaff, who is forgiven his roguish ways.

Slender and Doctor Caius reappear, chagrined. Both men erred on the color of Anne's dress (Slender thought it was white; Caius thought it was green) and ran off with boys instead of Anne. Fenton arrives with Anne. The two of them are married and Anne's parents begrudgingly accept the fact.

# Commentary

Mistresses Page and Ford determine that wives can lead boisterous, vivid lives (i.e., be merry) without having to betray their husbands. Page understands this, but Ford takes some convincing. The romance of Fenton and Anne Page affirms the idea of romantic love as a means of transcending class.

*The Merry Wives of Windsor* also emphasizes the provincial mindset, by making fun of a community that in turn makes fun of outsiders. Slender's pretensions make him look like a fool. Justice Shallow, whose authority derives from the crown, ends up much the same. Sir Hugh Evans, the Welsh clergyman, is mocked for his foreign accent, as is Dr. Caius. Slender and Mistress Quickly depend on cliché, while Quickly hears sexual double entendres in Latin conjugations and declensions. The hostility of the locals to the aristocracy is clearly seen in Page's rejection of Fenton's request for Anne's hand and the continued abuse of the impoverished knight, Falstaff.

While the play celebrates the mistresses' autonomy (due in part to their husbands' wealth and social positions), the only woman who is "liberated" is Anne, who avoids a marriage chosen for her by her parents in favor of a partnership of her own choosing against their will.

# Famous Lines

"If there be no great love in the beginning, yet heaven may decrease it upon better acquaintance, when we are married and have more occasion to know one another: I hope, upon familiarity will grow more contempt" (Act I, Scene I).

"This is the short and the long of it" (Act II, Scene II).

"This is the third time; I hope good luck lies in odd numbers . . . There is divinity in odd numbers, either in nativity, chance, or death" (Act V, Scene I).

# 33 § *The Taming of the Shrew*

## Main Characters

**Katherina**—The shrew of the title. Also called Kate.

**Petruchio**—A gentleman from Verona.

**Bianca**—Kate's younger sister.

**Baptista Minola**—One of the wealthiest men in Padua. Father of the two girls.

**Lucentio**—A young student from Pisa. In love with Bianca.

**Tranio**—Lucentio's servant.

**Gremio and Hortensio**—Suitors for Bianca.

**Grumio**—Petruchio's servant.

## Introduction

*The Taming of the Shrew* is an early comedy, loosely termed "romantic" along with *Much Ado About Nothing* and *A Midsummer Night's Dream* among others. The plays are lighthearted and often slapstick in style, filled with disguises and deception, and end happily. This is in sharp contrast to the later comedies that are much darker, and filled with cynicism and a sometimes bitter irony.

*The Taming of the Shrew* is clearly a young playwright's work, and focuses more squarely on marriage than almost any other of the early comedies. While the other plays end with a marriage, *The Taming of the Shrew* takes this almost as a starting point, following the early days of married life.

### Elizabethan Marriages

The average sixteenth-century playgoer was interested in discussions about marriage, in part because Henry VIII's separation from the Catholic Church in 1536 was brought about by wrangling over a divorce. (Shakespeare dealt with this subject more directly in his play *King Henry VIII*. Henry named himself "defender of the faith" a title still held by British monarchs, and formed the Church of England in order to get his own way.) The births of Mary and Elizabeth, his daughters, who became queens of England after Henry died, were directly responsible for this break with the Pope, who refused to grant Henry's request for a divorce so that he could remarry and produce a male heir. Henry desperately wanted a son. His eventual male heir, Edward was sickly most of his short young life, and did not last long as king.

**FACTS**

The plot was familiar to Elizabethan audiences, being drawn from popular ballads and folktales such as *A Merry Jest of a Shrewde Curste Wyfe* published in 1550. In the ballad the woman is thrashed to a bloody pulp and then wrapped in the salted skin of an old horse.

This recent history would be very much on the minds of an Elizabethan audience. Great pain, death, and turmoil had resulted from the break with Rome. Unless you were a determined king of England willing to suffer excommunication, the late sixteenth and early seventeenth centuries offered few ways out of an unhappy marriage, so the resolution of marital disputes was a very hot topic in the popular literature of the era.

Elizabethan marriages were still being made along medieval lines—they were far more often made for money, land, or power than for love. A woman had few options for survival set adrift from the rule and support of a man, either her father or her husband, and less often her brother, and the fact that Queen Elizabeth I never married was cause for great concern to Elizabethans because of its potential to undermine the power structure of society.

## The Shrew

Of particular worry among married men, were "shrews" or "scolds," that is, cantankerous or gossipy wives, who resisted or undermined the natural authority of their husbands. A large number of sermons, plays, and pamphlets of the time address related topics: the taming of shrews by their husbands or the public punishment of scolds (by repeated dunking in a river, for example). Some of this literature is very diplomatic, and some is clearly misogynistic. It's difficult to sometimes tell (perhaps deliberately so) what is meant as parody, and what is being presented as an ideal. This is also true for *The Taming of the Shrew*. Shakespeare's own marriage, at least at first, is thought not to have been the greatest, and he spent many years of it living apart from his family in London, while they stayed on in Stratford.

## Viewing from a Distance

The main part of *The Taming of the Shrew* is set in Padua, a city in northern Italy. To Elizabethan England, Italy was a beautiful country of rich food, loose women, and generally materialistic and pleasurable living. It became a favorite setting of Shakespeare and his contemporaries for plays involving deceit, money, beautiful women, cross-dressing, or anything worth taking a little sinful pleasure in—but at a very safe distance from England.

This idea of "viewing from a distance" is particularly true of *The Taming of the Shrew* because it has an "outer" and an "inner" play. The frame or outer play is actually set in the English countryside, and consists of only the first two scenes, called the Induction where, a group of English actors prepare to present the inner play, the story of Kate and Petruchio.

SSENTIALS

*The Taming of the Shrew* should not be confused with *The Taming of a Shrew* published in 1594. That version has three sisters and Sly, a drunk appearing as a Chorus throughout. It was probably reconstructed from the faulty memories of actors and was a pirated or stolen play, called a Bad Quarto.

## The Outer Play

Outside an alehouse somewhere in England, a beggar named Christopher Sly is arguing with the hostess of the alehouse. The hostess leaves to fetch the local authorities, and Sly passes out, drunk.

A passing lord decides to have some fun with the sleeping beggar. The lord decides to see if, with the right surroundings, he can convince a beggar that he is really of high birth. So he orders his servants to take Sly back to his house and treat him as if he were a lord.

At the house, the servants place Sly in the lord's bed with fine clothes and jewelry, and the lord disguises himself as one of the serving men. When Sly awakes, they present him with good wine and food and tell him that he is their master. He protests that he remembers being a poor tinker (an itinerant mender of pots). They tell him this memory is the result of a madness he has been in for fifteen years. They put on quite a show, pleading and wailing in feigned distress at his continued illness, but Sly is still skeptical.

However, when his "wife" is brought in—a male page dressed up as a woman—he is finally convinced. The servants are overjoyed that his "memory" has returned, and wish to entertain him. As luck would have it, a group of players happen to be in town, and prepare to put on a play for the enjoyment of Sly and his wife.

The "play within a play" forms the main action of *The Taming of the Shrew*. The text only returns to Sly briefly after this Induction, and never concludes his story.

## The Play within a Play

Lucentio arrives in Padua with his manservant Tranio to study at the university. Baptista, a wealthy merchant of Padua, has two daughters: Katherina and Bianca. Lucentio falls in love with Bianca, and becomes one of several suitors for the hand of the younger and kinder daughter. Lucentio and Tranio (his servant) switch clothes, and thus disguised, Lucentio will offer his services as a tutor for Bianca in order to get closer to her.

However, because of her older sister Katherina's shrewish disposition, Bianca's father has declared that no one will marry Bianca until Katherina has a husband. The suitors are beside themselves. Enter Petruchio, in Padua to visit his friend Hortensio (one of Bianca's suitors). Petruchio is attracted to Katherina's large dowry, and Hortensio sees a potential solution to his problem, which will put him in good stead with Baptista.

Despite all the warnings he gets about the fiery Kate, Petruchio claims that he finds her charming and pleasant. The marriage is arranged, and Petruchio immediately sets out to tame Kate. He shows up late to his own wedding, constantly contradicts whatever she says, calling the sun the moon, refuses to give her food until she agrees with him, and so on. Finally, an exhausted Kate is "tamed" into docility.

ESSENTIALS

The matches of Kate and Petruchio and Lucentio and Bianca become contrasting versions of marriage. It is interesting to compare the concept of love and partnership in more mature men and women in *The Taming of the Shrew* with Benedick and Beatrice in *Much Ado About Nothing*.

Lucentio wins Bianca's heart and Hortensio happily marries a rich widow in Padua. Petruchio and Kate return for Bianca's wedding. During the wedding feast, Petruchio makes a bet with the other two new husbands that he has the most obedient wife. Knowing her previous behavior the men take the bet, only to discover that Petruchio really has "tamed" his wife. In a complete turnabout, Kate gives Bianca a lecture on how to be a good and loving and obedient wife.

## Commentary

When you watch *The Taming of the Shrew*, it's important to remember the context of the play. In Elizabethan times marriages were made for the convenience of fathers far more often than because the potential bride and groom loved each other. People were married without ever having met previously. Spouses hoped to learn to love their partner once they were wed. There's no guarantee that "love at first sight," brings greater happiness in marriage than the slowly developed, consistent love of a couple who learn to live with and for each other.

The fatal, overpowering passions of *Romeo and Juliet* are not the best basis for a marriage, Shakespeare suggests. Rather, marriage should be more pragmatic, allowing a man and woman to create a peaceful, supportive union. Petruchio and Kate end up being well matched. Only a happy-go-lucky, persistent, self-assured man like Petruchio could break through Kate's defenses. It becomes clear that Kate wants a man—the right man—to say "no" to her. Few, including her father have been able to do so.

She is shocked when Petruchio is late for their wedding, and her reaction is not anger at being stood up, but fear she will die a lonely old maid. She wants a relationship of mutual respect. But to get there she must rethink her whole attitude toward men. Petruchio's attempts to stifle and humiliate her are meant only to force her to stop blindly lashing out. She must see him for who he is and what he can give her.

The result is that Kate can enjoy her married life, find an equal partner, and, as she finally reveals near the end of the play, love her husband in her married life without feeling she has somehow lost her earlier independence that brought her only anger and distress—and it is this revelation that she tries to teach her younger sister at the end of the play.

## Famous Lines

"I'll not budge an inch" (Induction, Scene I).

"And thereby hangs a tale" (Act IV, Scene I).

"Such duty as the subject owes the prince,
Even such a woman oweth to her husband" (Act V, Scene II).

"Who wooed in haste, and means to wed at leisure"
    (Act III, Scene II).

# 34 ♦ *The Tempest*

## Main Characters

**Prospero**—Once the duke of Milan, overthrown by his brother, Antonio.

**Alonso**—The king of Naples.

**Gonzalo**—A well-meaning elderly counselor of Alonso.

**Ferdinand**—The prince of Naples and Alonso's son.

**Miranda**—Prospero's daughter.

**Ariel**—A spirit Prospero rescued from imprisonment and now controls.

**Sebastian**—Alonso's brother.

**Antonio**—Prospero's brother.

**Trinculo**—Alonso's jester.

**Stephano**—Alonso's butler.

**Caliban**—Prospero and Miranda's slave. The son of a powerful witch.

**Adrian and Francisco**—Lords who attend Alonso.

**Boatswain, Master, and Sailors**—Seamen.

## Introduction

*The Tempest* is considered Shakespeare's last major play (written around 1611) and is a romantic comedy. It was likely performed at court as part of the celebration surrounding the marriage of Princess Elizabeth, the daughter of the King James I. It contains an unusual amount of "spectacle"—dances, songs, costumed plays-within-the-play—which would have made it especially appropriate as royal entertainment.

Shakespeare seems to have retired from full-time playwriting after *The Tempest*, although he likely collaborated with others, chiefly John Fletcher, on at least three more plays. As a result, some scholars consider *The Tempest* to be a farewell from a great playwright to his audience and a final, symbolic celebration of the magic of theater. Many people consider Prospero a stand-in for Shakespeare, since he gives up his magic and manipulation of the natural and unnatural world (read, playwriting) at the play's conclusion.

## The Survival of the *Sea-Venture*

In early June 1609, nine ships carrying around 600 people to strengthen the new English colony in Virginia, set out from England. The *Sea-Venture* was the lead ship and carried Sir Thomas Gates, the newly appointed governor of the colony, and Sir George Somers, the admiral of the Virginia Company. On July 25 a violent storm (probably a hurricane) overtook the ships and raged for several days. When the storm had subsided, four of the nine ships found each other and proceeded on to Virginia. Three more eventually made it into port. The *Sea-Venture* never showed up and was presumed to be lost.

**FACTS**

The setting of *The Tempest* draws on chronicles brought back from the early colonization of the American continents by travelers and explorers. Although the magic island of *The Tempest* is supposedly somewhere in the Mediterranean, it actually incorporates many myths and stories about the Bermudas and other American islands.

The news, when it reached England by the fall, created a public sensation. But unknown to the rest of the world, the battered ship had run aground on Bermuda, with all aboard making it safely ashore. The Bermudas had a reputation as a place of devils and wicked spirits, but the colonists found it to be very pleasant, and they lived there for the next nine months while building a new ship out of native wood under Somers's guidance.

They set sail on May 10, 1610, and reached Jamestown, Virginia two weeks later. A ship carrying Governor Gates and others left Jamestown two months later and reached England in September. The news of their survival caused another public sensation.

## The Tale Told

Several accounts of the wreck and survival of the *Sea-Venture* were rushed into print in the fall of 1610. The first of these, *A Discovery of the*

*Barmudas*, was written by Sylvester Jourdain, who had been aboard the *Sea-Venture* and had returned to England with Gates. A month later *A True Declaration of the Estate of the Colonie in Virginia* was published. This was edited together from various documents as a piece of pro-Virginia propaganda on behalf of the Virginia Company, the consortium of investors who had underwritten the trip. More important than either publication was William Strachey's *True Reportory of the Wrack, and Redemption of Sir Thomas Gates Knight*. Shakespeare almost certainly read the pamphlets and used them in writing *The Tempest*.

**ESSENTIALS** Though it was not officially published until 1625, Strachey's account is dated July 15, 1610, and was circulated among those in the know. Shakespeare had connections to the Virginia Company and Strachey, and it is highly likely that he had access to Strachey's account in manuscript form prior to publication.

A number of later adaptations include John Dryden's *The Enchanted Island,* Thomas Shadwell's opera (1674), and Henry Purcell's score (1690). An 1821 performance of *The Enchanted Island* included music by Purcell, Mozart, and Rossini. It is also the basis of W. H. Auden's long poem, *The Sea and the Mirror*.

## The Play

Prospero, a sorcerer and the rightful duke of Milan, lives on an enchanted isle with his daughter, Miranda. Twelve years earlier, the duke's brother, Antonio, and Alonso, the king of Naples, conspired to usurp his throne. Prospero and Miranda were set adrift in a boat and eventually washed up on the island. Using his magic, Prospero freed a spirit called Ariel from a tree.

As the play begins, Prospero has discovered that a ship carrying home his old enemies from a wedding is sailing nearby. Prospero conjures a storm to wreck their ship. The survivors make it to shore in scattered groups. Among these is Ferdinand, the son of Alonso, who meets Miranda. The two teenagers fall in love.

Meanwhile, Antonio, Alonso, Sebastian, and Gonzalo search the island for Ferdinand. As they do, Antonio plots with Sebastian to murder Alonso. However, Ariel thwarts the plot. Elsewhere on the island, Stephano and Trinculo encounter the island's other native inhabitant, Caliban, son of the witch Sycorax. After the three drink together, Caliban convinces the two servants to help him kill Prospero. He even promises Miranda to Stephano. Ariel keeps Prospero apprised of what the various groups are doing.

SSENTIALS    The numerous film adaptations of *The Tempest* include at least one classic—the 1956 sci-fi movie, *Forbidden Planet.* Those who like interesting "art films" may find Peter Greenaway's *Prospero's Books*, starring Sir John Gielgud, interesting.

Prospero makes Ferdinand work to win Miranda's love, and while that is going on, creates a magical banquet for Antonio and Alonso, which vanishes whenever they try to eat. He also sends Ariel to torment them for their crimes against him.

During a masque to celebrate the upcoming marriage of Miranda and Ferdinand, Prospero decides it's time to put an end to Caliban's plot and sends Ariel to punish them as well. The spirit does this by setting other island spirits on them in the shape of hunting dogs that chase them around the island.

Finally, Prospero confronts his brother and Alonso, revealing his true identity as the rightful duke of Milan. He demands that Antonio restore his throne; he also rebukes Sebastian for plotting against his own brother. He reveals Ferdinand as alive and well, playing chess with Miranda. Restored to his natural authority, Prospero abandons his magic and releases Ariel and Caliban from their servitude.

## Commentary

*The Tempest* is simply not a play to be read—it must be seen or at least heard. With this, his last great play, Shakespeare decided to pull out all the stops. It is an inherently visual spectacle, which unfolds in a series of exotic, otherworldly, and sometimes "invisible" characters that the audience can see but other characters cannot. It is best described as a multisensory theatrical experience, with sound and music used to complement a somewhat simple story of retribution, and a lyrical text that is lush with exotic images.

*The Tempest* does not have the bitterness of the later tragicomedies, and yet it does combine elements of a pastoral (the city folk forced to live as natives in the country) and tragedy (Prospero's revenge) with romantic comedy (the young lovers Miranda and Ferdinand). As in *Measure for Measure*, one of the problem plays, *The Tempest* also poses profound questions that defy easy resolution. The extraordinary thematic complexity of the play is far too involved to try to summarize effectively here.

**FACTS**

Modern critics often read the Caliban subtext from a postcolonial viewpoint, examining what the play can tell us about European colonization of the Americas in particular, and colonization in general. It is a play of great lyricism and heart that deserves careful and serious study.

Among other things, the play challenges our concepts of reality and illusion and our senses. On one level it is a self-conscious performance overtly orchestrated by the Shakespearelike "puppet-master" Prospero—the master illusionist, as he and his creator take their final bow. There are a number of themes, notably nature versus civilization or art. From certain perspectives, however, *The Tempest* tackles an overarching question: What is humanity?

## Famous Lines

"I would fain die a dry death" (Act I, Scene I).

"My library
Was dukedom large enough" (Act I, Scene II).

"Fill all thy bones with aches" (Act I, Scene II).

"Full fathom five thy father lies;
Of his bones are coral made;
Those are pearls that were his eyes:
Nothing of him that doth fade
But doth suffer a sea-change
Into something rich and strange" (Act I, Scene II).

"There's nothing ill can dwell in such a temple:
If the ill spirit have so fair a house,
Good things will strive to dwell with 't" (Act I, Scene II).

"Misery acquaints a man with strange bedfellows" (Act II, Scene II).

"Deeper than e'er plummet sounded" (Act III, Scene III).

"Our revels now are ended. These our actors,
As I foretold you, were all spirits, and
Are melted into air, into thin air:
And, like the baseless fabric of this vision,
The cloud-capp'd towers, the gorgeous palaces,
The solemn temples, the great globe itself,
Yea, all which it inherit, shall dissolve,
And, like this insubstantial pageant faded,
Leave not a rack behind. We are such stuff
As dreams are made on; and our little life
Is rounded with a sleep" (Act IV, Scene I).

"Where the bee sucks, there suck I;
In a cowslip's bell I lie" (Act V, Scene I).

# 35 ❧ *The Two Gentlemen of Verona*

## Main Characters

**Proteus**—Valentine's supposed best friend and one of the title gentlemen of Verona.

**Valentine**—The other title gentleman of Verona.

**Julia**—Proteus' beloved, and mistress to Lucetta.

**Silvia**—Daughter to the duke and beloved of Valentine.

**Duke of Milan**—Silvia's father.

**Lucetta**—Julia's servant.

**Launce**—Proteus's servant.

**Speed**—Valentine's page.

**Thurio**—A rival for Silvia's hand.

**Sir Eglamour**—The gentleman who helps Silvia escape the duke's court.

**Antonio**—Father to Proteus and master to Panthino.

**Host**—Houses Julia.

**Crab**—Launce's dog.

**Panthino**—Antonio's servant.

## Introduction

Critics are not certain exactly when *The Two Gentlemen of Verona* was written. Some believe *The Two Gentlemen of Verona* may be Shakespeare's first play. It is clearly not one of his best and is the work of a young writer. Authors such as Geoffrey Chaucer, Francis Bacon, John Lyly, and George Peele had undertaken similar debates between romantic love and male friendship prior to Shakespeare's own attempt to tackle the subject in *The Two Gentlemen of Verona*.

Some historians believe that the play was begun in 1592 and finished in 1593 for a specific performance date, which might explain the seeming addition of Launce and Crab, the inconsistent references to Milan and

Verona as the setting, and to Silvia's father, who is at times called the duke and at others the emperor.

**FACTS**

The first historical mention of *The Two Gentlemen of Verona* is in 1598, though the presence of certain theatrical techniques and themes in the play suggests that it was a precursor to other early works such as *As You Like It* and *Twelfth Night*.

While the date of the play's composition may be uncertain, its literary ancestors are not. The most significant source for the play is the story of Felix and Felismena, from Portuguese writer Jorge de Montemayor's work *Diana*. Shakespeare may have either read *Diana* in a French translation or seen a version of it performed at court in 1585. In the original play, Silvia's equivalent is killed off and Valentine does not exist. As was often his way, Shakespeare changed the original story to create a happier, more symmetrical ending.

## The Play

Valentine's father sends him to take up a position in the duke of Milan's court, and his friend Proteus reluctantly goes with him because he doesn't want to leave his beloved Julia. Once in Milan, Valentine falls for the duke's daughter, Silvia. However, Silvia is betrothed to Thurio, a wealthy courtier, although she clearly prefers Valentine. The two decide to elope, and Valentine confides in Proteus.

Proteus, however, also falls for Silvia, and in order to get Valentine out of the way, and get in her father's good graces, Proteus betrays his friend's plan to the duke. Valentine is banished, Silvia is imprisoned, and Proteus becomes a confidant of the duke.

Valentine comes across a band of outlaws and is elected their leader. Meanwhile, Julia, disguised as a boy page, enters Milan looking for Proteus, who is trying unsuccessfully to court Silvia. Silvia still loves Valentine. Julia, in disguise, becomes a page to Proteus, and ends up being an intermediary between Proteus and Silvia. Silvia finally seizes an opportunity to escape, and goes in search of Valentine. In the forest, Valentine's outlaws capture her.

The duke, Proteus, and Thurio set off to rescue Silvia, and Proteus recovers Silvia before the outlaws can take her to Valentine. As Proteus makes one last attempt to convince Silvia to love him, he and Valentine meet up again.

The two men eventually make peace with each other, and in a gesture of reconciliation, Valentine offers Silvia to Proteus, which causes Julia (who is still disguised as a page) to faint. Proteus finally recognizes her, much to his shame. The duke and Thurio now arrive on the scene. Thurio backs off his claim to Silvia when challenged by Valentine, and Valentine gets Silvia with the duke's approval. Proteus and Julia are reconciled, and the duke grants a pardon to the outlaws.

## Commentary

*The Two Gentlemen of Verona* is about the conflict of loyalty and passion. While the play eventually decides that friendship is more important (that is, the love of friends is purer than romantic love), the twists and turns that each character takes in order to reach that conclusion involve a number of other issues.

**FACTS**

The servants Launce, Speed, and Lucetta act as foils to their respective masters Proteus, Valentine, and Julia. The servants give us clues about their masters. Launce's pragmatic reasoning about love, for example, shows us that Proteus is more concerned with social position and money than romance.

By offering a view that challenged the works of other such established writers as Chaucer, Lyly, and Francis Bacon, with a certain hubris the young Shakespeare attempted to stand out from the accepted moral stance of the great writers of his time. The shame of it is that he threw down the gauntlet with a play that does not match the quality of work Shakespeare was later known for.

The forest (and countryside in general) plays an important role in Shakespeare's plays. From the magic of Prospero's deserted island, to the fairy-filled forest of Athens in *A Midsummer Night's Dream*, social status there becomes irrelevant. People are judged on their merits, not on their parentage. Such a breakdown encourages a rebellion that can include cross-dressing and even same-sex romance. When, for example, Proteus realizes he can't have Silvia, suddenly "Sebastian" (Julia) is attractive to him. Valentine's friendship with Proteus, and how they eventually resolve the contentious issue of Silvia, further reinforces the idea of gender-bending, and skirts the issue of homosexuality.

## Famous Lines

"That man that hath a tongue, I say, is no man,
If with his tongue he cannot win a woman" (Act III, Scene I).

"Is she not passing fair?" (Act IV, Scene IV).

"Come not within the measure of my wrath" (Act V, Scene IV).

# 36 ⚯ *The Two Noble Kinsmen*

## Main Characters

**Theseus**—Duke of Athens.

**Palamon**—Nephew of the king of Thebes.

**Arcite**—Nephew of the king of Thebes.

**Pirithous**—An Athenian general.

**Artesius**—An Athenian captain.

**Valerius**—A noble of Thebes.

**A Jailer**—Oversees the imprisonment of Palamon and Arcite.

**A Doctor**—Ordered by Theseus to tend to the wounds of Palamon and Arcite.

**Gerrold**—A schoolmaster.

**Hippolyta**—Wife of Theseus.

**Emilia**—Theseus's sister.

**Three Queens**—Their husbands were killed by Creon, ruler of Thebes.

**Jailer's Daughter**—In love with Palamon and frees him from the jail.

## Introduction

Based on Chaucer's *Knight's Tale*, *The Two Noble Kinsmen* was written at the end of Shakespeare's career, as a collaboration with the rising young dramatist John Fletcher. Chaucer's story of Palamon and Arcite was based on Boccaccio's *Teseide*. Boccaccio in turn based his work on material by Statius. Richard Edwards wrote *Palamon and Arcyte* as early as 1566, and it was performed before Elizabeth I by Oxford students on the occasion of the queen's visit to the university in that year. The account of this lost comedy, published in Nichols's *Progresses of Elizabeth,* suggests that it was a very different kind of play from *The Two Noble Kinsmen.* Nothing is known of the *Palamon and Arsett* mentioned by Henslowe as having been acted at the Newington theater in 1594.

    *The Two Noble Kinsmen* was the first published in 1634 in quarto format, although scholars date it sometime around 1613. The title page ascribes the play to "the memorable Worthies of their time; Mr. John Fletcher, and Mr. William Shakspeare" (sic) at the Blackfriars Theatre. Most modern critics accept this attribution.

Because the play was excluded from the 1623 First Folio some critics dispute Shakespeare's role in the play's composition. However, *Pericles* was also excluded from the First Folio, and *Troilus and Cressida* was included in only some editions, having been stitched into the binding between *King Henry VIII* (another coauthored play) and *Coriolanus*, and is subsequently absent from the title pages of those editions. When the second Beaumont and Fletcher folio was published in 1679, an additional eighteen plays were included, including *The Two Noble Kinsmen*.

It was not included in a complete Shakespeare edition until 1841 (*The Pictorial Shakespeare*) and only during the twentieth century has it been included in most of the major modern collections of Shakespeare's works: the Oxford, Riverside, Arden, Norton, Cambridge, and Penguin editions.

**FACTS**

Curiously, of all the single edition versions of the play in the twentieth century, only one, the Regents Renaissance Drama edition (edited by Richard Proudfoot, 1970), bears the names of both Shakespeare and Fletcher on the front cover.

## The Play

*The Two Noble Kinsmen* is essentially an adaptation of Chaucer's *Knight's Tale*. In this story, the two kinsmen are Palamon and Arcite, who are captured while fighting for Thebes against Athens. While imprisoned, the two cousins find themselves attracted to Emilia, Theseus's unmarried sister-in-law. Their professed "eternal friendship" is severely tested as the two cousins woo her. Theseus finds out what's going on, exiles Arcite from Athens and leaves Palamon in jail.

Once he is free, Arcite disguises himself as a peasant in order to keep an eye on Emilia. Meanwhile, the jailer's daughter has fallen in love with Palamon and helps him to escape and hide in the forest.

He runs into Arcite again, and the two men resume their argument over Emilia. They decide to fight a duel for her. However, as they prepare for the duel, the two cousins are discovered by Theseus. He condemns both to death, but after pleading from both Emilia and her sister Hippolyta, the duke decides to banish them both.

**SSENTIALS** | *The Two Noble Kinsmen* is a play that needs to be seen in order that the masque-like splendor of some of its scenes may be fully realized. It contains elements of classic legend, medieval romance, Elizabethan comedy, and Jacobean masque, and in the union of these varying elements, we can recognize the genius of a dramatist who could subdue all things to harmony.

Both Palamon and Arcite refuse. Theseus tells Emilia she must choose between them, and the loser will be put to death. Emilia, however, can't make up her mind, so Theseus declares that the matter will be settled by combat after all. In one month, Palamon and Arcite will fight for Emilia's hand, and the loser will be executed.

Meanwhile, the jailer's daughter has gone mad because of her unrequited love for Palamon. Theseus pardons the jailer, realizing he had no part in Palamon's escape, and forgives his deranged daughter. A doctor tries to help restore her sanity her by getting her fiancé to pretend he's Palamon.

The time for the contest comes about, and Arcite defeats Palamon. However, while Palamon awaits execution, a messenger arrives bringing news that Arcite's fatally injured himself in a horse-riding accident. Arcite gives Emilia's hand to Palamon before he dies.

## Commentary

Neglected until recently by directors and teachers, the play deserves to be better known for its moving dramatization of the conflict of love and friendship. While one of the kinsmen braces himself for execution, the shocking accident that frees him seems to makes a nonsense of the belief that we are responsible for our own fates. This concept is reinforced by Theseus's closing speech in the last scene, where he tries to convince us that Palamon had the better right to the lady because he saw her first. The enduring impression the play leaves is that humans are but puppets of fortune.

*The Two Noble Kinsmen* follows Chaucer's *Knight's Tale* closely, but the dramatists, deferring to the seventeenth-century taste for a realistic subplot to a romantic theme, added the story of the jailer's daughter. The play has problems, however. Palamon and Arcite are not particularly distinguished from each other; Theseus is a stilted and a vacillating figure; and Emilia is a poor copy of Chaucer's "Emelye the sheene." Finally, the subplot reminds us of a poorly revisited Ophelia (in *Hamlet*).

The authorship is clearly a problem. But to the play's credit, it's tough to say who wrote what exactly. Critics are agreed that one of the two authors was Fletcher, and that to him may be allotted most of Acts II, III, and IV, including the whole of the underplot, with the possible exception of the two prose scenes, but only a small, and comparatively unimportant, part of the main story.

The whole of the first act, the first scene in act III, and almost the whole of the last act are clearly not by Fletcher, and the choice of authorship seems to fall to Shakespeare. The profusion of striking metaphors, the profound thoughts, and the extreme conciseness of writing the scenes bear a marked resemblance to Shakespeare's later plays.

# 37 ❧ *The Winter's Tale*

## Main Characters

**Leontes**—The king of Sicilia.

**Hermione**—Leontes's queen.

**Perdita**—The daughter of Leontes and Hermione.

**Polixenes**—The king of Bohemia, and Leontes's boyhood friend.

**Florizel**—Polixenes's only son and heir.

**Camillo**—A Sicilian nobleman.

**Paulina**—A noblewoman of Sicily.

**Autolycus**—A roguish peddler.

**Shepherd**—He finds Perdita as a baby and raises her as his own daughter.

**Antigonus**—Paulina's husband.

**Clown**—Perdita's adopted brother.

**Mamillius**—The young prince of Sicilia.

**Cleomenes**—A lord of Sicilia.

**Dion**—A Sicilian lord.

**Emilia**—One of Hermione's ladies-in-waiting.

**Archidamus**—A lord of Bohemia.

## Introduction

*The Winter's Tale* is one of Shakespeare's last plays, written and performed around 1611. It joins *Pericles*, *Cymbeline*, and *The Tempest* in a list of genre-defying plays that are usually referred to as tragicomedies or bitter comedies.

There is no one source for *The Winter's Tale*, although Shakespeare relied heavily on *Pandosto*, a 1588 prose romance by Robert Greene, a university-trained London writer who in 1592 wrote a pamphlet accusing a young Shakespeare of being an untalented, "upstart Crow" who stole from other writers (which makes this borrowing somewhat ironic). The story of the abandoned royal baby probably comes from popular folklore, while

Hermione's resurrection at the end of the play is obviously from the Greek myth of Pygmalion, in which a sculptor's work comes to life.

## The Play

Leontes's friend Polixenes of Bohemia thinks he should return to his kingdom after spending time with his old school friend. Leontes asks his wife, Hermione, to try to persuade Polixenes to stay longer. Because Hermione succeeds, Leontes starts to think she is having an affair with Polixenes. His jealousy gets the better of him, and Leontes decides to kill Polixenes.

**ESSENTIALS**

The play has been a favorite of directors and audiences since it was first presented. In a number of productions the roles of Hermione and Perdita have been played by the same actress, notably Dame Judi Dench in 1969. Other productions have starred Patrick Stewart, Sir Ian McKellen, and Jeremy Irons.

Camillo, however, warns Polixenes and the two men escape to Bohemia. Leontes has Hermione tried for adultery, despite the fact that the Delphic oracle proclaims her innocent. While in prison, Hermione gives birth to a daughter, which Leontes orders killed. He is persuaded to save the child's life, and orders Antigonus to abandon the baby in the desert. Antigonus does so, but is devoured soon after by a bear. (This gives rise to one of Shakespeare's classic stage directions: "Exit, pursued by a bear.")

Leontes son, Mamillius, dies from grief over his mother's predicament. Hermione is next reported dead by her maid, Paulina. The shock seems to bring Leontes to his senses. He is overcome by grief and guilt and goes into seclusion.

The abandoned baby, Perdita, is found by a shepherd, who raises her as his daughter. Sixteen years later, Florizel, Polixenes's son meets Perdita, and the teenagers fall in love. Polixenes, however, is not happy that his son is in love with a peasant girl, so Florizel and Perdita decide to flee to Sicilia, aided by old Camillo.

Florizel and Perdita are welcomed at the court of Leontes. Polixenes follows them, and reconciles with Leontes. Perdita is revealed to be a princess, and Leontes and Polixenes are delighted that their children are in love.

Leontes's happiness is tempered by the bitter memory of Hermione's death. Paulina takes Leontes and the court to see a statue of the queen which magically comes to life. It seems the queen has been hiding for the past sixteen years. Thus Leontes is finally reunited with his wife, daughter, best friend, and closest advisor, Camillo. Even Paulina regains a husband when Leontes agrees to marry her to Camillo.

## Commentary

*The Winter's Tale* is perhaps Shakespeare's best tragicomedy. It is set in an imaginary world where ancient Greek oracles coexist with Renaissance sculptors, and offers an *Othello*-like tragedy that magically culminates in the all's well that end's well finale of *A Midsummer Night's Dream* or *The Tempest*.

 **ESSENTIALS** Leontes is both Othello and Iago. His paranoia underlines the terrifying destructive power of the whims of princes, and emphasizes subtly the need for the middle classes (through the growth of the power of parliament and the guilds) to take more control of their own lives.

The play is almost seasonal in structure. The first half is wintry and chilly, emotionally cold, and dominated by a fit of jealous madness and rage that seems so destructive even an innocent child may not escape.

But sixteen years pass, and Leontes's madness passes. The second half of the play is spring-like, and the destruction the king's madness created is ploughed under so that through coincidence, goodwill, and the magic of new life springing forth from previous hard and barren ground, a statue of his dead wife comes to life and embraces him.

The problem plays deal with death and the power of evil, and in *The Winter's Tale*, we are given an ending where death is literally banished from the stage.

Like *King Lear*, this play deals with the anarchy unleashed because of the main character's self-absorbed madness. When Leontes is told that there is "nothing" between Hermione and Polixenes, he declares, "Why, then the world and all that's in 't is nothing." When he finally comes to his senses, all Leontes can offer by way of explanation for his behavior is, "I have drunk, and seen the spider."

If Leontes is a tragic hero, Perdita is clearly a fairy-tale princess reared among commoners who falls in love with a prince and discovers her nobility quite naturally. The miracle of Hermione's resurrection at the play's close is an appropriate ending to a play about death (winter) and rebirth (spring).

## Famous Lines

"They say we are
Almost as like as eggs" (Act I, Scene II).

"To unpathed waters, undreamed shores" (Act IV, Scene IV).

# 38 ⑤ *Timon of Athens*

## Main Characters

**Timon**—A wealthy man who enjoys giving gifts to his friends and sharing his wealth.

**Apemantus**—One of Timon's guests.

**Alcibiades**—An acquaintance of Timon.

**Flavius**—One of Timon's servants.

**Lucullus, Lucius, Sempronius, and Ventidius**—Timon's fair-weather friends.

**Lucilius, Flaminius, and Servilius**—Timon's servants.

**Caphis, Varro's servant, Isidore's servant**—Servants of creditors who demand payment of their loan.

**Poet**—One of Timon's hangers-on.

**Painter**—One of Timon's hangers-on.

**Jeweler**—One of Timon's hangers-on.

**Fool**—The Fool appears with Apemantus outside Timon's house while servants of creditors wait for their payments.

**Bandits**—Thieves Timon meets in the wilderness.

**Senators**—Members of the Athenian Senate.

**Lords**—Among Timon's many friends who attend his feasts and accept his gifts.

## Introduction

*Timon of Athens* was probably written between 1605 and 1608, but is not known to have been produced, probably because, as many scholars argue, it was never finished. An alternative theory is that it focused on too controversial a topic for the years directly after James I's accession to the English throne in 1603.

In the early part of the seventeenth century there was growing condemnation of an almost profligate spendthriftness by the English aristocracy, most of whom could not afford the lifestyles they tried to maintain. Nobles constantly competed to outlavish one another, but lacked the cash to back up their behavior. As a result, a new credit market arose.

Some scholars think Shakespeare coauthored this play with a dramatist named Thomas Middleton. Nevertheless some Shakespearean characteristics are unmistakable, such as the story's derivation from Plutarch's *Lives of Noble Greeks and Romans*, one of Shakespeare's favorite sources.

James I was well known for such profligate behavior, giving his friends expensive gifts and generally spending money on fashionable things until he had incurred huge deficits in the royal treasury. Much of the aristocracy followed his example. The play draws attention to the irresponsible behavior of the upper classes, a criticism which no doubt contributed to keeping the play from being sponsored or performed.

## The Play

Timon is a generous aristocrat in Athens. Everyone loves him because of his generosity. He just hasn't wanted to hear what his steward Flavius has been trying to tell him. When Timon finds creditors knocking on the door, Flavius is finally able to tell him that he is bankrupt.

Timon then sends his servants to his "friends," only to find no one will lend him money to repay his debts except his steward, who gives what little he has to his master. Incensed at this betrayal, Timon invites everyone to one last feast. The only dish, to everyone's surprise, is warm water. Timon then denounces not only his former comrades but also humankind as a whole.

In the meantime, Alcibiades, a captain of Athens, is banished for pleading for the life of one of his men, under sentence of death by the senate. Alcibiades seriously considers turning his army against Athens in revenge.

He hears about Timon, who was living as a hermit in the forest, digging for roots to eat when he stumbled upon a buried trove of gold.

Alcibiades decides to visit Timon, who in turn offers Alcibiades gold if he will sack Athens. Alcibiades accepts his offer and marches on Athens.

Timon receives more visitors, some of whom are bandits. Timon pays them gold to wreak havoc on Athens. The bandits accept the gold, but Timon's ranting, ironically, convinces them to quit thieving. Timon also sends away his only loyal friend, his former steward, Flavius, but with gold in his pockets and more kindness than he has shown to anyone else.

**FACTS**

Despite his presumed goodness at the start of the play, Timon is a self-absorbed character who sets himself up as a god of generosity and when he loses his wealth through his own foolishness, becomes a god of vitriol and revenge, cursing humankind with the same kind of enthusiasm with which he earlier praised it.

Alcibiades takes Athens. Knowing he is a friend of Alcibiades, the Athenians beg Timon for help. Timon offers them a tree outside his cave—on which they can hang themselves. The senators ingratiate themselves with Alcibiades by giving up his enemies and those that refused to help Timon when he was in debt. Alcibiades agrees, vowing peace in Athens. A soldier enters with the sad news that Timon has died alone in his cave.

## Commentary

*Timon of Athens* focuses exclusively on the question: Is material well-being inextricably linked to love and friendship? It is, in some ways almost a proto-Marxist play and has a number of things to say to counter what some critics see as an American buy-now-pay-later mentality.

### A Poor Judge of Character

Timon enjoys sharing his wealth, but doesn't pick his friends very well. Almost certainly, the only reasons they have stuck around is the hope that Timon will give them a gift. Apemantus may think Timon's friends are all worthless flatterers, but he hangs around as well, although without eating or accepting gifts, just to see how long things will go on before they come crashing to a halt.

Timon likes his friends' affection and seems to get some form of status merely from spending. Perhaps he believes his generosity will solidify his friendship with the various Athenian lords who surround him. He is astonished to see the intangible bonds of "friendship" disintegrate when he needs more loans from his friends.

## Possession and Financial Gain

Apemantus takes the opposite tack to Timon at every stage. He believes people are naturally greedy and that generosity is an attempt to control and influence others and gain a return later. Yet both men believe that possessions, or lack thereof, determine how we think of ourselves.

Like the earlier play *The Merchant of Venice*, *Timon of Athens* concerns itself with the connection between ties of affection and monetary bonds. Timon must discover how much friendship has to do with self-interest, how material goods compare to intangible feelings, and how much people are esteemed for their personal characteristics versus their possessions.

The play is almost exclusively about financial exchanges between men (there is no significant female part), and in a certain light it suggests such dealings are almost depraved roles. The Fool at one point actually draws parallels between those who go to creditors and those who go to prostitutes. The play draws on the ancient portrait of moneylending as a depraved form of unnatural "breeding" of money for interest.

## Friends: Fair-weather or True?

Timon begins the play as a generous but foolish man, and ends it as an angry and foolish man. He takes the behavior of a few people he should have realized were fair-weather friends as a sign that the whole of humanity is rotten. Yet he fails to see that many people who come to see him in his cave prove his assumption false. Flavius, who echoes Timon's philosophy of generosity but in a sensible way, shares his remaining funds with Timon's servants, proving himself an honorable man; Apemantus and Timon argue, but clearly enjoy each other's company; and Alcibiades, in a subplot involving a condemned friend, which may have been one of the casualties of an unrevised play, prepares to attack Athens in order to rehabilitate Timon's honor in the city. At the end of the play Timon learns from the senators that many Athenians want to make amends for the way Timon has been treated. Still he rejects them.

When Alcibiades arrives at the gates of Athens with his army, the senators convince him not to attack by saying that those who were cruel to Timon and to Alcibiades make up only a small portion of the population, and will be easy to single out and punish. The play suggests that the wholesale villainy Timon thought made up the world is really only limited to some badly chosen friends.

## Famous Lines

"Here's that which is too weak to be a sinner,—honest water, which ne'er left man i' the mire" (Act I, Scene II).

"Every man has his fault, and honesty is his" (Act III, Scene I).

"Nothing emboldens sin so much as mercy" (Act III, Scene V).

"We have seen better days" (Act IV, Scene II).

"Life's uncertain voyage" (Act V, Scene I).

# 39 ♦ *Titus Andronicus*

## Main Characters

**Titus Andronicus**—General of Rome and tragic hero of the play.

**Tamora**—Queen of the Goths, mother of Chiron and Demetrius.

**Aaron**—Tamora's Moorish lover.

**Lavinia**—The only daughter of Titus Andronicus. In love with Bassianus.

**Marcus Andronicus**—Roman tribune. Brother of Titus Andronicus.

**Saturninus**—The eldest son of the late emperor of Rome.

**Bassianus**—The younger brother of Saturninus.

**Lucius**—Titus's only surviving son.

**Chiron and Demetrius**—Goth princes. Sons of Tamora.

**Young Lucius**—Titus's grandson, and Lucius's son.

## Introduction

Elizabethan written accounts testify to audiences with particularly bloody tastes, and *Titus Andronicus* was received with great applause, remaining a favorite for over a decade. However gruesome we find *Titus Andronicus* today, it's worth recalling that competing with the burgeoning theater, blood sports such as public bearbaiting were very popular in Elizabethan times. The play was hugely popular when it opened.

### Saving Shakespeare's Good Name

In 1687, some one hundred years after the first performance of *Titus Andronicus*, Edward Ravenscroft adapted the play for a different audience and called it *The Rape of Lavinia*. In an introduction to his more refined version, he wrote, "I have been told . . . that it was not originally [Shakespeare's], but brought by a private author to be acted, and [Shakespeare] only gave some Master-touches to one or two of the principal parts of characters. This I am apt to believe, because 'tis the most incorrect and indigested piece in all his works. It seems rather a heap of Rubbish than a structure."

What's particularly interesting about Ravenscroft's comment is his need to try and rescue Shakespeare's good name. It's as though an overtly brutal pornographic early novel by Samuel Beckett surfaced and scholars felt compelled to justify something they would otherwise condemn with disdain as low popular trash. *Titus Andronicus* is an Elizabethan *Texas Chainsaw Massacre.* Yet, knowing the author, we can't but think its massive excess seems to be less an imitation of the Elizabethan revenge drama than a parody of that form.

FACTS

During Elizabethan times, those found guilty of treason were publicly hung, cut down alive, and disemboweled (drawn), and their bodies then cut up or "quartered" and sent off to different parts of the realm; heretics were publicly burned alive.

In some ways this account gives some sense of the history of *Titus Andronicus.* Shakespeare's admirers halfheartedly try to deny his authorship of what is probably his worst play. The debate has gone on for centuries. In 1614, Ben Jonson claimed it was as popular a play as Thomas Kyd's equally bloody *The Spanish Tragedy.* Samuel Johnson theorized that Shakespeare "play-doctored" someone else's work.

If scholars acknowledge the hand of the great master in this work at all, they usually point to his youth as an excuse. Shakespeare would have been about twenty-six when he wrote *Titus Andronicus,* and it marked his first attempt at writing tragedy. This controversy rages despite the fact that Meres publicly named Shakespeare as the play's author in *Palladis Tamia* (1598), and that the play is included in the First Folio.

## Sources

The play was likely written between 1590 and 1593. While there is no clear main source for the story, critics think that they included *Hecuba* by Euripides, *Metamorphoses* by Ovid, and *Thyestes and Troades* by Seneca. A tutor to Emperor Nero, Seneca wrote plays that described the grisly horror of murder in elaborate detail. When Elizabethans began translating Seneca's works from Latin in 1559, writers relished them and wrote plays "in the classical style" imitating them. Shakespeare appears to have seasoned *Titus Andronicus* and later, *Macbeth* and parts of *King Lear* with some of Seneca's ghoulish spice.

The poetry of *Titus Andronicus* displays definite Shakespearean traits, and in the character of Aaron we see the seeds of Othello, Iago, and Richard III, while Tamora can be seen as an early version of Margaret in the *King Henry VI* plays. It is the only Shakespeare play, ironically, for which we have a contemporary illustration, by Henry Peacham, which shows characters in a mix of Roman and Renaissance costumes.

## The Play

Titus, a Roman general, returns to Rome after a victorious campaign against the Goths. In tow as captives are Tamora and her sons, one of whom, Alarbus, is sacrificed by Titus's sons. Saturninus, the newly declared Roman emperor, is feuding with his younger brother, Bassianus. Lavinia, Titus's daughter, chooses Bassianus over Saturninus, and the emperor is seduced by the captive Queen Tamora, who is plotting with her Moorish lover, Aaron, to get revenge against Titus.

**FACTS**

Before performing a bloody play such as *Titus Andronicus*, Elizabethan actors would fill vessels such as pig's bladders with blood and hide them under their costumes. Onstage, they had only to pound a fist against the bladder to release the blood.

Demetrius and Chiron come across Bassianus in the woods, then rape and mutilate Lavinia, leaving her without a tongue to speak or hands to write. Aaron now frames Titus's sons (Quintus and Martius) for Bassianus's murder, and they are condemned to death. Titus's remaining son, Lucius, tries to rescue his brothers and is banished from Rome.

Aaron tells Titus that the emperor will spare Quintus and Martius if Titus cuts off a hand and sends it to him. Titus does so. However, his hand is returned to him along with the heads of his two sons. Lucius, meanwhile, raises an army of Goths to sack Rome.

Titus finally is able to communicate enough with a half-crazed Lavinia to discover that Demetrius and Chiron were responsible for attacking her. Titus kills them, and serves them up as a pie!

When Tamora and Saturninus arrive to try to convince Titus to call off Lucius and his Goths, Titus serves them dinner, featuring pie as the main course. In the middle of the feast, Titus kills Lavinia to put her out of her misery, reveals the secret ingredient of his pie, then butchers Tamora. Saturninus in turn slays Titus. Lucius, newly arrived, kills Saturninus.

Lucius is elected emperor of Rome and orders Aaron (who refuses to ask forgiveness for his crimes) buried up to his chest and left to starve, and Tamora to be left unburied for the scavengers to feast on.

## Commentary

*Titus Andronicus* falls between two stools: it is neither history (not based on real events) nor Roman play with elements of a tragedy, because it is clearly a melodrama. The play is best described as Elizabethan revenge tragedy, a genre defined by a hero who doggedly pursues vengeance and perishes at his moment of success. *Titus Andronicus* also features one of the few genuinely evil characters in Shakespearean literature, Aaron the Moor. Aaron orchestrates all of the evil in the play, and his only regret is that he wasn't able to commit more evil. And yet even this personification of evil has one soft spot, his newborn son.

Titus is a paradoxical character. His behavior is hard for us to understand, but we can admire his concepts of honor and justice. As Rome's greatest general, Titus will allow nothing to compromise his honor or that of his family, even if he has to kill one of his sons to maintain it.

The revenge tragedy is not just about Titus getting revenge on those who wronged him and his family. It is also about Tamora getting revenge on Titus because his sons killed her son at the start of the play. She pushes Titus to the point where he has been stripped of all he holds dear, but fails to administer the *coup de grace* leaving him a wounded and dangerous creature.

While *Titus Andronicus* is clearly an archetypal gore-filled Elizabethan revenge tragedy, the story of *Hamlet* has a superficial resemblance to *Titus Andronicus.* Yet clearly, the more mature playwright with years of theatrical experience and experience of real personal tragedy (the death of his young son) who wrote *Hamlet,* decided to revisit a popular genre in order to turn it on its head and put the genre to rest. In *Hamlet* he is not content with just piling up the bodies. Instead, the horror of *Hamlet* is a spiritual one, and it takes the expectations of an audience for a genre play like *Titus Andronicus* and forces them to consider what all this violence and blood does to our souls.

## Famous Lines

"Sweet mercy is nobility's true badge" (Act I, Scene II).

"The eagle suffers little birds to sing" (Act IV, Scene IV).

# 40 § *Troilus and Cressida*

## Main Characters

**Troilus**—A prince of Troy. The younger brother of Hector and Paris.

**Cressida**—A beautiful young Trojan woman.

**Hector**—A prince of Troy.

**Ulysses**—One of the Greek commanders.

**Pandarus**—Cressida's uncle.

**Thersites**—A deformed slave serving Ajax.

**Achilles**—The greatest of the Greek warriors.

**Ajax**—A Greek warrior.

**Agamemnon**—A Greek general; brother of Menelaus.

**Diomedes**—A Greek commander.

**Paris**—A prince of Troy.

**Menelaus**—A Greek commander.

**Helen**—Menelaus's wife.

**Calchas**—A Trojan priest, and Cressida's father.

**Aeneas**—A Trojan commander.

**Nestor**—The oldest of the Greek commanders.

**Cassandra**—A Trojan princess and prophetess; she is considered mad.

**Patroclus**—A Greek warrior. Achilles's best friend, and maybe his lover.

**Priam**—The king of Troy, and the father of Hector, Paris, and Troilus, among others.

**Antenor**—A Trojan commander.

**Helenus**—A prince of Troy.

**Andromache**—Hector's wife.

## Introduction

*Troilus and Cressida* is one of Shakespeare's later plays, written shortly after *Hamlet* but before the other great tragedies. It is a sort of anti-*Romeo and Juliet*. Composed around 1602, it was probably performed in the winter of 1602–03, but no record of the performance survives, and the play itself was not published in a collection for six more years.

The genre classification of *Troilus and Cressida* has been in dispute from the beginning. Labeled a history in an early folio, it is not really tragedy, and is sometimes grouped with the so-called "problem comedies" *Measure for Measure* and *All's Well That Ends Well*. All three share a dark, bitter wit and a pessimistic view of human relations.

It's important to remember the popularity of Greek and Roman mythology in Shakespeare's time. The story of Troy was a well-known one and the events of the play, including the denouement, would have been expected from the beginning—Cressida's treachery and Hector's death would have been as predictable as the sinking of the *Titanic* is for moviegoers today.

Sources for the play include classical mythology and Homer's *Iliad*, which contains the Achilles-Hector story. The romance of Troilus and Cressida is principally derived from Chaucer's great fourteenth-century epic, *Troilus and Criseyde*. Typically, Shakespeare took only the bare bones of this story, combined with other medieval retellings of the tale, and emphasized the Elizabethan idea of Cressida's falseness over Chaucer's more sympathetic interpretation of her.

## The Play

The Trojan War is in its seventh year. The Greeks besieging Troy are bickering among themselves. When Hector, a Trojan hero, issues a challenge to fight any Greek in one-on-one combat, Ulysses arranges for Ajax to be the Greek champion. Ulysses hopes to spur Achilles out of his lethargy, and thus reinvigorate the Greek armies.

Calchas deserts Troy for the Greek encampment. In exchange for intelligence about the Trojan forces, Calchas asks the Greeks to exchange a Trojan prisoner for Cressida. Agamemnon, commander of the Greek army, agrees to this, and Cressida is soon parted from Troilus, who is devastated.

Once inside the Greek encampment, Cressida meets—and flirts—with all the Greek generals. Hector and Ajax battle each other to a standstill and eventually call a truce. The Trojan and Greek generals dine together at a feast.

Diomedes has been courting Cressida since her arrival in the Greek camp. While accompanying Ulysses, the heartbroken Troilus sees Cressida give Diomedes the love token Troilus gave her when she left Troy. He vows to kill Diomedes in battle.

During the battle next day, Hector slays Achilles's friend (and perhaps lover) Patroclus. When Achilles meets Hector on the field of battle the next day he is so incensed he has his men kill Hector while he is unarmed and resting. Troy has suffered a grave defeat, and an enraged Troilus hurls curses at Achilles and Pandarus alike from the city walls.

## Commentary

*Troilus and Cressida* is one of Shakespeare's more difficult plays. It's a romance set against the backdrop of an interminable war that is draining the humanity out of all who are engaged in it.

The play has a cast of generally unsympathetic characters but as in any great tragedy, it tackles the broad theme of conflict between an individual's interests and those of the state—in this case, the conflict between the romance of the title characters and the wartime politics that puts Cressida in the Greek camp where she is forced to make the best of her situation.

The play's general pessimism is matched only by that in *Timon of Athens*. Heroes such as Achilles and Ajax are presented as self-absorbed thugs, and the central romance of Troilus and Cressida is reduced to a roll in the grass that passes for love amid boredom and bloodshed. In the words of the archcynic Thersites, "all the argument is a whore and a cuckold" which rather sums up the Trojan War.

Structurally, the play feels disjointed. Shakespeare uses anticlimax throughout the play, so that scenes that we think will be critical turn out to be letdowns. This is especially true in the duel between Hector and Ajax, which ends in a draw, and again in the final battle, in which the events we expect do not transpire: Troilus is not avenged for the loss of his beloved, and Hector does not have a climactic duel with his great adversary, Achilles, but is ambushed and killed while he's unarmed.

SSENTIALS    Some critics have suggested that this play was performed only once, or not at all—possibly because some of the characters in the Greek and Trojan armies were thinly disguised caricatures of contemporaries, either of other playwrights or of members of King James I's court.

The play is almost defiantly philosophical. The argument between Hector and Troilus over the value of fighting to keep Helen in Troy is rich in insight, while Ulysses, one of the play's most interesting characters, discusses the role of order in society. Thersites is another interesting character. For all his abusiveness to the people around him, he ends up being the only moralist, even if that morality is delivered in bitter language about a futile situation made worse by uncaring, scheming heroes.

## Famous Lines

"The common curse of mankind,—folly and ignorance"
(Act II, Scene III).

"All lovers swear more performance than they are able, and yet reserve an ability that they never perform; vowing more than the perfection of ten, and discharging less than the tenth part of one" (Act III, Scene II).

"The end crowns all,
And that old common arbitrator, Time,
Will one day end it" (Act IV, Scene V).

# 41 § *Twelfth Night*

## Main Characters

**Viola (Cesario)**—A young woman.

**Count Orsino**—A powerful nobleman in the coastal country of Illyria.

**Olivia**—A wealthy lady.

**Sebastian**—Viola's lost twin brother.

**Malvolio**—Lady Olivia's straitlaced steward.

**Feste**—A clown; in the service of Olivia.

**Sir Toby Belch**—Olivia's uncle.

**Sir Andrew Aguecheek**—A friend of Sir Toby.

**Maria**—Olivia's witty, clever, servingwoman.

**Antonio**—A gentleman who rescues young Sebastian.

## Introduction

*Twelfth Night* was written in 1601 around the middle of Shakespeare's career. Many critics consider it one of his great comedies, along with *As You Like It*, *Much Ado About Nothing*, and *A Midsummer Night's Dream*.

QUESTIONS?

**What does "twelfth night" refer to?**
Twelfth night refers to the last night of Christmas celebrations that were very popular in Elizabethan times—usually January 6—which is also known in the church calendar as Epiphany, a day given to madcap fun, disguises, and pranks.

*Twelfth Night* is about illusion, deception, disguises, madness, and perhaps homosexuality—it is certainly concerned with the extraordinary things we'll do in the name of love. It's a fun, entertaining play, and one of the most accessible of the several movie adaptations is, arguably,

Trevor Nunn's 1996 version starring Helena Bonham Carter. Music has been written for and about the play including an opera composed by Smetana, and works by Brahms, Schubert, and Sibelius.

# The Play

Viola and her twin brother Sebastian are shipwrecked in a violent storm off the coast of Illyria and lose contact, with each thinking the other is dead. Viola disguises herself as a boy named Cesario and becomes a page in the service of Duke Orsino.

## Lost in Love

Olivia is in mourning for her father and brother and not interested in being courted. Orsino, however, is determined to woo her. He sends Cesario to Olivia with love letters. Cesario insists on being allowed to see Olivia. Olivia finally agrees, and on meeting the boy messenger takes a fancy to Cesario.

She sends her steward, Malvolio, after Cesario with a ring she purports Cesario left behind by mistake. Viola finds herself in a bind: She realizes to her dismay that Olivia has fallen for Cesario—and Viola herself has a stirring of affection for Orsino who is still besotted with Olivia.

Sebastian (Viola's twin) is rescued by Antonio and they become fast friends. At some risk to himself, because he ran afoul of the duke, Antonio helps Sebastian.

Back in Olivia's house, Sir Toby Belch (her uncle, who has shades of Falstaff about him) has hoodwinked a foppish wealthy friend, Sir Andrew Aguecheek, into supporting him by convincing him that Olivia might be interested in marrying him. Malvolio is a pompous and bossy steward who has a running feud with Sir Toby. With the help of Maria, Olivia's maid, and Feste, a clown, Sir Toby plots to bring Malvolio down a peg or two.

Maria writes a love letter to Malvolio that makes him think Olivia has fallen for him. Malvolio's self-importance makes him fall for the trick, which eventually leads to his being locked up as a madman.

## Confusion Abounds

Meanwhile, Sir Toby is egging Sir Andrew into a duel with Cesario. Olivia is now in love with Cesario, even though Cesario continues to press Orsino's cause. As Cesario and Sir Andrew prepare for a duel that neither wants, Antonio happens upon the scene. Believing Viola to be Sebastian, he intervenes and is arrested. Viola, of course, does not recognize Antonio who now thinks his newfound friend has abandoned and betrayed him.

Sir Andrew encounters Sebastian, thinking he is Cesario. This time Cesario doesn't back down when Aguecheek challenges him, and resoundingly beats him. Olivia intervenes just in time, and mistakes Sebastian for Cesario and continues to press her suit for him. A bemused Sebastian agrees to marry her.

Antonio is brought before the Duke for questioning, and Viola relates the events of the duel. Pointing to Cesario, Antonio tells everyone how he dragged "this man" from the surf, saving his life. Olivia now enters, searching for her new husband whom she mistakes for Cesario. Adding to this confusion, Sir Toby and Sir Andrew enter claiming that Cesario has violently assaulted them.

In the middle of Viola's denials, Sebastian appears. The brother and sister recognize one another and are reunited. Sebastian helps to clear the confusion as to who fought and married whom. At the end, Orsino and Viola pledge their love, Olivia and Sebastian remain happily married, and Olivia rebukes Sir Toby and Maria for their abuse of Malvolio, who vows his revenge upon the whole lot. Sir Toby agrees to marry Maria to make up for getting her in trouble, and all, except the disgruntled Malvolio, live happily ever after.

## Commentary

*Twelfth Night* is one of Shakespeare's "transvestite comedies," a category that also includes *As You Like It* and, to a lesser degree, *The Merchant of Venice*. These plays feature female protagonists who, for one reason or another, have to disguise themselves as young men.

It's worth remembering that in Shakespeare's day, all the parts were played by men, so Viola would actually have been a boy pretending to be a girl pretending to be a boy. Some contemporary critics have also found a great deal of interest in the homoerotic implications of these comedies.

**ESSENTIALS** Many scholars think the play was first performed on January 6, 1601 at the Whitehall for an Italian nobleman, Duke Orsino of Bracciano. Others think it was first performed on February 2, 1602.

*Twelfth Night* is the only Shakespeare play to have an "alternative" title: *Twelfth Night: or, What You Will* although critics are not quite sure what the play's two titles mean. *Twelfth Night* is considered to be a reference to the twelfth night of the Christmas celebration, a holiday celebrated as a festival in which everything was turned upside-down— much like the topsy-turvy world of Illyria.

## Famous Lines

"If music be the food of love, play on;
Give me excess of it, that, surfeiting,
The appetite may sicken, and so die.
That strain again! it had a dying fall:
O, it came o'er my ear like the sweet sound
That breathes upon a bank of violets,
Stealing and giving odor!" (Act I, Scene I).

"We will draw the curtain and show you the picture"
    (Act I, Scene V).

"He does it with a better grace, but I do it more natural"
    (Act II, Scene III).

"Is there no respect of place, persons, nor time in you?"
    (Act II, Scene III).

"My purpose is, indeed, a horse of that color" (Act II, Scene III).

"She never told her love,
But let concealment, like a worm i' the bud,
Feed on her damask cheek: she pined in thought,
And with a green and yellow melancholy
She sat like patience on a monument,
Smiling at grief" (Act II, Scene IV).

"I am all the daughters of my father's house,
And all the brothers too" (Act II, Scene IV).

"Some are born great, some achieve greatness, and some have
greatness thrust upon 'em" (Act II, Scene V).

"Love sought is good, but given unsought is better" (Act III, Scene I).

"Still you keep o' the windy side of the law" (Act III, Scene IV).

"Out of the jaws of death" (Act III, Scene IV).

"For the rain it raineth every day" (Act V, Scene I).

# APPENDIX A
# *Resources for Further Study*

## Reading Resources

All these are available at Amazon.com or from your local bookseller.

*Acting Shakespeare* by John Gielgud.

*Acting with Shakespeare: The Comedies* by Janet Suzman.

*Adaptations of Shakespeare: A Critical Anthology* edited by Daniel Fischlin and Mark Fortier.

*Clues to Acting Shakespeare: Skills Clarified for the Actor, Student, and Reader* by Wesley Van Tassel.

*Cleopatra* by Michael Grant.

*Lectures on Shakespeare* by W.H. Auden.

*William Shakespeare: The Man Behind the Genius: A Biography* by Anthony Holden.

*Brightest Heaven of Invention: A Christian Guide to Six Shakespeare Plays* by Peter J. Leithart.

*The Cambridge Companion to Shakespeare* edited by Margreta De Grazia and Stanley W. Wells.

*Coined by Shakespeare: Words and Meanings First Used by the Bard* by Jeffrey McQuain and Stanley Malless.

*A Companion to the Shakespearean Films of Kenneth Branagh* by Sarah Hatchuel.

*The Arden Shakespeare Complete Works* edited by Richard Proudfoot, Ann Thompson, and David Scott Kastan.

*A Shakespeare Glossary* by C.T. Onions.

*A Dictionary of Shakespeare* by Stanley Wells and James Shaw.

*Shakespeare Lexicon and Quotation Dictionary* by Alexander Schmidt.

*The Arden Dictionary of Shakespeare Quotations* compiled by Jane Armstrong.

*Daily Life in Elizabethan England* by Jeffrey L. Singman.

*Shakespeare's England: Life in Elizabethan and Jacobean Times* by Ron Pritchard.

*The Reader's Encyclopedia of Shakespeare* edited by Oscar James Campbell and George Quinn.

*From Shakespeare to Existentialism* by Walter Kaufmann.

*The Cambridge Companion to Shakespeare on Film* edited by Russell Jackson.

*A History of Shakespeare on Screen: A Century of Film and Television* by Kenneth S. Rothwell and Kenneth J. Rothwell.

*Interpreting Shakespeare on Screen* by Deborah Cartmell.

*Orson Welles, Shakespeare, and Popular Culture* by Michael Anderegg.

*Shakespeare in the Movies: From the Silent Era to Shakespeare in Love* by Douglas C. Brode.

*Shakespeare, the Movie: Popularizing the Plays on Film, TV, and Video* edited by Lynda E. Boose and Richard Burt.

*The Friendly Shakespeare: A Thoroughly Painless Guide to the Best of the Bard* by Norrie Epstein.

*Shakespeare's Mystery Play: The Opening of the Globe Theatre 1599* by Steve Sohmer.

*The Purpose of Playing: Shakespeare and the Cultural Politics of Elizabethan Theatre* by Louis Montrose.

*Shakespeare's Globe Rebuilt* edited by J.R. Mulryne and Margaret Shewring.

*Shakespeare's Theatre* by Andrew Langley.

*Staging in Shakespeare's Theatres* by Andrew Gurr and Mariko Ichikawa.

*Welcome to the Globe: The Story of Shakespeare's Theatre* by Peter Chrisp (children's book).

*William Shakespeare & the Globe* by Aliki.

*Understanding Hamlet* by Don Nardo.

*Understanding Hamlet: A Student Casebook to Issues, Sources, and Historical Documents* by Richard Corum.

*What Happens in Hamlet* by John Dover Wilson.

*Henry V, War Criminal? and Other Shakespeare Puzzles* by John Sutherland, et al.

*The Children of Henry VIII* by Alison Weir.

*Thy Father Is a Gorbellied Codpiece: Create over 100,000 of Your Own Shakespearean Insults* by Barry Kraft.

*Shakespeare and the Jews* by James Shapiro.

*Understanding Shakespeare's Julius Caesar* by Thomas J. Derrick.

*The Lives of the Kings and Queens of England* by Antonia Fraser.

*Shakespeare's Kings: The Great Plays and the History of England in the Middle Ages: 1337–1485* by John Julius Norwich.

*Understanding Macbeth: A Student Casebook to Issues Sources, and Historical Documents* by Faith Nostbakken.

*The Military Campaigns of the Wars of the Roses* by Philip A. Haigh.

*The Merchant of Venice: Choice, Hazard and Consequence* by Joan Ozark Holmer.

*The Merchant of Venice Study Guide* by Bethine Ellie.

*Bulfinch's Mythology* by Thomas Bulfinch.

*Dictionary of Classical Mythology* by John Edward Zimmerman.

*Greek Gods and Heroes* by Robert Graves.

*The Greek Myths* by Robert Graves.

*Heroes, Gods and Monsters of the Greek Myth* by Bernard Evslin.

*Mythology: Timeless Tales of Gods and Heroes* by Edith Hamilton

*Othello: A Guide to the Play* by Joan Lord Hall (ed.).

*Understanding Othello: A Student Casebook to Issues Sources, and Historical Documents* by Faith Nostbakken.

*Romeo & Juliet Study Guide* by Bethine Ellie.

*Understanding Romeo and Juliet* by Thomas E. Thrasher.

*Understanding Romeo and Juliet: A Student Casebook to Issues Sources, and Historical Documents* by Alan Hager (ed.).

*Shakespeare After Theory* by David Scott Kastan.

*Shakespeare: The Invention of the Human* by Harold Bloom.

*Shakespearean Tragedy: Lectures on Hamlet, Othello, King Lear & Macbeth* by A.C. Bradley.

*Shakespeare's Women in Love* by Alice Griffin.

*Shakespeare's Sonnets: Critical Essays* edited by James Schiffer.

*The Art of Shakespeare's Sonnets* by Helen Hennessy Vendler.

*Tempest: Complete Study Edition* edited by Sidney Lamb.

*Twelfth Night: A User's Guide* by Michael Pennington.

*Understanding The Merchant of Venice: A Student Casebook to Issues Sources, and Historical Documents* by Jay L. Halio.

# Shakespeare on Film

There is nothing that compares to watching a wonderfully envisioned and acted version of a Shakespeare play. Type in Shakespeare at the Internet Movie Database (*www.imdb.com*) and you will get many listings for Shakespeare on DVD and videotape going back to a silent version of *King John* in 1899, directed by Sir Herbert Beerbohm Tree. Most of this is available for rent or purchase. A great resource to start with is your local library, many of which now have movie rental sections and can get interlibrary loans for movies they don't have, in some cases.

When watching Shakespeare on film, you will enhance your experience if you pay attention to the following ten viewers' clues:

1. Things happen in a live performance that are sometimes unrehearsed and unscripted. But everything in a film is meant to be there. If something stands out, chances are it was supposed to, so pay attention. In general, ask yourself why a director would use that music or focus on that thing?

2. Watch the film a couple of times and then follow it with a copy of the original play on your lap. Try and spot which scenes have been cut or merged, and which lines cut or reordered. Play performances are often rearranged and edited as well, but not to the same degree. What is the director trying to tell you about the play? To really see the difference a director can make, watch two different versions of the same play.

3. Who's in the cast? Are they popular actors? Do they specialize in something? For example, is Ice T playing Othello? How does this affect the way you see this character? Is the director relying on star appeal? Shock appeal? Can you explain any of the director's casting decisions?

4. Where is the film set? In what era? Does the play need a historically "accurate" setting for example, Renaissance England rather than Fascist Italy in the 1930s for Richard III?

5. What do the costumes tell you? Are they being used to convey a general impression or to establish a historical era or both?

6. How knowledgeable are we expected to be about the original play? Have any subplots or characters been dropped for this film? Why?

7. Has the genre of the film been changed? *Hamlet* became Disney's *The Lion King; The Tempest* became the 1956 sci-fi classic *Forbidden Planet.* What does this change tell you about the play you hadn't thought of before?

8. What does the music in the film tell you about it? Music speaks to the emotional undercurrent in the story. How does the score affect how you experience the dialogue? Is it intrusive?

9. What did this film teach you about this play? What would you change?

10. When a new film comes out, watch how it's promoted. Catch interviews with the cast and the director. What they thought they were doing, and what actually ended up on film may be very different.

The following is a partial list of films of Shakespeare plays, of dramas inspired by his plays, or about Shakespeare, that are worth watching.

*The Taming of the Shrew* (1929), featuring Douglas Fairbanks and Mary Pickford.

*Romeo and Juliet* (1935), directed by George Cukor.

*A Midsummer Night's Dream* (1935), directed by Max Reinhardt and William Dieterle.

*As You Like It* (1936), directed by Paul Czinner.

*Swinging the Dream* (1938), featuring Louis Armstrong and Benny Goodman (based on *A Midsummer Night's Dream*).

*Henry V* (1945), directed by Lawrence Olivier.

*A Double Life* (1948), directed by George Cukor, starring Ronald Coleman (based on *Othello*).

*Macbeth* (1948), directed by Orson Welles.

*Hamlet* (1948), directed by Lawrence Olivier.

*Othello* (1952), directed by Orson Welles.

*Julius Caesar* (1953), directed by Joseph L. Mankiewicz.

*Romeo and Juliet* (1954), directed by Renato Castellani.

*Richard III* (1955), directed by Lawrence Olivier.

*Forbidden Planet* (1956), directed by Fred M. Wilcox (based on *The Tempest*).

*West Side Story* (1961), starring Natalie Wood and Richard Beymer (based on *Romeo and Juliet*).

*Hamlet* (1964), starring Richard Burton and directed by Bill Colleran and John Gielgud.

*Hamlet* (1964), directed by Grigori Kozintsev.

*Chimes at Midnight* (1965), directed by Orson Welles (a fictional biography of Falstaff, lifted from the histories).

*Othello* (1965), starring Lawrence Olivier, Maggie Smith, and Frank Finlay.

*The Taming of the Shrew* (1967), starring Elizabeth Taylor and Richard Burton, and directed by Franco Zeffirelli.

*Romeo and Juliet* (1968), directed by Franco Zeffirelli.

*King Lear* (1970), directed by Peter Brook.

*King Lear* (1970), directed by Grigori Kozintsev.

*Macbeth* (1972), directed by Roman Polanski (Bitter Moon).

*Antony and Cleopatra* (1974), starring Patrick Stewart and Ben Kingsley, and directed by Trevor Nunn and John Schoffield.

*Comedy of Errors* (1978), starring Judi Dench and Francesca Annis, and directed by Philip Casson and Trevor Nunn.

*Richard II* (1978), starring Derek Jacobi, John Gielgud, and Wendy Hiller.

*Hamlet, Prince of Denmark* (1980), starring Patrick Stewart, and directed by Rodney Bennett.

*The Merry Wives of Windsor* (1982), starring Ben Kingsley, and directed by David Hugh Jones.

*The Tempest* (1982), directed by Paul Mazursky.

*Ran* (1985), directed by Akira Kurosawa (based on *King Lear*).

*King Lear* (1987), directed by Jean-Luc Godard.

*Henry V* (1989), directed by Kenneth Branagh.

*Rosencrantz and Guildenstern Are Dead* (1990), featuring Richard Dreyfuss (based on *Hamlet*).

*Romeo and Juliet* (1990), starring Francesca Annis, Vanessa Redgrave, and Ben Kingsley, and directed by Armando Acosta II.

*Hamlet* (1991), directed by Franco Zeffirelli.

*Prospero's Books* (1991), directed by Peter Greenaway (based on *The Tempest*).

*As You Like It* (1992), directed by Christine Edzard.

*Much Ado about Nothing* (1993), directed by Kenneth Branagh.

*Othello* (1995), directed by Oliver Parker.

*Richard III* (1995), directed by Richard Loncraine, and featuring Sir Ian McKellen.

*Hamlet* (1996), starring Kenneth Branagh, Richard Attenborough, Judi Dench, Billy Crystal, and Kate Winslet, and directed by Kenneth Branagh.

*Twelfth Night* (1996), starring Helena Bonham Carter, Nigel Hawthorne, Ben Kingsley, Imogen Stubbs, and Mel Smith, and directed by Trevor Nunn.

*Looking for Richard* (1996), directed by Al Pacino.

*Romeo and Juliet* (1996), featuring Leonardo DiCaprio and Claire Danes.

*Shakespeare in Love* (1998), starring Gwyneth Paltrow, Geoffrey Rush, and Judi Dench, and directed by John Madden.

*10 Things I Hate About You* (1999), starring Julia Stiles and Heath Ledger, and directed by Gil Junger (based on *The Taming of the Shrew*).

*A Midsummer's Night's Dream* (1999), starring Calista Flockhart and Michelle Pfeiffer, and directed by Michael Hoffman.

*Titus* (1999), directed by Julie Taymor, and starring Anthony Hopkins and Jessica Lange.

*Othello* (1999), featuring Lawrence Fishburne and Kenneth Branagh.

*Love's Labour's Lost* (2000), directed by Kenneth Branagh.

# Shakespeare on the Web

There are quite literally thousands of Web sites about Shakespeare. Below are a handful of sites that are interesting and useful. They have been categorized by topic to help you find your way around. No doubt your search will find many more.

## Complete Texts

*www.ipl.org/reading/shakespeare/shakespeare.html*
*www.groundling.com//Edward3/index.shtml*
*http://shakespeare.about.com/mbody.htm*
*www.chemicool.com/Shakespeare/*
*http://theplays.org/*
*http://htf-puppy.mit.edu/research/shakespeare/sea.html*
*www.btinternet.com/~steveaj/Shakespeare/works.htm*

## Summaries and Plot Guides

A.C. Bradley's Shakespearean Tragedy:
  *www.clicknotes.com/bradley/welcome.html*
All Shakespeare:
  *www.allshakespeare.com/index.php*
Shakespeare Resource Center—Synopsis Index:
  *www.bardweb.net/plays/index.html*
Shakespeare Magazine:
  *www.shakespearemag.com*
SparkNotes Shakespeare:
  *www.sparknotes.com/shakespeare/.dir/*
The Seven Ages Shakespeare's Life:
  *http://web.uvic./shakespeare/Library/SLTnoframes/life/lifesubj.html*
The Shakespeare Classroom:
  *www.jetlink.net/~massij/shakes/*

Shakespeare Play Summaries-Synopses:
  *www.unc.edu/~monroem/shakespeare/shakespeare.html*
Shakespeare Study Guide with Plot Summaries:
  *http://zekscrab.users.50megs.com/Cummings/Shakespeare*

## Shakespeare Performed

Romeo & Juliet: *www.romeoandjuliet.com*
IMS William Shakespeare, HarperAudio:
  *http://town.hall.org/Archives/radio/IMS/HarperAudio/020994_harp_ITH.html*
Shakespeare Wired for Books:
  *www.tcom.ohiou.edu/books/shakespeare*
Village Story Tapes:
  *www.storytapes.net/index.html*
Shakespeare Film: *www.jetlink.net/~massij/shakes/films/movilist.html*
Lynch Multimedia—Shakespeare:
  *www.lynchmultimedia.com/shakespeare.html*
Shakespeare and the Globe Then and Now:
  *http://shakespeare.com/shakespeare/ind_.html*
The Play's the Thing audio files and information:
  *www.eamesharlan.org/tptt/audio.html*
Taste Shakespeare:
  *www.atasteofshakespeare.com*
Virtual Globe Theatre—Opening Page:
  *www.holycross.edu/departments/theatre/wrynders/globe/globe.htm*
The Official RSC Web site: *www.rsc.org.uk*
Shakespeare's Globe Theatre, Bankside, Southwark, London:
  *www.shakespeares-globe.org*
Shakespeare Film—Miami University: *www.mucmuohio.edu/~shakespeare/index2.html*

# APPENDIX B
# *How to Curse in Shakespeare*

Do you find yourself using curse words too often? Can't think any alternatives? You're still stuck in Anglo-Saxon times. Be modern: Think Elizabethan English.

Elizabethans took a delight in clever use of language and wove together words to make stinging but witty insults ("You mammering plume-plucked maggot!" for example). Certainly, Elizabethans used words like *fie* and swore by God's wounds ("Z'wounds" became "Zounds."), and if an occasion arose where they felt the only suitable expression would involve the "F" word, more often as not they would use the verb *swive*, which is completely gone from the language.

Name-calling was an art in Shakespeare's day and some of his best comes from family members insulting other family members. "Thou art a boil, a plague sore!" Lear screams at his daughter Goneril. "Thou toad," the duchess of York yells at her son Richard III.

Instead of just calling Falstaff a fat liar, Prince Hal calls him "A huge hill of flesh." And then goes on to call him:

> A trunk of humours,
> that bolting-hutch of beastliness, that swollen parcel
> of dropsies, that huge bombard of sack, that stuffed
> cloak-bag of guts, that roasted Manningtree ox with the
> pudding in his belly.

To create your own curses, memorize some choice terms from the list below, two adjectives and a noun minimum per curse, please. For example, try "Thou bawdy bat-fowled barnacle," or to sound more modern, try "You surly sheep-biting puttock."

Combine words from each of the three columns below.

| Adjective | Adjective | Noun | Adjective | Adjective | Noun |
|---|---|---|---|---|---|
| artless | base-court | apple-john | mewling | idle-headed | lewdster |
| bawdy | bat-fowling | baggage | paunchy | ill-breeding | lout |
| beslubbering | beef-witted | barnacle | pribbling | ill-nurtured | maggot-pie |
| bootless | beetle-headed | bladder | puking | knotty-pated | malt-worm |
| churlish | boil-brained | boar-pig | puny | milk-livered | mammet |
| clouted | clay-brained | bum-bailey | rank | onion-eyed | minnow |
| cockered | clapper-clawed | bugbear | reeky | plume-plucked | miscreant |
| craven | common-kissing | canker-blossom | roguish | pottle-deep | moldwarp |
| currish | crook-pated | clack-dish | ruttish | pox-marked | mumble-news |
| dankish | dismal-dreaming | clotpole | saucy | reeling-ripe | nut-hook |
| errant | dread-bolted | death-token | spleeny | rough-hewn | pigeon-egg |
| fawning | earth-vexing | dewberry | spongy | rude-growing | pignut |
| fobbing | elf-skinned | flap-dragon | surly | rump-fed | pumpion |
| frothy | fen-sucked | flirt-gill | tottering | shard-borne | puttock |
| froward | fat-kidneyed | flax-wench | unmuzzled | sheep-biting | rascal |
| gleeking | flap-mouthed | foot-licker | vain | spur-galled | ratsbane |
| goatish | fly-bitten | fustilarian | venomed | swag-bellied | scut |
| gorbellied | folly-fallen | giglet | villainous | tardy-gaited | skainsmate |
| infectious | full-gorged | haggard | warped | tickle-brained | strumpet |
| loggerheaded | half-faced | hedge-pig | wayward | toad-spotted | varlot |
| lumpish | hasty-witted | horn-beast | whoreson | wart-necked | vassal |
| mammering | hedge-born | hugger-mugger | weedy | unchin-snouted | whey-face |
| mangled | hell-hated | joithead | yeasty | weather-bitten | wagtail |

Need more? Look up Shakespearean insults on the Internet. Or you can always read Shakespeare's plays and then make them up. For references on such terms, try *Shakespeare's Bawdy* by Eric Partridge; *Shakespeare's Insults: Educating Your Wit* and *Insults for Teachers*, both by Wayne F. Hill and Cynthia Öttchen; and more generally, *Opus Maledictorum: A Book of Bad Words and Talking Dirty* by Jeremy Ellis.

# *Index*

# We Have EVERYTHING!

Everything® **After College Book**
$12.95, 1-55850-847-3

Everything® **American History Book**
$12.95, 1-58062-531-2

Everything® **Angels Book**
$12.95, 1-58062-398-0

Everything® **Anti-Aging Book**
$12.95, 1-58062-565-7

Everything® **Astrology Book**
$12.95, 1-58062-062-0

Everything® **Baby Names Book**
$12.95, 1-55850-655-1

Everything® **Baby Shower Book**
$12.95, 1-58062-305-0

Everything® **Baby's First Food Book**
$12.95, 1-58062-512-6

Everything® **Baby's First Year Book**
$12.95, 1-58062-581-9

Everything® **Barbeque Cookbook**
$12.95, 1-58062-316-6

Everything® **Bartender's Book**
$9.95, 1-55850-536-9

Everything® **Bedtime Story Book**
$12.95, 1-58062-147-3

Everything® **Bicycle Book**
$12.00, 1-55850-706-X

Everything® **Breastfeeding Book**
$12.95, 1-58062-582-7

Everything® **Build Your Own Home Page**
$12.95, 1-58062-339-5

Everything® **Business Planning Book**
$12.95, 1-58062-491-X

Everything® **Candlemaking Book**
$12.95, 1-58062-623-8

Everything® **Casino Gambling Book**
$12.95, 1-55850-762-0

Everything® **Cat Book**
$12.95, 1-55850-710-8

Everything® **Chocolate Cookbook**
$12.95, 1-58062-405-7

Everything® **Christmas Book**
$15.00, 1-55850-697-7

Everything® **Civil War Book**
$12.95, 1-58062-366-2

Everything® **Classical Mythology Book**
$12.95, 1-58062-653-X

Everything® **Collectibles Book**
$12.95, 1-58062-645-9

Everything® **College Survival Book**
$12.95, 1-55850-720-5

Everything® **Computer Book**
$12.95, 1-58062-401-4

Everything® **Cookbook**
$14.95, 1-58062-400-6

Everything® **Cover Letter Book**
$12.95, 1-58062-312-3

Everything® **Creative Writing Book**
$12.95, 1-58062-647-5

Everything® **Crossword and Puzzle Book**
$12.95, 1-55850-764-7

Everything® **Dating Book**
$12.95, 1-58062-185-6

Everything® **Dessert Book**
$12.95, 1-55850-717-5

Everything® **Digital Photography Book**
$12.95, 1-58062-574-6

Everything® **Dog Book**
$12.95, 1-58062-144-9

Everything® **Dreams Book**
$12.95, 1-55850-806-6

Everything® **Etiquette Book**
$12.95, 1-55850-807-4

Everything® **Fairy Tales Book**
$12.95, 1-58062-546-0

Everything® **Family Tree Book**
$12.95, 1-55850-763-9

Everything® **Feng Shui Book**
$12.95, 1-58062-587-8

Everything® **Fly-Fishing Book**
$12.95, 1-58062-148-1

Everything® **Games Book**
$12.95, 1-55850-643-8

Everything® **Get-A-Job Book**
$12.95, 1-58062-223-2

Everything® **Get Out of Debt Book**
$12.95, 1-58062-588-6

Everything® **Get Published Book**
$12.95, 1-58062-315-8

Everything® **Get Ready for Baby Book**
$12.95, 1-55850-844-9

Everything® **Get Rich Book**
$12.95, 1-58062-670-X

Everything® **Ghost Book**
$12.95, 1-58062-533-9

Everything® **Golf Book**
$12.95, 1-55850-814-7

Everything® **Grammar and Style Book**
$12.95, 1-58062-573-8

Everything® **Guide to Las Vegas**
$12.95, 1-58062-438-3

Everything® **Guide to New England**
$12.95, 1-58062-589-4

Everything® **Guide to New York City**
$12.95, 1-58062-314-X

Everything® **Guide to Walt Disney World®, Universal Studios®, and Greater Orlando, 2nd Edition**
$12.95, 1-58062-404-9

Everything® **Guide to Washington D.C.**
$12.95, 1-58062-313-1

Everything® **Guitar Book**
$12.95, 1-58062-555-X

Everything® **Herbal Remedies Book**
$12.95, 1-58062-331-X

Everything® **Home-Based Business Book**
$12.95, 1-58062-364-6

Everything® **Homebuying Book**
$12.95, 1-58062-074-4

Everything® **Homeselling Book**
$12.95, 1-58062-304-2

Everything® **Horse Book**
$12.95, 1-58062-564-9

Everything® **Hot Careers Book**
$12.95, 1-58062-486-3

Everything® **Internet Book**
$12.95, 1-58062-073-6

Everything® **Investing Book**
$12.95, 1-58062-149-X

Everything® **Jewish Wedding Book**
$12.95, 1-55850-801-5

Everything® **Job Interview Book**
$12.95, 1-58062-493-6

Everything® **Lawn Care Book**
$12.95, 1-58062-487-1

Everything® **Leadership Book**
$12.95, 1-58062-513-4

Everything® **Learning French Book**
$12.95, 1-58062-649-1

Everything® **Learning Spanish Book**
$12.95, 1-58062-575-4

Everything® **Low-Fat High-Flavor Cookbook**
$12.95, 1-55850-802-3

Everything® **Magic Book**
$12.95, 1-58062-418-9

Everything® **Managing People Book**
$12.95, 1-58062-577-0

Everything® **Microsoft® Word 2000 Book**
$12.95, 1-58062-306-9

Everything® **Money Book**
$12.95, 1-58062-145-7

Everything® **Mother Goose Book**
$12.95, 1-58062-490-1

Everything® **Motorcycle Book**
$12.95, 1-58062-554-1

Everything® **Mutual Funds Book**
$12.95, 1-58062-419-7

Everything® **One-Pot Cookbook**
$12.95, 1-58062-186-4

Everything® **Online Business Book**
$12.95, 1-58062-320-4

Everything® **Online Genealogy Book**
$12.95, 1-58062-402-2

Everything® **Online Investing Book**
$12.95, 1-58062-338-7

Everything® **Online Job Search Book**
$12.95, 1-58062-365-4

Everything® **Organize Your Home Book**
$12.95, 1-58062-617-3

Everything® **Pasta Book**
$12.95, 1-55850-719-1

Everything® **Philosophy Book**
$12.95, 1-58062-644-0

Everything® **Playing Piano and Keyboards Book**
$12.95, 1-58062-651-3

Everything® **Pregnancy Book**
$12.95, 1-58062-146-5

Everything® **Pregnancy Organizer**
$15.00, 1-58062-336-0

Everything® **Project Management Book**
$12.95, 1-58062-583-5

Everything® **Puppy Book**
$12.95, 1-58062-576-2

Everything® **Quick Meals Cookbook**
$12.95, 1-58062-488-X

Everything® **Resume Book**
$12.95, 1-58062-311-5

Everything® **Romance Book**
$12.95, 1-58062-566-5

Everything® **Running Book**
$12.95, 1-58062-618-1

Everything® **Sailing Book, 2nd Edition**
$12.95, 1-58062-671-8

Everything® **Saints Book**
$12.95, 1-58062-534-7

Everything® **Selling Book**
$12.95, 1-58062-319-0

Everything® **Shakespeare Book**
$12.95, 1-58062-591-6

Everything® **Spells and Charms Book**
$12.95, 1-58062-532-0

Everything® **Start Your Own Business Book**
$12.95, 1-58062-650-5

Everything® **Stress Management Book**
$12.95, 1-58062-578-9

Everything® **Study Book**
$12.95, 1-55850-615-2

Everything® **T'ai Chi and QiGong Book**
$12.95, 1-58062-646-7

Everything® **Tall Tales, Legends, and Outrageous Lies Book**
$12.95, 1-58062-514-2

Everything® **Tarot Book**
$12.95, 1-58062-191-0

Everything® **Time Management Book**
$12.95, 1-58062-492-8

Everything® **Toasts Book**
$12.95, 1-58062-189-9

Everything® **Toddler Book**
$12.95, 1-58062-592-4

Everything® **Total Fitness Book**
$12.95, 1-58062-318-2

Everything® **Trivia Book**
$12.95, 1-58062-143-0

Everything® **Tropical Fish Book**
$12.95, 1-58062-343-3

Everything® **Vegetarian Cookbook**
$12.95, 1-58062-640-8

Everything® **Vitamins, Minerals, and Nutritional Supplements Book**
$12.95, 1-58062-496-0

Everything® **Wedding Book, 2nd Edition**
$12.95, 1-58062-190-2

Everything® **Wedding Checklist**
$7.95, 1-58062-456-1

Everything® **Wedding Etiquette Book**
$7.95, 1-58062-454-5

Everything® **Wedding Organizer**
$15.00, 1-55850-828-7

Everything® **Wedding Shower Book**
$7.95, 1-58062-188-0

Everything® **Wedding Vows Book**
$7.95, 1-58062-455-3

Everything® **Weight Training Book**
$12.95, 1-58062-593-2

Everything® **Wine Book**
$12.95, 1-55850-808-2

Everything® **World War II Book**
$12.95, 1-58062-572-X

Everything® **World's Religions Book**
$12.95, 1-58062-648-3

Everything® **Yoga Book**
$12.95, 1-58062-594-0

# Visit us at everything.com

Everything® is a registered trademark of Adams Media Corporation.

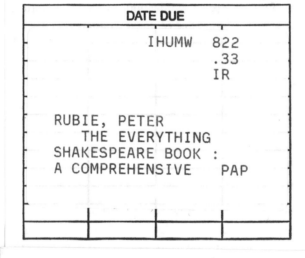